CAIRNS CASTLE, Mid Calder, N.B.

From a Photo.]

A HISTORY

OF THE

FAMILY OF

CAIRNES OR CAIRNS

AND ITS CONNECTIONS.

BY

H. C. LAWLOR.

LONDON:
ELLIOT STOCK, 62 PATERNOSTER ROW, E.C.
1906.

Cavalier Books

Typeset and printed by R. Carswell and Son, Belfast 1906.
First published by Elliot Stock, 62 Paternoster Row, London 1906.
Reprinted and republished by Cavalier Books, Milwaukee 2015.
Cover Images from *Chapter X: Armorial Bearings, Crests, Seals, &c.*

ISBN-13: 978-0-692-34546-7
ISBN-10: 0692345469

IN PIAM

MEMORIAM

J. H. L.

PREFACE.

IT is now a good number of years ago since some of my relatives, both in Australia and at home, expressed a desire to know something of the history of our ancestors. In accordance with this desire, my late father obtained a copy of the MS. pedigree of the Cairnes family in the Office of the Ulster King of Arms, of which he supplied several transcripts to members of the Cairnes family and others interested.

A perusal of this document whetted the appetite of some of the recipients for more information. As I have inherited both from my father and from my mother's father, a love and veneration for things ancient, I gladly volunteered to endeavour to elucidate something of the history of the persons whose mere names appeared in the Ulster Office Pedigree. My original intention was only to write a short memoir of the Irish family of Cairnes, but so engrossing did the subject become to me, that, having pretty well exhausted the Irish family, I began inquiries as to its progenitors, the Scottish family. One discovery led to another, and my original intention to write a memoir of the Irish branch gradually developed into an effort to write a history of the whole family. I have spared no pains to make my work as complete as possible. Few will believe the amount of labour this has entailed. It has been, although always a pleasure to me, a vast undertaking. This is because almost the whole book has had to be compiled at first hand from original sources. True, the Ulster Office Pedigree to which I have referred formed a groundwork for a small section of the book, but on carefully examining old records, family papers, &c., I found this to contain several errors, and therefore to be unreliable. With this exception the history of the family as chronicled in these pages is the result of original research. I have deemed it best in all cases to give my authorities in footnotes. These, it will be noted, are in most cases from original records, or from verified sources. Hence I can place the volume in the hands of the subscribers with the belief that it will be found reliable as a work of reference. At the same time, I am quite conscious that the book has many defects. I can only crave my readers' forgiveness for these and plead that I have done my best, and that it is my first attempt at writing a book.

It will probably be said by some critics, "Who are these Cairneses or what have they done to warrant their family history being written?" I admit they have no claim to be included among the greater noble families of these kingdoms; yet I think that anyone who reads these pages will acknowledge that they contain the history of a noble family. In the six hundred years covered by this work the family has supplied many prominent and useful members to the State, the Church, the Army and the Bar. It has produced none but good citizens, whether of high or low degree. In the many hundred books, public records and private documents I have perused in the preparation of my book, I have never found the name of Cairnes sullied by unworthy or dishonourable conduct.

In this age, when it is becoming fashionable in some quarters to pretend to despise noble and ancient lineage, it is a pleasure to find even such a radical reformer as the late Mr. Gladstone expressing his sympathy with those who venerate the memory of their forebears, in the following words—"There is no greater folly circulating upon the earth at this moment, or at any other time, than the disposition to undervalue the past, and to break those links which unite human beings of the present day with the generations that have passed away and have been called to their account."[1]

I have endeavoured above all things to be accurate in all my statements. I have no desire to exaggerate or to minimise the merits of anyone, nor have I endeavoured to raise either the family of Cairnes or any member of it to a higher position than is warranted by absolute and verified facts.

If the book should be judged to have any merit, I must candidly admit that the credit will rightly belong more to others than to

[1] Speech of Mr. Gladstone at Mold, August, 1873, quoted by Miss M. A. Hickson, in *Old Kerry Records*.

myself, and I take this opportunity of expressing my gratitude to those who have helped me. Foremost among these I desire most sincerely to thank my brother Professor Hugh Jackson Lawlor, D.D. All through the printing of the book, he carefully went through the proof-sheets, supplementing my narrative with most valuable information on various historical matters, and in many cases going to vast trouble in searching up records to authenticate or disprove doubtful points. To the Rev. John Cairns, M.A. of Dumfries, also, I am under a heavy debt of gratitude. In addition to his intimate knowledge of Scottish topography, particularly of the Lothians and Berwickshire, he is thoroughly conversant with Scottish History. He placed all the information he possessed freely at my disposal, and it is chiefly owing to his help and that of his brother the Rev. W. T. Cairns, that I was enabled to get together the facts contained in Chapter I. and parts of Chapters II., III., and IX. I have also to acknowledge the early encouragement and help given me by Erskine Beveridge, Esq., LL.D. of Dunfermline.

No words of mine can adequately express the extent of the kindness of Mr. Maitland Thomson of the Register House. He gave me full advantage of his inexhaustible knowledge of the Scottish Records, and extracted therefrom endless notes bearing on the subject of my book, without which I should have been unable to write Chapters IV. and VIII. and parts of Chapters I. and III.

For much information regarding the Armorial bearings of the Cairnes family and its connections, I am indebted to Sir James Balfour Paul, the Lyon King of Arms of Scotland, and Mr. Grant the Lyon Clerk, and to Sir Arthur Vicars, the Ulster King of Arms, and Mr. G. D. Burtchaell.

I must also warmly thank those who placed their private papers at my disposal and otherwise supplied me with information. Among these I desire especially to mention Mrs. Lawlor and Miss Cairnes of Kingstown, Lord Rossmore, Messrs. R. D. Percival, Walter Ovens, Philip Crossle, and Robert Stavely, the late Lady M'Clure, Canon Maddison, Mr. R. D. Robinson Douglas, D.L., Miss Hamilton of Craighlaw, Earl Cairns, Mr. Charles E. Green, Mr. James Gourlay, Mrs. C. Waldie Cairns, and others whose names I have mentioned in footnotes referring to the subjects on which they have assisted me with information.

Not the least interesting portions of this book are the reproductions of old Family Portraits. The greater number of these together are at Rossmore, and I have to thank their noble owner for his hospitality while there getting all these photographed. I am similarly indebted to Sir Henry Bellingham for giving me the opportunity of having those at Castlebellingham photographed. My mother, Mrs. Lawlor, has also a number of the family portraits which she got photographed for me. I have also to thank Miss Stiven, Mrs. Brinsley, the Earl of Rosebery, Mr. R. Gun Cuninghame of Mount Kennedy, and Mr. G. Gun Mahony of Kilmorna, for facilities granted me in reproducing portraits in their possession. In the list of illustrations below the present possessor of each of the portraits is stated.

In conclusion, I must bear tribute to the care and patience exercised by Messrs. R. Carswell & Son of Belfast, who have executed all the illustrations, lithographs, printing and binding in connection with this work, and to the unfailing courtesy of Mr. Elliot Stock of London, the publisher.

H. C. LAWLOR.

Killyfaddy,
Windsor Avenue,
Belfast,
22nd October, 1906.

TABLE OF CONTENTS.

CHAPTER VII.

CHAPTER VIII.

CHAPTER IX.

CHAPTER X.

APPENDICES.

LIST OF ILLUSTRATIONS.

LIST OF PEDIGREES.

ERRATA.

Page 6, Note 4,
For "Lynn MSS." read "Armorial MSS. of Sir David Lindsay."

" 65,
Among the sons of William Cairnes of Orchardton, insert George of Muretoun.

" 83, Line 2,
For "Elchin," read "Echlin."

" 87, Line 1,
For "Cadwaller," read "Cadwallader."

" 89, Line 14, and on Portrait facing,
For "Cunningham," read "Cuninghame."

" 116, Line 10,
For "Elizabeth," read "Esther."

CHAPTER I.

William Carnys of that Ilk—The Castle and Estate of the Carnys—Stephen Crichton—George Crichton, heir of the Carnys, Earl of Caithness and Lord High Admiral of Scotland—The Siege of Blackness Castle—The Crichtons of Strathurd.

IN the Parish of Mid-Calder, Midlothian, some fourteen miles from the capital, are the ruins of an ancient castle, an illustration of which forms the frontispiece of this volume. The castle and the surrounding estate derive their name from the two pointed and stoney hills known respectively as Easter and Wester Cairn, which are prominent features of the locality, rising each to a height of 1,840 feet.

The castle is prettily situated on the right bank of the Water of Leith, about five miles from Kirknewton Station on the Caledonian Railway. It was originally of a style frequently met with in castles of the period, consisting of two square and unornamented towers rising, probably, in their perfect state, to a height of sixty or seventy feet. To-day but one of the towers remains, standing about forty feet high, with little more than the foundations of the second tower abutting thereon. The latter, a smaller tower than the other, was merely a wing of the main structure. It was standing in 1855, but fell since then. The basement consists of a vaulted dungeon or cellar, entered by a doorway under a circular arch. This room communicated by a door with a similar room in the smaller tower, but neither had internal communication with the upper or living portion of the castle.

This was entered by a square-headed doorway approached by a staircase now gone.

A careful examination of the building suggests that the basement storey is of much earlier date than the upper portion. Dr. Sommers, in an account of the Parish of Mid-Calder published in 1838, refers to a tradition that the Castle of the Cairns "was founded by Sir William *(sic)* Crichton, Lord High Admiral of Scotland, who had a possession in the Parish of Cramonde." He, of course, refers to Sir George Crichton of Carnys, and if the tradition be founded on fact, it would place the date of the building of the castle about 1440.

It will be shown in the following pages that this Sir George Crichton, besides inheriting the Cairns estate also inherited Barnton, in the Parish of Cramond, on the death of his father Stephen Crichton, in 1427. Stephen had married the heiress of Duncan de Carnys of that ilk about the year 1390, so that Sir George became the heir of the family of Carnys through his mother, thus inheriting the estates of Carnys, Parish of Mid-Calder, Barnton, Parish of Cramond, Easter and Wester Whitburn in Linlithgowshire, and other lands.

The tradition referred to by Dr. Sommers, taken in conjunction with the difference in the style both of the masonry and architecture between the basement and upper storeys of Cairns Castle, suggests that the original castle, of which the basement is the remnant, dates from the fourteenth or even the thirteenth century.

The date at which the ancestor of George Crichton's mother, the heiress of the family of Cairns of that ilk, became possessed of the estate cannot now be ascertained. It is quite within the bounds of possibility that he was in possession of the property as early as 1060 to 1100, which is said by some authorities to be the approximate period when it became the

CAIRNS CASTLE.

custom for the head of a house to assume a definite surname, derived from the land in his possession ; at any rate, whether this was the period or not, in conformity with this custom, the owners of this estate derived their surname therefrom, and we find in 1349[1] it was in possession of William de Carnys.[2]

It is regrettable from the historian's point of view that owing to the terrible and bloodthirsty wars, both between Scotland and England, and among the Scottish chieftains themselves, in which castles, towns, and even whole baronies were devastated and laid waste, hardly a State record exists of date prior to 1300. From that date they are more plentiful, though many are missing and some that exist are undecipherable.

In 1363 William de Carnys must have been a man of considerable importance, as we find by a charter of 35 David II. that he was then owner of the Baronies of East and West Whitburn in Linlithgow, in addition to his family estate of Carnys. The charter referred to is merely a grant to William de Carnys and his son Duncan of a modification of the terms upon which they held Whitburn. Formerly the feofee had been obliged to attend regularly when required at the Court of the Constable of Linlithgow, but it was conceded by this charter that henceforth he need only attend three times a year at the three principal assizes.[3]

[1] Attached to a charter belonging to Lord Torpihchen, but not in the Register of the Great Seal, is the signature as a witness of William de Carnys.

[2] The plural termination "ys" or "is" is of frequent occurrence. During the three centuries following 1350, the name gradually changes, and appears as de Carnys, de Carnis, de Cairnis, Cairnis, Cairnes, and Cairns.

[3] Reg. Mag. Sigilli. Vol. I. David II. p. 33.—"Concessio facta Willelmo de Carnys, et Duncano filio suo—Apud Edynburch XXVI die Septembris anno immediate supradicto (*i.e.* 1363)—Conceditur Willelmo de Carnys et Duncano de Carnys, filio suo et heredi quod ubi ipsi tenebantur in communi secta ad curiam constabularii de Lynlithcu pro terris suis de Esterquhytburne et Westirquhitburn de cetero teneantur tantum in tribis sectis per annum ad tria placita constabularii praedicti capitalia apud Lynlithcu tenenda."

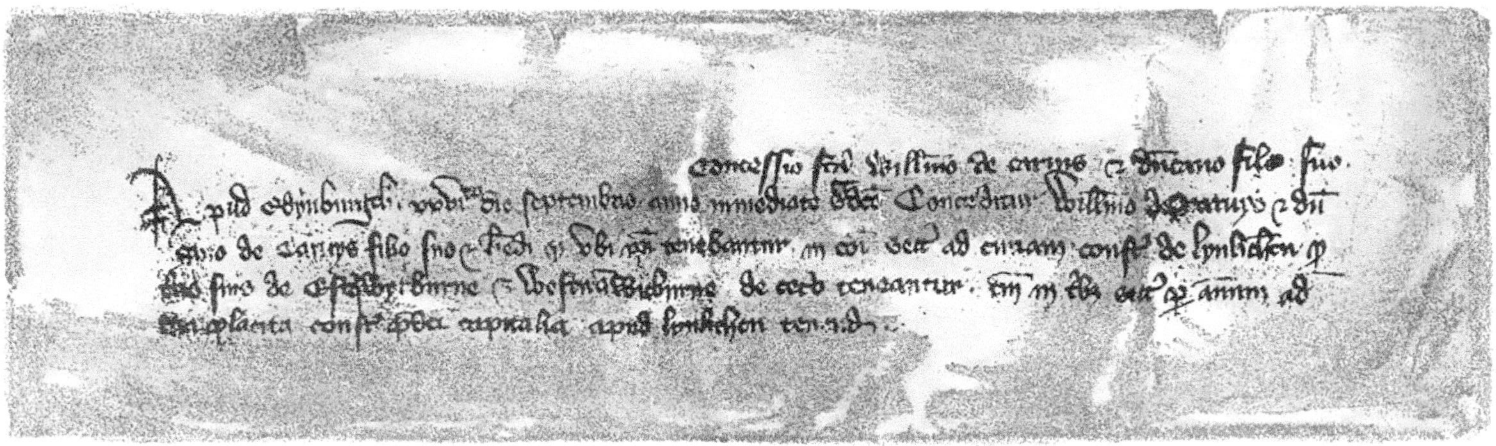

CHARTER OF THE BARONIES OF EAST AND WEST WHITBURN, LINLITHGOWSHIRE, TO WILLIAM AND DUNCAN DE CARNYS, A.D. 1363.

Though not mentioned so far as we can trace in any of the records prior to 1349, frequent mention is made of members of the family in the various State documents referring to Linlithgow and Edinburgh during the succeeding forty years. The influence of William de Carnys secured for his sons positions of importance, his second son John becoming Custumar of Linlithgow,[1] while William his third son was Constable of Linlithgow,[2] and afterwards of Edinburgh Castle.[3] A younger son Alexander, an ecclesiastic, eventually became Provost of Lincluden Abbey, and owing to his skill in diplomacy was several times selected during the Regency of the Duke of Albany as Special Ambassador to both the English and French Courts.[4]

Of the eldest son Duncan little is known. Assuming that he was of age, or a little over, at the date of the charter, he must have been born about 1340. Whom, or when, he married is not recorded. That he was dead in A.D. 1417 is probable. The records throw no light upon the life of this Duncan de Carnys or his family, or even the estate, for the forty years following 1363. In the Register of the Great Seal, however, under date A.D. 1418, appears the record of a charter issued at Stirling Castle, one of the witnesses to which signs himself Stephen de Crechtoun de Carnys. In 1427, George de Crechtoun, son and heir of Stephen de Crechtoun de Carnys, assigned by charter certain lands in the Barony of Cramond to Edward Crechtoun of Krettelhouse, showing that his father Stephen was dead in

[1] Exchequer Rolls of Scotland, 1369.

[2] Ibid.

[3] Ibid., 1372.

[4] There were probably two other sons, Thomas and Richard. See Chap. IX.

this year. Again, under date 1452, we find this George de Crechtoun de Carnys Earl of Caithness, owner of the lands of Carnys, and East and West Whitburn,[1] the estates belonging to William de Carnys of the 1363 charter, which he had inherited by direct descent.[2] Any doubt as to the clearness of the genealogy is removed by reference to the quarterings of the arms of George de Crechtoun de Carnys, Earl of Caithness. The arms of Carnys of that ilk were "Gules, three martlets or"[3]; these the Earl quartered 2nd and 3rd on his shield with those of Crechtoun 1st and 4th[4], thus proving beyond question that his mother was the heiress of the house, and only surviving child of its head, Duncan de Carnys.

The Stephen de Crechtoun de Carnys mentioned above was the second son of William de Crechtoun, the eldest son being John de Crechtoun, father of the famous William de Crechtoun or Crichton, Chancellor of Scotland during the minority of James II. Stephen's eldest son George, Lord High Admiral of the Kingdom, was therefore first cousin of the Chancellor.

It is not within the scope of such a work as this to make more than passing reference to what is fully recorded in every history of Scotland. The unseemly and deadly rivalry between Sir Alexander Livingston and the Chancellor Crichton for the actual possession of the person of the young King—who, as the intrigues of these two mountebanks were alternately successful, was bandied about from one to

[1] See note below p. 11.
[2] Exchequer Rolls of Scotland, vol. V., p. cii.
[3] Records in the Office of the Lyon King of Arms. See Chap. X.
[4] Lynn MSS.—Nisbet's Scottish Heraldry, vol. I., p. 279.

the other—is too well known to be recounted in detail. Suffice it to say that in his cousin the Admiral, the Chancellor had an able, and probably not less unscrupulous assistant. For his reward he secured for himself grant after grant of lands all over Scotland.[1] Of course, on the other hand, he suffered some misfortunes when the rival faction gained ascendency. Thus on 20th August, A.D. 1443, William Earl Douglas, Lord of Galloway, whom it suited at the time to form an alliance with Sir Alexander Livingston, who had secured for the moment the custody of the young King, proceeded with a large host and laid siege in the King's name to the Castle of Barnton (Barnton adjoined Carnys), the property of the Admiral. After an assault lasting four days, the castle capitulated and was levelled to the ground.[2] No mention is made of the fate of the inmates. It was probably not considered worthy of record! In the November following a council was held at Stirling, to which both the Chancellor and the Admiral were summoned. They deemed it wiser not to appear, and in their absence were outlawed and attainted.[3]

We next find these two worthies in the following year with an army, harrying and plundering the lands of Earl Douglas and his ally Sir John Forrester of Corstorphine, carrying off horses and cattle and any stray valuables they could find, burning the Granges of Abercorn and Strabrock; while Douglas in retaliation stormed and burned the Admiral's Castle of Blackness (Linlithgow).[4]

[1] Enumerated in detail in charter of 1452. Note on p. 11 below.

[2] Asloan MS., quoted in preface to vol. V. Exchequer Rolls of Scotland.

[3] Ibid.

[4] Ibid.

Sir William Crichton's successor in the office of Chancellor was James Kennedy, Bishop of St. Andrews, a nephew of James I., and a prelate whose singleness of purpose and purity of character, combined with great wisdom, stand out in bright relief in an age when such qualities were indeed rare. Having the good of the King and State deeply at heart, he viewed with dismay the coalition between Livingston and the powerful and ambitious Earl Douglas; the more so as it was understood that the utterly unscrupulous and equally ambitious David, third Earl of Crawford, was secretly allied to the same party. Kennedy therefore made advances to the ex-Chancellor Crichton, who was also joined by James Douglas, Earl of Angus. Alarmed at the thus recruited strength of the Crichton faction, the Earl of Crawford, joined by Alexander Ogilvy of Innerquharity and some of the Livingstons, with a large following, proceeded to retaliate upon the Bishop. They made an inroad on his territories, laying waste his lands, burning his granges, and carrying off rich booty to their own strongholds. Upon which the sacrilegious Earl and his abettors were solemnly excommunicated by the Bishop for the space of one year.[1]

Within the year a quarrel arose between the Lindsays and the Ogilvys, and exactly twelve months from the sentence of excommunication the rival families with their friends and retainers met in a sanguinary battle at Arbroath (23rd January, 1446). Both sides fought with desperation and the field was strewn with dead. The Lindsays won the day, with the loss, however, of their chief, the Earl of Crawford, who was killed early in the fray. Ogilvy of Innerquharity, severely

[1] Asloan MS.

wounded, was carried to the Castle of Finhaven, where his cousin, the widowed Countess of Crawford, smothered him with a down pillow as he lay in bed. It is related that for four days the body of the Earl lay on the battlefield, as no one dare bury him, until the Bishop sent the Prior of St. Andrews to remove the curse of excommunication[1].

By 1448, when the young King had reached his eighteenth year, the Crichtons had regained the Royal favour and their former power. Sir William again became Chancellor of Scotland, and he, with the Bishop of Dunkeld, was sent to France on the most delicate mission of choosing a wife for the King.[2] In the selection of a suitable lady he was advised by Charles VII., who, there being no French Princess of suitable age, sent the envoys to the Court of Philip the Good of Burgundy, who recommended his kinswoman Mary, daughter of Arnold Duke of Gueldres. This lady, whom the Chancellor reported to James as "jam nubilem et formosam," was eventually selected ; and after duly completing the matrimonial arrangements in the form of a treaty, signed at Brussels in 1449, preparations were made for the arrival of the prospective bride.[3] In June, 1449, the Princess of Gueldres, with a large suite, "in thirteen great shippis and ane craike," set sail from Flanders, escorted by the Chancellor Crichton, the Bishop of Dunkeld, and the Lord of Campvere. They were received with great state on their arrival at Leith on the 18th of June, and the marriage contract having been ratified under the

[1] Asloan MS.

[2] Stevenson's Letters and Papers illustrative of the Wars of the English in France, I., p. 227.

[3] Harleian MS. 4637, vol. III., f. 5. Treaties Philip and James.

Great Seal, the ceremony took place on the 3rd of July, followed immediately by the coronation of the King and Queen at Edinburgh. To this ceremony all the leading Barons of the Realm were summoned, and a great State banquet was given at Holyrood. This feast lasted no less than five hours, during which course after course was disposed of, and "strong drinks were as plentiful as sea water." It is specially recorded with much gravity, as an incident most creditable to the Church, that "a legate, a mitred abbot, and three bishops sat at a table by themselves drinking out of the same cup, *without spilling any*"! [1]

Within a month of the Chancellor's return he had the gratification of seeing the final overthrow and downfall of his enemies the Livingstons. The aged Sir Alexander and all his sons, the eldest of whom was Lord Chamberlain of Scotland, together with several of their influential kinsmen, were, by the King's warrant, suddenly arrested and thrown into the dungeons of the castle of Sir George Crichton de Carnys at Blackness.[2] The real reason for this act is utterly unaccounted for, the nominal charges upon which they were tried and found guilty being crimes long since condoned and forgotten. There can be little doubt, however, that the return of the Chancellor Crichton, and the entire success attending his mission, brought him into a position of the closest favour and friendship with the King and Queen—a position which he would not scruple to use to pay off old scores with his enemies. The fact of the prisoners

[1] Pinkerton I., 432. The various expenses in connection with the reception of the Princess on landing and her marriage are noted in detail in the Exchequer Rolls.

[2] Asloan MS. pp. 25-42.

being placed in the custody of the Admiral Crichton in Blackness Castle increases the likelihood of this assumption being correct.

As a result of the trial of the Livingstons before a Parliament, held at Edinburgh in January, 1450, the aged Sir Alexander Livingston, his eldest son James the Lord Chamberlain, his kinsman James Dundas of Dundas, and others of his friends and followers were attainted and thrown into Dumbarton Castle, and Alexander, youngest son of Sir Alexander Livingston, and his cousin Robert Livingston the Comptroller, were removed from the trial and forthwith executed, while every State official who owed his appointment to the Livingstons was dismissed from his post.

This wholesale forfeiture to the Crown of the estates of these attainted landowners placed enormous tracts of land within the gift of King James, and, as may readily be surmised, the two Crichtons were not behindhand in grasping the good things fortune put in their way. During the two years, 1450-52, charters granting them immense estates appear in the Register of the Great Seal, and in the latter year their various grants were confirmed by charters annexing and consolidating their various estates, and incorporating them into Earldoms. Sir George Crichton de Carnys, Lord High Admiral of Scotland, was created Earl of Caithness,[1] and

[1] Reg. Magni Sigilli, vol. II., No. 587.—"Rex cum matura deliberatione in plano Parliamento, &c. Confirmavit Georgeo de Creichtoun, comiti de Caithness, regni admirallo, *et assignatis ejus*, Baroniam de Rochenes, alias Blackness nuncupatum, Baroniam Strathmount, dimedietatem Baronie de Quhitburne, terras de Davidstoun et de le wra, Vic. Linlithgw; terras de Carnys, Berentoun, Boltoun, Carnyhill, Aldinstoun et Brethertoun, Vic. Edynburgh; Baroniam Tybbris, Aumornesse et le Monches, Vic. Dumfries (sic); Terras de Ballingredane, Vic. Wigton; terras dominicas de Tullybothy, cum molendino earundem,

Sir James Crichtoun, of Frendraught, eldest son of the Chancellor, "was beltit Earl of Moray."[1]

The Earls Douglas and Crawford, firm and fast allies, also benefited to a considerable extent by grants of the forfeited lands, and this notwithstanding the fact that they had been active supporters of the Livingstons, and that they had been guilty of various acts of lawlessness and rebellion, as well as being in secret communication with the English Court.[2]

These Earldoms, accompanied by the charters confirming them in their enormous estates, placed the Crichtons on a pinnacle of power which their ambition, insatiable as it was, could hardly have hoped for. Yet within two years of the receipt of their honours, the Chancellor, his son the newly created Earl of Moray, and George Earl of Caithness, had rendered account of their conduct to a higher Power than their King, all three dying in 1454—5. Of the descendants of the Chancellor, the Lords Frendraucht, it is not within the scope of this work to relate the history,[3] but the final years in the life of the Earl of Caithness, representative in the female line of the family of Cairns of that ilk, are sufficiently remarkable to be worthy of mention. He had

Vic. Clackmannan; terras de Fynnart, Vic. Renfrew, terras de Grestoun et de Gillishauch, Vic. Peblis—quas omnes idem Geo. resignavit, et quas Rex dicto Comitatui de Catnes, et regalitati ejusdem comitatus, annexuit et incorporavit — Tenend. de Rege, in liberam egalitatem, &c. Redend. unam rubeam rosam apud Brathule, nomine albe ferme, Test., &c. . . . . apud Edynburgh, 8 July, 1452.

[1] Asloan MS. pp. 11-49.

[2] Pell's Issue of the Rolls of England, 11th December, 30 Henry VI.

[3] The present descendants include the Marquis of Bute, the Maitland-Mackgill-Crichtons of Kankeilour, and probably the Earls of Erne. The last Lord Frendraucht accompanied James II. of England to France, where he died without issue, the title becoming extinct.

been twice married. The name of his first wife we do not find recorded, but he married secondly Janet Borthwick, widow of James Douglas, Lord Dalkeith. By his first wife he had a son James; by his second wife he had a daughter, Janet. She seems to have been born either before or during the subsistence of her mother's marriage with Lord Dalkeith, and for that reason to have been counted illegitimate. The term "filia naturalis" may not in every case mean an illegitimate daughter, but the persistent way in which Janet is so called in the charter quoted below,[1] leads unavoidably to the conclusion that such is the meaning of the phrase in the present instance. To his daughter the Earl granted the lands of Barnton in 1453, and next year she became the wife of John, son and heir apparent of Robert, Lord Maxwell.[2]

As will have been noted in the charter set forth on page 11, the lands of the Earldom were granted, not to the Earl and his heirs, as is usually the case, but to the Earl and his *assignees.* Evidently to the astonishment of his son and natural heir, and everyone else, the Earl in 1453 appointed the King as his immediate assignee, without reserving even his own liferent. The reasons for this

[1] Reg. Mag. Sigilli, vol. II. No. 594, Rex confirmavit Georgio Comiti de Catnes et Jonete [Comitisse de Catnes, spousa ejus, terras de Bernetoun, Vic. Edynburgh, quas dicti Georgius et Jonet] apud civitatem S. Andree personaliter resignaverunt. Tenend, dicto Georgeo et Jonete, et eorum alteri diutius viventi, et heredibus inter ipsos legitime procreatis, quibus deficientibus, Jonete filie naturale dictorum Geo. et Jon, et heredibus ejus, semper et quosque dictus Geo. aut sui assignati persolverit aut persolverint predicte Jonete, filie sue naturale uno die inter solis ortum et occasum, in ecclesia parochiali Beati Egidii de Edynburgh super summo altari ejusdem summam 300 marcas. . . . Jan., 1453.

[2] Tybberis is also mentioned in Exchequer Rolls (vol. V. pref., p. civ.) as passing to Janet Maxwell, but we cannot find corroboration of this in the Reg. Mag. Sigilli. The Editor also asserts that Barnton and Tybberis passed to her descendants by inheritance. This also appears inaccurate, as we find Barnton shortly afterwards passing to another family of Maxwell, and Tybberis to the Maitland family.

extraordinary assignment cannot be discovered,[1] and the act was certainly most unpalatable to his eldest son James. In May, 1453, the son, thus excluded and deprived of the succession, took violent possession of his father's late castle of Blackness, into the dungeon of which he cast his father. He, however, was closing the stable door after the steed had gone, as we find the King, now the owner of the Earl's estates, proceeding forthwith in person to recover the fortress.

In the Exchequer Rolls appear ample preparations for the siege. They tell us it lasted three weeks, and that not only the King, but also the Queen was present, and that the castle was invested by both land and sea. One Laurence Poke was paid £12 for the services of himself, his ship, and his crew.[2] Twelve blocks (or twelve stones?) of iron were provided at a cost of thirty-two shillings by one Andrew Wright, and paid for out of the Customs of Linlithgow.[3] These were probably battering rams or possibly cannon balls. For various implements for the siege, brought up by sea, £10 13s. 4d. was paid to Richard Forbes.[4] £6 15s. was paid to John Dalrymple for Beoun wine and crossbows for the Queen's use (sic).[5] John Park received

[1] Sir Bernard Burke in his "Extinct Peerages" seems to have fallen into an inaccuracy in stating that a condition of the charter was the appointment of the King as assignee. As will be seen, there is nothing in the wording of the charter to this effect.

[2] Exchequer Rolls, vol. V., p. 610, Accounts of the custumars of Edinburgh, 1454, "Et Laurencio Poke et nautis suis, pro servicio suo et nautarum suorum cum nave ejusdem per viginti dies ad obsidionem castri suprdicti, testantibus dominis supradictis, mandatum Regis super compotum xij Li."

[3] Exchequer Rolls, V., 623.

[4] Ibid., 610.

[5] Ibid., 616—"Pro Vino de Beoun empto et recepto ab eodem ad usum Regine, et pro certis arcubus missis ad Blackness ad usum Regine."

thirty-six shillings for hire of horses for the Queen.[1] The King's Serjeant was also paid fifty-three shillings and four pence for his great labours and expenses at the siege.[2]

After twenty days' siege, the hero of Blackness capitulated on honourable terms. He was allowed a free pardon for his offence, and granted forthwith lands in the Barony of Strathurd, with succession on his father's death to the ancient estates of the Cairns family, though not to those acquired by fresh grants.

The Earl died in 1454, when his son and heir succeeded to the Carnys and other estates. We find in the Exchequer Rolls of the several years following, references to sums of money due by him as heir, which sums were deficiencies in the accounts of the Sheriffdom of Linlithgowshire held by his father. After repeated applications, these debts were remitted by the King. His name occurs several times in the Register of the Great Seal,[3] where he is described as a Knight. His wife's name was Levenax. By her he had two sons, Sir James, his heir, and Andrew; and two daughters, Margaret and Marion;[4] he had also a natural son, Archibald.

He was succeeded by his son Sir James Crichton of Carnys, who was in 1493 appointed Coroner for the County of Perth.

The next in succession was his eldest son, Sir John Crichton of Carnys. In 1529 he and Elizabeth Lyoun, his wife, had a Charter from James V., of lands in Clack-

[1] Exchequer Rolls, V., 674.
[2] Ibid., p. 649.
[3] Reg. Mag. Sigilli, 1472 and 1491.
[4] Ibid., 1492.

mannan, which were united, and consolidated into the Barony of Strathurd. From this property Sir John henceforth took his designation. He married secondly Janet Sinclair.[1] He sold the ancient family estate of Carnys to John Tennent, in whose family it remained for about 150 years.[2] It is now the property of William H. Hamilton, Esq., W.S., whose father acquired it by purchase in 1869.

Sir John Crichton of Strathurd was living in 1547.[3] His heirs remained in possession of Strathurd for many generations.

---

1 Reg. Mag. Sigilli., 1535.

2 M'Call's "History of Mid Calder," p. 103.

3 Records of the Privy Council of Scotland, 1547.

TABLE I.

PEDIGREE OF
THE FAMILY OF CARNYS OF THAT ILK.
AND OF
CRICHTON OF CARNYS.

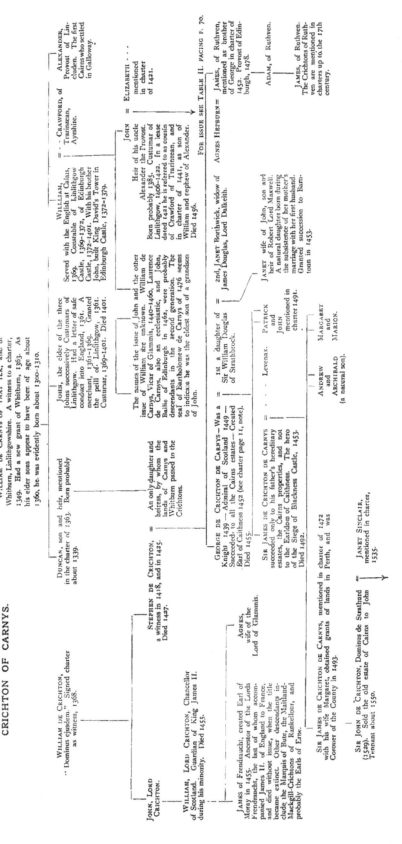

WILLIAM DE CARNYS OF THAT ILK, also of Whitburn, Linlithgowshire. A witness to a charter, 1349. Had a new grant of Whitburn, 1363. As his elder sons appear to have been of age about 1360, he was evidently born about 1300-1310.

WILLIAM DE CRICHTON, "Dominus ejusdem." Signed charter as witness, 1368.

DUNCAN, son and heir, mentioned in the charter of 1363. Born probably about 1339.

JOHN, the elder of the three Johns successively Custumars of Linlithgow. Had a letter of safe conduct into England, 1361. A merchant, 1361-1369. Granted the peill of Linlithgow, 1361. Custumar, 1369-1401. Died 1401.

WILLIAM, Served with the English at Calais, 1369. Constable of Linlithgow Castle, 1369-1372, of Edinburgh Castle, 1372-1401. With his brother John, built King David's Tower in Edinburgh Castle, 1372-1379. = - - CRAWFORD, of Trarinzean, Ayrshire.

ALEXANDER, Provost of Lincluden. The first Cairns who settled in Galloway.

JOHN, LORD CRICHTON.

STEPHEN DE CRICHTON, a witness in 1418, and in 1425. Died 1427. = An only daughter and heiress, by whom the lands of Carnys and Whitburn passed to the Crichtons.

The names of the issue of John and the other issue of William are unknown. William de Carnys, Vicar of Glammis, 1440-1460, Laurence de Carnys, also an ecclesiastic, and John, Bailie of Edinburgh in 1462, were probably descendants in the second generation. The seal of Bartholomew de Carnys of 1476 seems to indicate he was the eldest son of a grandson of John.

JOHN Heir of his uncle Alexander the Provost. Born probably 1385. Custumar of Linlithgow, 1406-1422. In a lease dated 1421 he is referred to as cousin of Crawford of Trarinzean, and in charter of 1441, as son of William and nephew of Alexander. Died 1456. = ELIZABETH - - - mentioned in charter of 1421.

FOR ISSUE SEE TABLE II. FACING P. 70.

WILLIAM, LORD CRICHTON, Chancellor of Scotland. Guardian of King James II. during his minority. Died 1455.

JAMES of Frendraucht, created Earl of Moray in 1455. Ancestor of the Lords Frendraucht, the last of whom accompanied James II. of England to France, and died without issue, when the title became extinct. Other descendants include the Marquis of Bute, the Maitland-Mackgill-Crichtons of Rankeilour, and probably the Earls of Erne.

AGNES, wife of the Lord of Glammis.

GEORGE DE CRICHTON DE CARNYS—Was a Knight 1439 — Admiral of Scotland 1449 — Succeeded to all the Cairns estates — Created Earl of Caithness 1452 (see charter page 11, note). Died 1455. = 1st a daughter of Sir William Douglas of Strathbrock. = 2nd, JANET Borthwick, widow of James Douglas, Lord Dalkeith.

AGNES HEPBURN = JAMES, of Ruthven, mentioned as brother of George in charter of 1452. Provost of Edinburgh, 1478.

ADAM, of Ruthven.

JAMES, of Ruthven. The Crichtons of Ruthven are mentioned in charters up to the 17th century.

SIR JAMES DE CRICHTON DE CARNYS succeeded only to his father's hereditary estates, the Cairns properties, and not to the Earldom of Caithness. The hero of the Siege of Blackness Castle, 1453. Died 1492. = - - - Levenax.

PATRICK and JOHN mentioned in charter 1491.

JANET wife of John, son and heir of Robert Lord Maxwell. A natural daughter born during the subsistence of her mother's marriage with her first husband. Granted succession to Barntoun in 1453.

SIR JAMES DE CRICHTON DE CARNYS, mentioned in charter of 1472 with his wife Margaret, obtained grants of lands in Perth, and was Coroner of the County in 1493.

ANDREW and ARCHIBALD (a natural son).

MARGARET and MARION.

SIR JOHN DE CRICHTON, Dominus de Strathurd (1529). Sold the old estate of Cairns to John Tennant about 1550. = JANET SINCLAIR, mentioned in charter, 1535.

CHAPTER II.

Some contemporary Scottish History.

A CHAPTER devoted to a brief account of the Earls of Douglas, Lords of Galloway, who were overlords of the branch of the Cairns family settled in Galloway in the first half of the fifteenth century, may be thought somewhat beyond the proper compass of this work; but as, owing to the almost kingly position of the house of Douglas during this period, the history of the Earls from about 1400 to 1456 is practically a history of Scotland, such a chapter may serve to convey in a measure to the reader the condition of society generally in Scotland at the time.

The opening year of the fifteenth century was the last in the life of the celebrated Archibald the Grim, Earl Douglas and Lord of Galloway, a man whose extraordinary sagacity and unparalleled valour, combined with immense ambition, had raised him practically to kingship in Galloway. Although illegitimate by birth, such was his influence that he not only compelled Robert II. to formally ratify his legitimacy, but two years later demanded and obtained from Robert III. the hand of Margaret, Princess Royal of Scotland, for his eldest son and heir. Head of a house whose members had intermarried on no less than twelve occasions with the Royal families of Scotland or England, his acknowledgment of the King of Scotland as his overlord, if existing, was merely nominal. Such was his power in Galloway that he had compelled all the barons in that territory to surrender their charters of land to him, in all cases forcing them to accept fresh tenures from himself, on condition of fealty and military service. He was thus able at any time to bring together a formidable army and navy, which he on several occasions did in his incursions into the border counties, and even into Ireland and the Isle of Man, whence his followers brought spoil, no doubt amply sufficient to reconcile them to having to acknowledge him as their Lord Paramount. He habitually assembled his baronage in his local Parliament, in which laws were discussed, framed, and promulgated. Being ready for war secures peace, and the territories of the Earl were enjoying such a spell of quiet under his system of administration, that on his death, in 1401, his eldest son and successor, Archibald, the 4th Earl, a born warrior, could find no one near home to fight with. But in the following year we find him at the head of a Scottish army on an expedition, hardly of international importance, but of the character of a border fray of unusual dimensions. The expedition ended disastrously at the Battle of Homildon Hill, where the Scots were utterly routed by Hotspur. We next find the Earl in league with Hotspur against Henry IV. of England. At the Battle of Shrewsbury in 1403, Hotspur was killed and Douglas taken prisoner. His captivity was prolonged, and fearing troubles at home in his absence, he obtained a letter of protection from Henry IV. to Alexander de Carnys, Provost of Lincluden, which secured the safety not only of the College and Abbey of Lincluden, but of the Earl's property. We shall, however, refer in detail to this letter, and to the Provost's intercourse with Henry IV. at this period, in a subsequent chapter.

During the Earl's captivity he was, "owing to the prompting of affection toward our beloved cousin," treated by Henry IV. more as a personal friend than as a prisoner, so that on his liberation on the payment of his ransom, the Earl desisted for a time from assailing the subjects of the English King. The reverses of the French armies against the English, however, were more than the warrior Earl could hear of with equanimity, and in 1422 he joined Charles VI. That King, elated on securing the services of so bold a warrior, created him Duke of Touraine and Lieutenant-General of the French forces. His honours were, however, but shortlived, as in 1424 he was killed at the sanguinary battle of Verneuil. His equerry, John de Carnys,[1] nephew to the Provost, escaped with his life.

Archibald Douglas was succeeded in the Earldom by his eldest son, also Archibald; but by his will the suzerainty of Galloway passed to his widow the Lady Margaret, in which she was confirmed by charter of James I. at the Castle of Threave. She ruled as Queen in Galloway for sixteen years, dying in the same year as her son the 5th Earl, 1439. She is recorded to have been a woman of marvellous ability, of sweet disposition, feared yet loved by all her dependents; withal a worthy upholder of the dignity and might of the house of Douglas. She was buried with great pomp. Her remains were conveyed from

[1] Charter at Lochnaw Castle, 1421. "John de Carnis, Scutifer Comitis." See ensuing chapter. Scutifer is, of course, literally a shield bearer

her Castle of Threave to the Abbey of Lincluden, which owed much to her piety and generosity, and there they were laid to rest in the chapel which she had munificently endowed. Her beautiful monument is in fair preservation still, and not far from it is the tomb of Alexander de Carnys the Provost of the Abbey, the close and faithful friend of her husband.

On the death almost simultaneously of the Princess Margaret and her son the 5th Earl, David the eldest son of the latter succeeded to the chieftainship of the house as 6th Earl. He was then only a little over fifteen, while his next brother William was thirteen; the youngest of the family, then under ten years old, was Margaret, known to fame as the Fair Maid of Galloway.

At this time, as recorded in the last chapter, the Government, during the childhood of King James II., was in the hands of his guardians, William Lord Crichton and Sir Alexander Livingston. Crichton at the moment had possession of his ward in Edinburgh Castle. These two, agreeing in nothing else, both foresaw with alarm for their own future the power that must in the course of a few years be in the hands of the young Douglas, and together planned what is probably the most fiendish piece of villainy recorded in history. Under pretence of friendship they invited the two brothers to Edinburgh to meet the young King, then about their own age; on the 24th November, 1440, they arrived at the Castle. During the progress of supper, at which the King was present, Livingston and Crichton suddenly arose, and in cold blood murdered the two boys with their own hands. Not all the pleadings and prayers, nor the bitter tears of the boy King served to stay the hands of the assassins, or save the lives of his playmates.

On the death of the 6th Earl, the titular Lordship of Galloway, with its vast possessions, passed to his sister the Fair Maid of Galloway, while the Earldom of Douglas passed to the next male heir, his granduncle James the Gross, younger son of Archibald the Grim, who thus became 7th Earl. Celebrated for little but his corpulency, he allowed nothing to disturb his peace of mind, and made no effective protest against the crime. He died in 1443, and was succeeded by his son William, 8th Earl.

Earl William, utterly unscrupulous and ambitious, crafty, clearheaded, and of iron will, cast longing eyes upon the Lordship of Galloway, now alienated from his Earldom. He lost no time in putting his wife out of the way, and, supported by the young King, applied to the Pope to sanction an unholy marriage with the Fair Maid of Galloway. His consent obtained, the marriage took place, though the bride at the time was only twelve years of age.

Having thus secured for himself through his wife, the Lordship of Galloway, he maintained the traditions of Archibald the Grim and the Princess Margaret by his wisdom and justice, and the firmness of his hand in the government of his territory. He assembled the Barons of Galloway and Annandale in his Parliament regularly as his grandfather had done, and so widely were his administrative powers recognised that he was appointed by the Council of Regency, Lieutenant General of Scotland during the King's minority—a position which he filled with dignity for several years. Holding himself above the unseemly squabbles of Livingston and Crichton, he nevertheless used his position of authority to build up for himself a power in the kingdom superior to that of Royalty itself. He formed with the Earl of Crawford, and others of lesser importance, a secret alliance, offensive and defensive, against all assailants, including even the King himself. To those who joined with him the Earl was a firm friend, enabling them to work their will upon outsiders. An example is found in the case of John de Auchinleck, a partisan of the Earl's. Having frequently raided the lands and property of the Colvilles of Ochiltree, and having been as often saved by Douglas from pursuit and revenge, he was at last met by Colville when outside the range of assistance from his patron. Old scores were soon settled, and Auchinleck slain. The Earl upon this at once proceeded to Ochiltree, grossly maltreated the tenants of Colville, whose castle he stormed, hanging him over his own gate.[1]

Hitherto Douglas had exercised his regal powers nominally on the King's behalf, and his rule had been

[1] A cadet of this family came to Ireland among the Scottish planters in 1609. His son Alexander, after graduating in Trinity College, where he obtained his D.D., was presented with the livings of Skerry and Rathcavan and Carnmoney. He speculated largely in landed property, one of his first purchases being a portion of M'Quillan's lands of Glenagherty, of which a portion is the present Galgorm estate of the Rt. Hon. John Young, D.L. At Galgorm he is said to have made the acquaintance of the Devil, with whom he made a most advantageous bargain by means of a trick. As a result of this bargain, or by other means, he accumulated a vast fortune, his son Sir Robert Colville inheriting his tastes as a land speculator, and purchasing large estates in Co. Down and elsewhere. These included the present Lord Londonderry's estate, which he purchased from the representatives of the last Earl of Mount Alexander. After the death of Sir Robert Colville, many of the scattered portions of his estates were sold, the remainder passing to his heiress, who married a member of the Moore family, from whom descend the Earls of Mountcashel.

Ochiltree passed from the Colvilles to the Stuarts, whose descendants, the lineal heads of this ancient and Royal family, are the Earls of Castlestuart.

popular, but latterly his arrogance got the better of his judgment. James II., now growing to manhood, desired to take upon himself the reins of government, but the Earl declined to submit to any control or to modify his conduct, finally defying and even insulting the King's emissaries. After several attempts on the part of the King, guided by the counsel of the good Bishop Kennedy, to bring the Earl to reason and submission, a crisis arose owing to the occurrence of a case similar to that of Colville of Ochiltree.

The partisans of Douglas having several times raided the lands of Sir John Herries, whose appeals for redress were all in vain, the latter at last took the law into his own hands, and making a counter raid upon his assailants, succeeded in recovering a part of his missing goods and cattle. A complaint was at once lodged with Douglas, who immediately summoned Herries to his court, where he was duly tried, and, with an utter mockery of justice, found guilty of stealing his own goods, and sentenced to execution. In haste the King's sheriff, M'Clellan of Bomby, dispatched messengers to the King, then at Stirling; with all speed they returned with a Royal mandate ordering the release of Herries. This Douglas treated with contempt, and forthwith ordered the sentence of his court to be carried out. Herries was hanged at Threave as a common malefactor. Against this barbarity and disobedience to the King, M'Clellan, as in duty bound, officially protested in the King's name. Enraged at his intervention, Douglas ordered his arrest. The sheriff, naturally defending himself from those sent to effect his arrest, a scuffle ensued, and one of Douglas's men was killed; whereupon M'Clellan shut himself up in his Castle of Raeberry, a fortress considered practically impregnable. The bribery of a sentry, however, enabled the Earl to gain admission, and he personally seized M'Clellan and bore him back to Threave where he cast him into his dungeon. Adam Lord Grey and his brother Patrick, maternal uncles of M'Clellan, and fellow-members with him of the Royal Household, were on duty at Court when the news arrived of their nephew's plight. They at once sought audience of the King and begged his assistance; he, thinking more of the necessity of saving his sheriff than of the insult to his own authority, wrote "ane richt sweit letter to ye Earl Douglas," not commanding this time, but imploring him to deliver up the person of his sheriff and servant M'Clellan to Sir Patrick Grey. Sir Patrick started in all haste with the letter and arrived at Threave just as the Earl was rising from table. On seeing him, Douglas divined his errand, but went to meet him with elaborate protestations of cordiality and welcome in the outer hall. Under the plea that it was ill talking between a full man and a starving, he gained time while Sir Patrick was dining to have M'Clellan's head cut off, before the messenger had been able to introduce the subject of his mission.

Having feasted his visitor right well he expressed himself honoured by a visit from the King's familiar servant, and on being handed the letter he assured Sir Patrick that any command or request of the King would be thankfully complied with, not only because of his loyalty to the King, but of his friendship to himself. Having reverently opened and read the Royal letter, he turned to Sir Patrick, and taking his arm, led him out to the green, where was spread a white cloth. This being raised, the Earl, affecting surprise, exclaimed " Sir Patrick, you are a little too late ; your sister's son wants his head, but his body is at his Majesty's service." Grey called for his horse, and having hastily mounted, he fiercely retorted " my Lord, as I live, you shall dearly pay for this day's work." The fleetness of his horse and the few minutes' start alone saved him from hanging on the oft used gallows knob of Threave[1].

On his arrival at Stirling Castle, where he laid this alarming news before his master, the King's rage knew no bounds. He saw the futility of the policy of conciliation which, notwithstanding Douglas's oft repeated offences, he had pursued towards him for several years[2]. He now saw clearly that unless he could bring Douglas to submission, his rule in more than name was at an end. Some counselled an appeal to arms in a determined effort to crush the powerful rebel at once, but James, doubting his power to successfully oppose such a combination as Douglas could command through his alliance with Earl Crawford and others, decided once more to endeavour to win him over by conciliatory means.

He wrote to the Earl, gently remonstrating with him on his disloyalty and begging him, under solemn promises of safety and assurances of personal affection, to come to him at Stirling to discuss matters. Under this promise, and possibly softened somewhat by the King's evident disposition

1 Agnew's "Hereditary Sheriffs of Galloway," vol. I., chap. XIV.

2 He had, in pursuance of this policy, granted Douglas rich tracts of forfeited estates, and shown him many marks of Royal favour, being judiciously blind to offences he could hardly punish.

towards him, the Earl arrived at Stirling Castle on the 20th of February, 1452. He was received with cordial welcome and pleasant words, and after a hearty supper the King dismissed all in attendance to talk with Douglas alone. He reminded him of the many favours he had hitherto shown him and held out hopes of more to come, and in memory of the loyalty of his forbears begged him to alter his conduct and give up his treasonable intrigues. At this point the Earl scornfully replied that nothing would make him break his engagements with his friends. "Then this must," replied the King, as, maddened with rage, he plunged a dagger into Douglas. The noise of the scuffle reached those outside the room. Sir Patrick Grey rushed in to find the murderer of his nephew in grips with the King, and without delay split his skull with his battle axe: and the others following him, the corpse of the Earl was heaved through the upper window into the courtyard below.

The news of the Earl's death spread like wildfire through the length and breadth of Scotland. An army from Galloway and Annandale, led by his brothers, was soon hammering at the gates; but though they many times outnumbered the garrison, the Castle held out. Trusted messengers sent out by Bishop Kennedy from St. Andrews, hastily assembled a host of the Gordons and others, who were in time to intercept a great army raised by the Earl of Crawford coming from the North to join the Galloway army at Stirling. Crawford was defeated, and the wily Bishop seizing the opportunity to bring his marvellous tact and diplomacy to bear, by promises of forgiveness and rewards, induced Earl Crawford to throw in his lot with the

King. The two armies thus united were augmented by thousands who hastened to join the Royal Standard, while the army of the Douglases began to melt away like snow in the sunshine.

Thus for ever was broken the power of the House of Douglas. At a Parliament held in Edinburgh in the June following, the assassination of Douglas was declared to be a legal act; the new Earl, James, brother of William, and his two brothers were attainted and declared enemies of the State, and the lands of the Earldom of Douglas forfeited to the Crown. Out of these the King rewarded many of his loyal followers, foremost among whom in Galloway were Sir Gilbert Kennedy, Sir Herbert Maxwell, and Sir Andrew Agnew, the latter at this time receiving also a charter conferring upon him and his heirs male for ever, the Sheriffdom of Galloway, a title held by his descendants for over three hundred years.

James, 9th Earl of Douglas, remained in hiding for some months and finally threw himself upon the mercy of the King, who was ever ready to forgive. He was received into favour, but the lands of the Earldom having been granted to others, he was Earl Douglas but in name. However, to remedy this, the King presented him with the hand of the lately widowed Fair Maid of Galloway who still enjoyed the titular Lordship thereof. This in spite of the indignant protests of the unfortunate lady, whose horror of the new marriage was entirely ignored. Being doubly within the prohibited degrees, a Papal dispensation had to be obtained from Pope Nicholas[1].

[1] It bore date February 26, 1451. The Fair Maid was then but 23 years old.

All having been now made comfortable for the Earl at home, the King conferred a further mark of favour upon him by appointing him special Envoy to the English Court, a piece of folly that can only be excused when we reflect that the King was possibly in utter ignorance of the fact that the Earl was in secret correspondence with the English with a view of securing the complete restoration of his house, if not of actually placing him upon the Throne of Scotland.

So secretly had Douglas matured his plans, and so swiftly had he acted, that the first intimation of treachery gained by James was the appearance of the Earl with his three brothers the Earls of Moray and Ormonde and Lord Balvany, with an immense host, at Stirling, where they laid siege to the Castle in which the King was holding his court. So unprepared were the inmates, that it is generally believed that had Douglas pressed home the assault without loss of time, he would have made himself master of the Kingdom. A fatal delay occurred, during which the astute Kennedy found opportunity to work individually upon the fears or the avarice of several of the Earl's followers, thereby secretly detaching them from his cause.

The delay was thus increased, while some of Kennedy's emissaries secretly escaped from the Castle and roused to action the nobles loyal to the King. An army was being hastily assembled from Wigton, Kirkcudbright, and Annandale when the Earl, hearing thereof, promptly raised the siege and fell upon the gathering army at Arkenholme. The battle was long and fierce, but ended in the utter route of the Douglases. The Earl of Moray was killed[1], and the Earl of Ormonde was made prisoner and executed, the heads of both being impaled for public view. Earl Douglas escaped to England, whence he never returned, and the youngest brother, Lord Balvany, escaped, probably finding refuge in England.

The Parliament of 1455 formally annexed the Lordship of Galloway to the Crown, all those who held their land under the Douglases being confirmed therein as holding direct from the Crown. The King made a State progress through the Lordship, receiving in person the homage of the landowners, which was everywhere joyfully accorded. The Castle of Threave, where was the Lady Margaret, evidently an unwilling rebel, alone held out against the King. The island fortress, with its walls of immense thickness, withstood all efforts of the besiegers. The small cannon of the period had no effect upon either the doors or the walls. The King's adherents, determined upon its downfall, subscribed to furnish such a piece of artillery as would have the desired power, and the services of a blacksmith, M'Min by name, being requisitioned, he succeeded in welding together that triumph of Scottish ordnance known as "Mons Meg."[2] This addition to the arms of the besiegers had the desired effect, and the Castle soon capitulated, its unhappy owner, the Lady Margaret Douglas, throwing herself on the King's mercy, which he readily extended to her. It is pleasant to relate

[1] The Earldom of Moray was conferred upon Sir James Crichton (son of the Chancellor), who had married the daughter of Douglas, Earl of Moray. See ante, p. 12.

[2] So says Agnew. Without presuming to dispute the accuracy of Sir Andrew Agnew's account of the origin of Mons Meg, it is undoubtedly open to controversy. Other writers record that it was made at Mons, in Belgium, in 1476, and this is usually accepted as correct.

that this celebrated lady had brighter days before her. Hitherto she had been held a prisoner by the brothers, the Earls William and James, to whom she had been successively married, against her will, for her possessions. She shortly afterwards married, not unwillingly, the King's half-brother, the Duke of Athole, by whom she had issue.

Before taking his departure from Galloway, the King conferred a charter on the town of Kirkcudbright[1], its first Provost being M'Clellan of Bomby, son of the victim of the 8th Earl Douglas. He also conferred rewards upon several of his followers who had assisted him at Threave, among these being John Cairnis, grand nephew and heir of the venerable Provost of Lincluden. The services rendered by Cairnis, and his rewards, will be referred to in the next chapter.

[1] "Hereditary Sheriffs of Galloway," vol., I. p. 274.

CHAPTER III.

The Sons of William of Carnys, 1360—1422.

WE must now revert to the family of William Carnys of that ilk, and of Whitburn in Linlithgowshire—referred to in chapter I. He had at least four sons, Duncan (his heir), John, William, and Alexander. It is also probable that Thomas, an ecclesiastic, and Richard, merchant in Edinburgh, were fifth and sixth sons respectively, but there is no direct evidence available. In 1365, John was one of the Bailies of Linlithgow, in which burgh he had established himself as a merchant. His choice of Linlithgow as his place of business was natural, owing to the influence of his family in the district. He had the honour of securing the King as one of his customers, and supplied him with two casks of wine at a cost of £13 6s. 8d.[1] In the same year he was paid eleven shillings and seven pence for "carriages made for the King's wardrobe." It thus seems evident his business as a merchant was of a miscellaneous kind. We find he received a charter from David II. of "the place called the Peill of Linlithgow, within the burgh of Linlithgow, he being obliged to build it against the

[1] Exchequer Rolls, 1365, vol. II., p. 221. No other payments to John de Carnys for wine for the King's use are recorded, and we fear he got no repeat orders. As it is certain David II. never became a teetotaller, we regret to have to infer that John de Carnys at the commencement of his career as a merchant, either charged His Majesty too much for his liquor, or worse still, supplied him with a bad article.

King's coming."[1] It seems uncertain whether he carried out this contract. No payments are recorded for the work in the Exchequer Rolls, but probably he was to be recompensed by rents of part of the lands surrounding the tower. The original Roll in which the charter was recorded is lost, so its terms can only be surmised.

That John Carnys was considered an expert architect of fortified buildings, whether his experience was gained in building the Peill of Linlithgow or not, is proved by his securing the contract for the erection of the Great Tower by the gate of Edinburgh Castle in 1372.

In 1369 he was appointed to the important position of Custumar of the Burgh of Linlithgow, the port of this town, Blackness, being then one of the important seaports of the Kingdom. The duties of this office were to collect the specified duties on all merchandise exported from or imported to the various custumar's districts. The custumar had considerable power in the levying of these duties, and made his annual returns in person before the Council. That the office was one of considerable emolument is evident from an enactment of the Parliament of 1363-4 appointing tronars, whose duties were to check the weights returned by the custumars and prevent fraud. They were paid by the weight of merchandise passed through the tron, or weigh house. Thus, while the custumar might have made a nice little income by making false returns of the weights, the tronar was there to see that he didn't.

[1] Robertson's Index of Lost Scottish Charters. Date a little uncertain, probably 1361. A "Peill" is a fortified tower. This charter is referred to in Bell's Castles of the Lothians, the date being referred to as 1350, a manifest error.

John de Carnys occupied the custumarship up to 1401, when he died. Annual returns of his office are recorded in the audits held before the Council from 1369 to 1401. The entries are all much alike, the amounts collected and disbursed of course varying. In the return for 1377, the custumar is referred to as "Esquire to the Earl of Carrick" (afterwards Robert III.).

The most interesting references to John de Carnys in the Exchequer Rolls, however, are the records in the Chamberlain's accounts of the payments made to him in connection with his contract for the building of the new tower near the gate of the Castle of Edinburgh. The items are given in detail, and amount in all to £736 13s. 0d. The payments extend from 1367 to 1379, a period of twelve years. The first payments on this account were to William de Guppyld in 1367. The work seems to have proceeded but slowly until 1372, when the payments were for the first time made to John de Carnys and occasionally to his brother William. From this date the payments, at any rate, became more rapid, and the building was completed in 1379. It was known as King David's Tower, and was at the time considered a masterpiece of fortification, and absolutely impregnable. It was the most striking feature of the whole castle. The introduction of cannon into warfare during the following centuries, however, entirely changed the requirements of fortification, and this massive tower, so long deemed indestructible, fell a victim to the artillery of the Earl of Morton at the siege of 1573. It was superseded by the half-moon battery still forming such an imposing background to the esplanade.

The records tell us of the death of John de Carnys in 1401. He was succeeded in the office of Custumar of Linlithgow by his nephew John, son of William. This John did not take up the active duties of the office until 1406; in the interim the returns were presented by "deputies of John de Carnys lately deceased." It is reasonable to believe that the office was being kept open for the coming of age of the young custumar. Of him we shall treat later.

Of the next member of William de Carnys' family, also William, apparently the third son, we have pretty frequent mention in the records. His name first appears, curious to say, in the accounts of the town of Calais in 1369. At this time the English and Scots were enjoying a period of friendship, and this young soldier, with many of his countrymen, volunteered for service under the King of England in his French wars. We cannot discover when William de Carnys enlisted in the English service, but in 1369 the treasurer of Calais paid to "Patrick de la Chambrè, William de Carnys, and William Egelyn (William de Eglintoun ?), Scotsmen in the King's service, for wages, forty shillings each, and twenty shillings each to their six vallets";[1] the period of service remunerated by this princely salary is not mentioned. In the same year William de Carnys retired from the English service to take up the important position of Constable of Linlithgow. The accounts of his constableship were returned somewhat intermittently, and present no feature of special interest. He joined with his brother John in the building of King David's

[1] Calendar of Documents relating to Scotland, Vol. IV., No. 165.

Tower, and in 1379, the year the tower was finished, he was promoted to be Constable of Edinburgh Castle. He held this position up to 1401, when he received a pension, but the year of his death is not recorded. He had at least one son, John, above named. It is very probable that both he and his brother John had other issue, but it is impossible to trace, among the several references to members of the family, ecclesiastics, burgesses, and bailies of Linlithgow and Edinburgh in the years following, from which of the two brothers, John or William, they descend. From the crescent in the fess point, and the label in the chief of the shield of arms of Bartholomew de Carnis, Bailie of Edinburgh in 1460, it may be with much probability inferred that he was an eldest son—that his father was then living—and that the latter was direct in descent from the second son of the head of his family, namely, from John de Carnys, second son of William of the 1363 charter.[1] The identity of John, the younger Custumar of Linlithgow, is proved by one of the Douglas charters, to which reference will be made hereafter. The various members of the family in Edinburgh, Linlithgow, and elsewhere, whose precise genealogy is uncertain, will be referred to in a separate chapter.

The fourth and eventually the most distinguished of the sons of William of the 1363 charter was Alexander, an ecclesiastic. Early in life he formed what proved to be a life-long friendship with the house of Douglas. In a most interesting document among the Douglas charters in possession of Lord Home, it is recorded that some time prior to

[1] See Chapter X. on Armorial Bearings and Seals.

the date of the document (which is undated, but was probably written about 1385), Archibald the Grim, Earl Douglas, had granted to the abbot and convent of Melrose Abbey the patronage of the living of Great Cavers, then in his gift. Notwithstanding this transference of the patronage, on the next vacancy occurring Earl Douglas presented Alexander de Carnys to the living. This rather high-handed action caused the resentment of the Abbot of Melrose, who insisted on presenting his own nominee, as he was entitled to do, and a serious dispute arose between Douglas and the ecclesiastics of Melrose.

A solution of the difficulty, however, was arrived at by the intervention of the Bishop of St. Andrews, referred to in the document as a relative of Alexander.[1] He offered him another living, which, although not so good, Alexander, with a desire to settle the difficulty, accepted. The alternative living is not referred to by name in the document, but a charter in the possession of the family of Maxwell of Terregles (also undated, but undoubtedly of date circ. 1400), is attested by "Eliseus, Provost of Lyncludane," and "Alexander de Carnys, Rector of Forest." From this we may infer that the living to which Alexander was appointed in lieu of Great Cavers, was that of Forest, unless he had held a living between the time of his resignation of the former and his appointment to the latter.

[1] It is unfortunate that the date of this document cannot be definitely fixed, as the uncertainty makes it impossible for us to determine to which Bishop of St. Andrews the Cairns family was related. William Landal occupied the See for the remarkably long period of forty-four years, 1341—1385; his successor was Walter Trail, 1385—1401. On the whole, the circumstances suggest that the compromise was effected by the latter. If this is correct, a relationship, of uncertain degree, existed between the families of Cairns and Trail.

Eliseus, Provost of Lincluden, still held that office in June, 1404, when letters of safe conduct were granted by Henry IV. of England to Sir John Herries, Sir William Borthwick, and "Elias, Provost of Lynclowden," with twenty attendants, coming into England for six weeks.[1] This Elias, or Eliseus, whose surname is not recorded, was the first Provost of the Abbey and newly-formed College of Lincluden. He does not appear in any of the records as Provost later than 1404, while Alexander de Carnys is first referred to as Provost in 1408. It seems probable, however, that he succeeded to the provostship in 1405; at any rate he had then been received into the confidence of the Princess Margaret of Douglas, for we find that in that year he, with Sir Thomas Murray and Sir William Douglas of Drumlanrig, was entrusted with a mission to England[2] to confer with, and open negotiations for the release of Earl Douglas, who had been a prisoner since the battle of Shrewsbury in 1403.

He returned on a similar journey in 1407.[3] This captivity of the Earl's lasted apparently no less than fifteen years, but during it he was most kindly treated by Henry IV., and was allowed on several occasions to return home for periods of some months, his place as prisoner being taken by many hostages of high importance. He was also allowed free intercourse, by confidential messengers, with his Countess and friends at home. While holding the Earl as his prisoner under heavy ransom, there are many

[1] Calendar of Documents relating to Scotland, IV. No. 658.

[2] Chancery Files, Bundle No. 487.

[3] Privy Seals (Tower), 9 Henry IV., File 10.

evidences of Henry IV.'s desire to cause him as little personal inconvenience as possible, and at the same time to secure that his estate and friends should not suffer by the absence of their natural protector. This kindly feeling is fully established in the following letter of safe protection under the King's sign manual, addressed to Alexander de Carnys from the Royal Castle at Pontefract, where the Court was sitting[1] :—

"REX universis et singulis capitaneis castellanis custodibus castrorum et aliorum fortaliciarum et eorum locorum tenentibus in marchiis regni nostri anglie versus partes Scocie ac aliis fidelibus et subditis suis tam infra libertates quam extra ad quos presentes litteræ pervenerint, salutem. Sciatis quod intuitu caritatis et ad specialem requisitionem dilecte consanguinei nostri Archebaldi Comitis de Douglas suscepimus et suscipimus per presentes in protectionem tuicionem et defensionem nostras speciales Magistrum Alexandrum de Carnys prepositum Ecclesie Collegiate de Lincludane in Scocia ubicunque ipsum prepositum infra regnum Scocie personaliter fore contegerit, ac dictum locum de Lyncludane et capellanes pauperes ibidem Deo servientes necnon terras predicte prepositi dicte Ecclesie circumjacentes una cum grangiis bladis catallis et aliis bonis et rebus suis quibuscunque tam ecclesiasticis quam temporalibus. Et ideo vobis et cuilibet vestrum mandamus quod eidem preposito ubicunque ipsum infra dictum regnum Scocie personaliter fore contigerit, aut dicte loco suo de Lyncludane seu Cappellanis et pauperibus ibidem Deo servientibus in personis terris grangiis bladis bonis catallis aut rebus quibuscumque

[1] Patents, 1-11 Henry IV., m. 5.

supra dictis non inferatis vel inferri permetatis injuriam molestiam dampnum violenciam impedimentum aliquod seu gravamen. Et si quid eis in aliquo premissorum forisfactum fuerit vel injuriatum id eis sine dilacione debite corrigi et reformari faciat. Proviso semper quod idem prepositus aut capellani et pauperes predicte Deo servientes sive tenente, sui infra dictum locum de Lyncludane aut dictas terras predicti prepositi commorantes et residentes quicquamquod in nostri regni seu populi nostri anglie dampnum prejudicium vel inquietacionem cedere valeat, non faciant attemptent seu prosequantur quovis modo. In cujus etc. pertriennium duratura. Teste Rege apud Castrum de Pount freyt xx. die Aprilis [1408].

"PER IPSUM REGEM."

Put into English this letter reads:—

"THE KING to all and singular the captains, castellans, and custodians of castles and other forts, and their deputies in the Marches of our Kingdom of England, lying towards Scotland, and to his other loyal and dutiful subjects either within or without his dominions to whom this present letter may come, greeting. Know ye, that being prompted by affection, and at the special request of our dearly beloved cousin Archibald Earl of Douglas, we have taken and do hereby take under our special protection, safe keeping and defence, Master Alexander de Carnys, Provost of the Collegiate Church of Lincluden in Scotland, wheresoever the said Provost may happen to be in person within the Kingdom of Scotland; also the said place of Lincluden and the poor chaplains serving God therein; also the lands of the said Provost round the church, with his granges, crops, cattle and goods of whatever sort whether ecclesiastical or temporal. Therefore we command you and each of you that ye neither inflict nor allow to be inflicted any injury, molestation, loss, violence, interference or any other hardship, upon the said Provost wheresoever he may be in person in the said Kingdom of Scotland, or upon the said place of Lincluden, or upon the chaplains and poor men serving God in the said place, either on their persons, lands, granges, crops, goods, cattle or property of any kind whatever aforesaid. And if any robbery or injury shall have been done to them in any of their premises, ye shall immediately make compensation and restitution. Provided always that the said Provost or chaplains and poor men serving God or dwelling in the said place of Lincluden, or sojourning or residing on the said lands of the aforesaid Provost, shall neither do nor attempt to do anything whatsoever that may result in any loss, prejudice, or disquiet to our Kingdom or our people of England. This (mandate) to remain in force for three years. In testimony whereof, &c., the King, at the Castle of Pontefract, this twentieth day of April [1408].

"BY THE KING'S OWN HAND[1]."

[1] "Per ipsum Regem"—by the King himself. The King usually affixed his sign manual only to the more important State documents, others merely bearing the Royal Seal, with the words, "by the King's command." It must be borne in mind that in giving the words of ancient charters, &c., we can in most cases only quote the official copies in the State Records. These were often condensed, being only intended for official reference. In issuing a charter under the Great Seal, or a Royal missive, only the original document issued bore the actual signatures and seals of the grantors or the witnesses thereto. Of the many thousand charters recorded in the Register of the Great Seal of Scotland, it is probably safe to say that not ten per cent. of the very early original documents exist, and not two per cent. are available to the ordinary historian. The State copies in the registers were made as each document was issued, and were engrossed, the earliest on great parchment rolls, the later

Thus placed under Royal protection, the College of Lincluden prospered under the provostship of Alexander de Carnys. The community increased, and grew to consist of eight prebendaries, twenty-four bedesmen, and a chaplain.[1] So renowned for his wisdom and tact had the Provost become, that in 1410 he was selected by the Regent Albany as one of three envoys sent to the English Court to conclude a peace. This mission consisted of Sir William Hay of Lochorwart, Sir William Borthwick, and the Provost of Lincluden. They met the English envoys at Hawdenstank, and a truce was concluded for one year[2], at the expiration of which (May, 1411) a further conclave took place, also at Hawdenstank[3], when an indefinite truce was concluded. The Scottish envoys on the second occasion were the Bishops of St. Andrews and Glasgow, the Earls of Douglas and March, Alexander de Carnys, and John Morton, with Sir William Hay, Sir William Borthwick, and Sir William Graham. The English Envoys were the Bishops of Durham and Bath, the Earls of Warwick and Westmoreland, the Baron of Hilton, with Sir Thomas

in book form. The writing is often cramped and almost impossible to decipher, and the difficulty in doing so is enormously added to by the use of extraordinary contractions of the Latin words, many of which are purely mediæval Latin. Through the herculean efforts of the Keepers of the Records in the three Kingdoms, many of the existing registers and documents have been published in readable form, with elaborate indices and most useful prefaces, rendering researches comparatively simple. Of the ancient Scottish State documents connected with the Cairnses, referred to in this work, the great majority are merely the official copies in the registers, the most important original being the Douglas charter of the estate of Cults to John de Carnys, nephew of the Provost. This interesting old parchment is in the charter chest at Lochnaw Castle, and is the property of Sir Andrew N. Agnew, Bart., M.P.

[1] McDowall. "Chronicles of Lincluden," p. 54.

[2] Scottish Documents, Chapter House, Box 95, No. 5M.

[3] Privy Seals (Tower), 12 Henry IV., File 4, and Miscellaneous Rolls, No. 459.

Grey and Sir Robert Umraville. The preliminaries of this most important meeting and the terms of truce had been provisionally drawn up beforehand by the Provost of Lincluden and the Bishop of St. Andrews, Sir John Stewart Lord of Lorne, and John Busby, Canon of Moray. Their letters of safe conduct from Scotland to England for this purpose were issued at Westminster in April, 1411[1], the final truce being concluded some time in May.

Towards the autumn the Provost was again chosen as ambassador, this time on a secret mission to the Court of France. The object of this mission is not recorded; there were three ambassadors, namely—The Lord John Stewart, Lord of Lorne, Master Alexander de Carnys, the Provost, and Master John Trotter.[2] It is probable they prepared to embark for France from Dumfries, close to Lincluden, and from our knowledge of the prevalence of westerly winds in autumn in that district, we can easily account for the fact that the ship in which they intended to sail was storm-bound and unable to undertake the voyage. As the matter for which they were proceeding to the French Court seems to have been urgent, and as the weather held out no hopes of their being able to proceed within reasonable time, a second embassy started from an eastern port and the originally appointed envoys were recalled.[3]

---

[1] Calendar of Documents relating to Scotland, Vol. IV., No. 801.

[2] A name still of distinction in Galloway.

[3] An interesting item appears in the Rolls of the Exchequer, vol. IV., p. 164.—"Et per solucionem factam domino Johanni Senescalli de Loorn, Magistro Alexandro de Carnys, preposito de Linclouden, et Magistro Johanni Trotter, ambassiatoribus ordinatis ad Franciam,

In 1410 the Provost was commissioner for negotiating a day of Border Trews[1], an office requiring no small amount of diplomacy; indeed all accounts tend to prove that he was "an able sagacious man with a diplomatic turn of mind."[1] That he had created this idea in his intercourse with the English Court seems to be borne out by a warrant issued by Henry V. in 1413 to his uncle the Bishop of Winchester, Chancellor, desiring him to see to the safety of Alexander de Carnys, Provost of Lincluden, with his attendants (8 in number) "coming to commune with the King in England." Issued at Westminster, 6th July.[2]

His last recorded journey to England was to secure the release, on payment of ransom, the nature of which he was to negotiate, of James Douglas, who had been taken prisoner, evidently in a border fray, by Sir John Plellyp. The letter of safe conduct for his journey for himself and eight attendants is dated from Westminster, 18th November, 1418.[3] He was at this time about sixty-eight years of age.

Of this remarkable, and, judging from all we know, upright and able ecclesiastic, we have no further record. The date of his death is not absolutely certain. It occurred

qui tamen diu expectantes ventum, in naulo navium ac pluribus expensis magnos fecerunt sumptus licet postmodum fuerunt ex magna causa revocati et non processerunt (pro ipsorum tamen sumptibus et expensis de receptis nichil reddiderunt)—£200." Considering the value of money at that period, these three ambassadors seem to have determined to provide for themselves pretty comfortably!

[1] Chronicles of Lincluden, p. 71.

[2] Privy Seals (Tower), 1 Henry V., File 2.

[3] Miscellaneous Rolls (Tower), No. 459. Rymer's Foedera, 1739–1745 Edition, vol. IX., 646.

in either 1421 or 1422. He was buried in the south transept at Lincluden. The monument erected to his memory, in the course of ages, when the venerable abbey of Lincluden fell into ruins, became buried in debris and was lost, and both it and the memory of the Provost passed for centuries from human ken.

The ruins of the ancient abbey and college were long an object of the keenest interest to antiquaries, but so terrible had been the ravages of time that practically all the interesting monuments and most of the exquisite heraldic and other sculptures lay buried many feet deep in rubbish, rendering the successful investigations of individuals impossible. In 1877 the Dumfries and Galloway Natural History and Antiquarian Society determined to make a strong effort to effect the partial restoration of the ruins, and with this end in view appointed a deputation of two of their members—Mr. J. Gibson Starke, of Troqueer Holm, and Mr. William McDowall, F.S.A., Scot.—to wait upon the landlord of the property, Captain Maxwell of Terregles, with a view to obtain his practical sympathy in their effort. They found him only too anxious to assist as far as lay in his power, but owing to the ground on which the abbey lies being let on lease to a tenant, the actual commencement of the restoration had to be deferred until the expiry of the lease. This occurred in 1882, when Captain Maxwell at once embraced the opportunity, and guided by the skilful advice and practical antiquarian knowledge of Mr. James Barbour, an eminent architect of Dumfries, Mr. William McDowall, and others, the work was carried out.

Of the many most interesting discoveries made in the course of the excavations, it is not within the province of this work to treat in any detail, but an extract from a paper read by Mr. Glover Anderson at a meeting of the Dumfries and Galloway Antiquarian Society in 1877, will not be out of place. Speaking of the abbey he said — "It was undoubtedly the richest work of architecture ever erected in the district ; for lofty solemn grandeur it may not have been able to compare with Sweetheart, but for pure yet lavish decoration there must have been few buildings in the south of Scotland worthy of comparison."

This paper was read, it will be noted, before the excavations were made, but the results of these more than justified all that Mr. Anderson had said.

Unfortunately it was discovered that falling stones and beams, and years of exposure to the weather, had played deplorable havock with most of the beautiful carvings with which the church had been adorned. The recumbent figure of the Princess Margaret, Countess Douglas, was found, but terribly mutilated, broken, and fallen from its place. The tomb itself, however, suffered less, and remains, even with its defects, a magnificent example of mediæval sculpture. Across the base of the monument are nine beautifully carved shields of arms, each set within an arched panel. All the shields are in good preservation, and display the arms of Bruce, Royal Scotland, Stuart, Douglas, and others[1].

---

[1] The late Mr. William McDowall, in his valuable work, *The Chronicles of Lincluden*, furnishes some most interesting information, not only about the many discoveries made during

A monument of less importance, but of much greater interest, so far as the subject of this work is concerned, was that discovered on the floor of the transept, namely, a flat stone, covering the remains of the second Provost of the College, Alexander de Carnys.

Unfortunately, like most of the monuments unearthed, this relic of past ages had suffered greatly from the causes already referred to. It was broken into three pieces, having been buried under the weight of a stratum of stones and rubbish four feet deep, which had accumulated on the floor. It was originally a massive slab of red sandstone, measuring eight feet by four. Round the sides runs an inscribed border, within which is a tree. Entwined round this is a scroll on which is incised in early English characters, "Qui me calcatis pedibus prece subveniatis." "Ye who tread upon me with your feet support me with prayer." The inscription round the border, so far as it can be deciphered, reads—"Hic jacet Magister Alexander de Carnys." The words following, those on the edge of the middle portion of the slab, cannot be made out, though a faint trace of the letters "ec," after an undecipherable space, suggests the following: "Qu (quondam) ecclesie Collegiate de Lyncluden Prepositus." On the opposite edge of the middle portion of the slab are numerals and letters, apparently "XIIII. Jul." The lettering on the bottom portion of the slab is hope-

the excavations referred to here, but also about the history of the abbey and college of Lincluden, and many details of local and national history akin to his subject. The author desires to acknowledge with gratitude the information with regard to Lincluden which he has obtained from this work, and also to thank Mr. Barbour for his kindness in supplying him with a rubbing of the tombstone of the Provost, taken when it was first discovered.

TOMB OF ALEXANDER DE CARNYS
PROVOST OF LINCLUDEN 1422.

lessly obliterated, but with what can be more or less clearly read and what can be inferred, the inscription translated would probably read

HERE LIES MASTER ALEXANDER DE CARNYS,
[SOME TIME PROVOST OF THE COLLEGIATE] CHURCH
[OF LINCLUDEN . . . .
WHO DIED] 14TH JULY [A.D. 1422].

The tree, from which is suspended a shield charged with a fesse, sculptured within the border, will be referred to in a later chapter dealing with the early armorial bearings of the Cairns Family.

CHAPTER IV.

The Cairnses in Galloway—John de Carnys, son of William the Constable—Heir of the Provost—His descendants, the families of Orchardton, Kipp, and Torr.

ALEXANDER DE CARNYS, the Provost of Lincluden, during the term of his office, accumulated a considerable property, not only in Kirkcudbrightshire, but elsewhere. By several charters to be referred to in detail in this chapter, we learn that he possessed the lands of Carsluthe adjoining the river Cree, the neighbouring property of Strothans, and a property called Gilchristcluych in Lanark. During his life he formally appointed as his heir his nephew John de Carnys, son of his brother William, and these properties were conveyed by him to John, the Provost retaining a life interest[1].

[1] In a most interesting document in the charter chest of Sir Andrew N. Agnew at Lochnaw Castle, a lease dated 1421 from John de Crauford de Trarinzean to John de Carnys, of the lands of Cults, Parish of Cruggleton, valuable genealogical information is found. John is therein mentioned by Crauford as his cousin and son of William de Carnys. He is mentioned in a confirmatory charter of the Countess of Douglas in the Register of the Great Seal (see below p. 54) as nephew to the Provost. These two references supply conclusive evidence of the consanguinity of the Provost with John the Custumar of Linlithgow and William the Constable of Edinburgh Castle. Without them, the fact that the Provost was a brother of William and John, however probable it might have appeared, could not be proved. The "cousinship" between Crauford of Trarinzean and John de Carnys also suggests that William de Carnys had married a Crauford. The estate of Cults, leased to John de Carnys, was resigned by Crauford in 1426, and re-granted to William Douglas of Leswalt, so that Carnys held under Douglas. An account of this William Douglas, and how he came to be styled "of Leswalt" and also "of Lochnaw," is given in the late Sir Andrew Agnew's "Hereditary Sheriffs," vol. I., pp. 230-240. Cults remained in possession of the direct heirs of John de Carnys until sold to a cadet of the ancient family of McDowall of Galloway by Alexander Cairnes in 1604, some years prior to his emigration to Ireland. The Cairnes family had held it under the Douglases until the sequestration of the estates of that house, when they became holders direct from the Crown.

Of this John de Carnys we find frequent mention in the Exchequer Rolls. As has been recorded in the last chapter, his uncle John held the office of Custumar of Linlithgow for the thirty-two years from 1369—1401. On his death in the latter year the vacant custumarship was not immediately filled, the returns being for several years made by Thomas Wylde as "deputy for John de Carnys deceased."

This peculiar arrangement is accounted for by the entries of 1406, when we find the late custumar's nephew John in the office, thus suggesting that through some influence not recorded, the appointment had been kept open for the nephew who was not immediately ready to step into his uncle's shoes. The reason for the appointment of the deputy was in all probability that the younger custumar was not of age in 1401, a probability supported by the fact that he died in or about 1456, which, were he just 21 in 1406, would fix the date of his birth as 1385 and his age at death about 75 or 76 years.

The office of custumar was one of considerable importance, and doubtless of respectable remuneration, but a careful study of the Exchequer Rolls of the first half of the fifteenth century shows that it was not in all respects an enviable position. During the Reign of Robert III., and more especially during the Regency of the Duke of Albany, the lawlessness of the more powerful of the nobility grew to proportions almost incredible. Not content with the spoils collected in border raids and from their weaker neighbours, it was no uncommon event for them to rob the stores of the custumars of the larger towns, those of

Edinburgh and Linlithgow being the most frequent victims. These offences the Regent, powerless to punish, was compelled to forgive. It grew to be of almost everyday occurrence for some of these nobles to ship the produce of their estates duty free, in defiance of the protests of the collectors of customs, and even to aid the local merchants who might be under their protection to do the same. Nor did these personages scruple, when it suited them, to incarcerate the custumars until they disbursed any balance in hand, or, while they kept them in durance vile, to collect the customs themselves, keeping the custumar under lock and key until they had collected enough for their immediate requirements. At the annual audits, these various shortages are entered as "arrears," and are often carried forward from audit to audit. The principal offenders were James, afterwards the 7th Earl Douglas, and his brother Archibald the 4th Earl, Walter de Haliburton, Sir William Crawford, the Earl of Orkney, and William of Borthwick.

The amounts entered as arrears from these depredations are, considering the then value of money, sufficiently alarming. In the annual audits the shortages in the Edinburgh accounts alone in 1409 come to £708 2s. 1d.; 1413, £634 10s. 11d.; 1414, £1,339 5s. 9d. (all due to seizures by Earl Douglas); 1415, £1,254 4s. 2½d. But in addition, the gross customs receipts, through forcible evasion of payment of customs, had gradually fallen, until in 1417 they amounted to only £1,336 5s. instead of probably £4,000, had all duties been paid.

Occasionally the Regent appears mildly to have asked the offenders for an explanation, which was usually forthcoming in the form of a contra account, some of the items of which suggest a sense of grim humour on the part of the claimants. In the audit of 1408 the contra account furnished by Douglas includes a heavy item for "his expenses in pillaging and setting fire to the town of Berwick!"

The customs accounts of Linlithgow tell a similar story. In 1414 the custumars William de Crauforde and John de Carnys appear by deputy at the audit held at Perth. Their statement sets forth that they had been seized by James Douglas and held by him prisoners in his castle at Abercorn. The total receipts were £388 0s. 4d.; payments, £255 2s.; "taken by James Douglas, £132 18s. 4d.;" balance, nil. In addition, Douglas had extorted £88 12s. 8d., and Walter de Haliburton £54 5s. 8d., direct from the merchants. The 1415 accounts were again presented by deputies, William and Norman Young, on behalf of Crauforde and Carnys the custumars, who apparently were still incarcerated at Abercorn. The receipts this year were £358 1s. 3d.; expenses, £75 13s. 10d.; taken by Douglas, £239 16s. 7d.; by Haliburton, £42 10s. 9d.; balance, nil. In 1416 the receipts came to £500 2s. 10d.; expenses, £304 8s. 2d.; taken by Douglas and Haliburton direct from "divers Burgesses of Linlithgow, several of whom they had been compelled to lock up at Abercorn," £194 14s. 8d.; balance handed to the Chancellor of the Exchequer, twenty shillings!

From 1416 to 1422 the accounts of the Customs of Linlithgow were presented by the Youngs, deputies for Carnys and Crauforde the custumars. The receipts and expenditure, of course, varied from year to year, but the balance due to the Exchequer each year found its way to the pockets of Douglas and Haliburton. The former usually got the lion's share ; but in this respect the year 1420 shows an exception, as Haliburton, alive to the fact that, evidently owing to a good year's trade, the customs receipts were heavy, seized the custumars, incarcerated them in his Castle at Furthra (or Fidra), and netted the respectable balance in hand of £235 8s. 3d.

It is worthy of note that while Douglas and Haliburton acted in the rapacious manner described, and even went so far as to imprison the custumars in order to attain their end, each year they paid them their commission in full on all customs received, as well as the tronar's fees.

Although James Douglas had imprisoned John de Carnys on several occasions when he deemed it necessary to have a free hand to rob the customs, it appears that he did so in a friendly sort of way, for many favours were conferred upon Carnys by James's brother Earl Douglas, and afterwards by his widowed Countess. In 1421 the Earl appointed Carnys his scutifer[1], a term literally meaning shield-bearer, but more applicable to the modern office of aide-de-camp. In 1422-3 Carnys resigned his position as Custumar of Linlithgow, to enter into possession of the Galloway property reverting to him on the death of his uncle Alexander, and probably to fulfil his duties as scutifer to Earl Douglas, who was preparing to join the French army.

The Earl sailed to France in 1423 and joined the French King who received him with the greatest honour, creating him Duke of Touraine and appointing him lieutenant-general

[1] The Lochnaw lease before referred to mentions John as "Scutifer Comiti de Douglas."

of his army. The Earl had with him no less than 10,000 soldiers[1], a welcome addition to the depleted ranks of Charles VII.'s army. A list of those in the Earl's train would be interesting reading were it forthcoming, but unfortunately no such list exists. That he was joined by many of the lesser nobles of Galloway and Annandale, and that he had with him as his aide-de-camp, John de Carnys, are undoubted. How many of his followers lost their lives with the Earl at the disastrous field of Verneuil, or how many of the ten thousand returned home to recount their adventures and misfortunes can never be known. Deprived by death of their leader, the Scottish contingent, sorely reduced in numbers, lost heart and interest in the venture in which they had embarked, and many of the survivors returned during the year following the battle of Verneuil.

In an entry in the Register of the Great Seal of 1440-41, recording the Royal confirmation of charters of the Princess Margaret Countess of Douglas, granted in her widowhood in 1425, we learn that among the survivors of the French expedition was the late Earl's scutifer John de Carnys. In that year he obtained from the Countess, now Duchess of Touraine, confirmation of the several charters previously granted him during the life of his uncle Alexander, of the lands held by him. As this entry is of considerable interest for many reasons, a copy of it will not be out of place. It supplies some explanation of the fact that the accounts of the Custumar of Linlithgow were presented by the deputy custumars the brothers Young from 1414 to 1422. While on one or two occasions during that period, the custumars

[1] Hollinshed.

themselves were suffering imprisonment by Douglas or Haliburton, thus necessitating the presentation of the accounts at the audit by deputy, we cannot think that the incarceration could have lasted during the whole eight years, and thus be the sole reason for the appearance of deputy custumars at the annual audits. In this charter we find that the Provost had, as early as 1416, conveyed part of his property to his nephew, so that it is most likely the latter, from this date forward, only paid occasional visits to Linlithgow, merely superintending the performance of his duties as custumar by the deputies.

The Charter in the Register of the Great Seal reads as follows :—

"Apud . . . .[1] Rex confirmavit cartam
"Margarete ducisse Turonie comitisse de Douglass, &c.
"[qua in pura viduitate confirmavit quondam cartam D.
"Arch. comitis de Douglas, &c. quondam sponsi sui (per
"quam dictus comes concessit Johanni de Carnis, et
"Elizabeth sponsa ejus—terras de Carsluthe super ripariam
"de Cree, in parochia de Kyrkdale, Constab. Kyrkcou-
"briche ;—quas terras M. Alexander de Carnis, avunculus
"dicto Johanni resignavit ; ac etiam terras de Strothanis
"adjacentes dictis terris de Carsluthe : — Tenend. dictis
"Joh. et Eliz. et eorum viventi et heredibus inter ipsos
"procreatis, quibus deficientibus, dicto Joh. et heredibus ejus
"quibuscunque. Reservato libero tenemento predicto M.
"Alex. pro toto tempore vitæ ejus ;—Reddend. annuatim 1
"den. argenti nomine albe ferme ;—Test. Joh. de Seton

[1] Place and date are omitted. The charter is inserted in the register between one dated 8th December, 1440, and one dated 5th January, 1441.

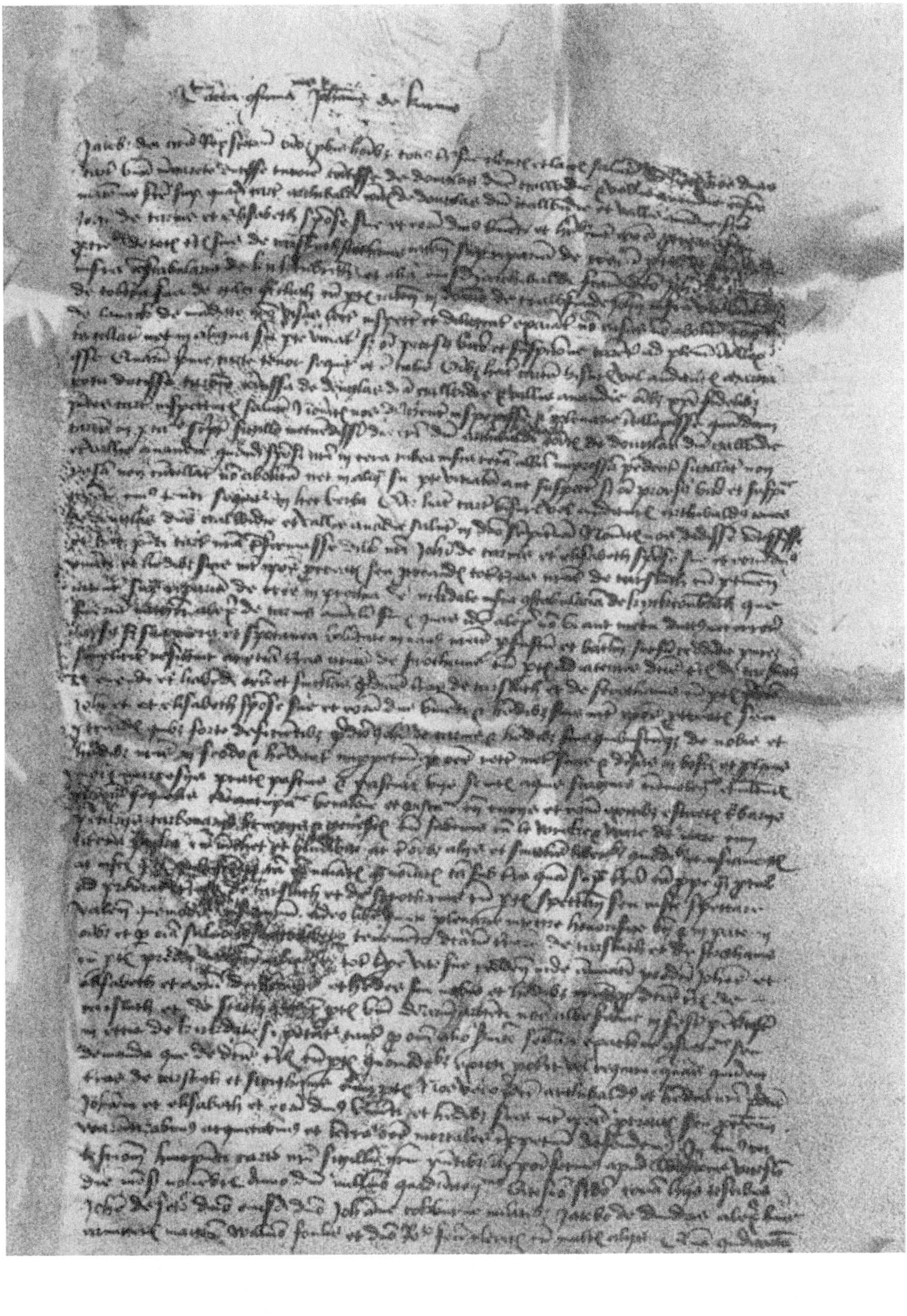

CHARTER TO JOHN DE CARNYS FROM THE CROWN OF HIS LANDS IN GALLOWAY, FORMERLY HELD UNDER THE EARLS DOUGLAS, A.D. 1440.

" dom ejusdem, D. Joh. Cokburne, militibus, Jac. de Dundas, " Alex. Hume armigeris, M. Will. Foulis et D. Rob. Feuer, " clericis ;—apud Wigtone, Nov. 20, 1422). Test. D. Herb. " Heris dom. de Terreglis, milite, Wil. de Douglas de " Anguse, Pat Johannis McLelane, dom. de Gillistone, " Alex. Mure, Joh. Levingstone, armigeris, M. Joh. McGil- " hauche, rectore de Kyrkandris. M. Gilb. Park et D. Will. " Brissone, clericis : — Apud Castrum de Trefe, Oct. 10, " 1425] : — Necnon cartam Archibaldi comitis de Douglas " &c. [qua concessit dicto Johanni et heredibus ejus,—terras " de Gilcristcluyche, in dominio de Craufurde-Johne, vic. " Lanark ; quas M. Alex. de Carnis prepositus eccles. Colleg. " de Lyncloudane resignavit : — Reddend. annuatim dicto " comiti 1 den. argenti, albe firme :—Salvo libero tenemento " prefato M. Alex. pro toto tempore vite ejus :—Test D. Wil. " de Borthwic dom ejusdem, Adam de Hepburne dom de " Halis, D. Wil. Collevile, et Joh. de Cokburne, militibus, " Rob. de Ramsay dom de Dalwolsy, Wil. de Borthwic filio " et herede D. Wil. de B. predicti, et M. Wil. de Fownys " clerico :—Apud Edinburghe Aug. 4, 1416] . . . . .[1]"

No record exists to show of what family was " Elizabetha ejus sponsa." It is probable she married her husband in 1422, and that the lands of Carsluthe and Strothans, which, it will be noticed, are granted to both husband and wife, with remainder to their lawfully begotten heirs, formed the marriage settlement.

Of John de Carnys, the Provost's nephew, we know

[1] This charter is without testing clause, and not quite complete. The above is extracted from the printed Kalendar, and the numerous contractions and abbreviations are by the Editor of the Kalendar. The original register is here reproduced.

but little after his return from France. He was certainly living in 1441, and almost certainly up to 1456. He made Galloway his home, though the actual place of his residence is not recorded. That he kept up some connection with Linlithgow is suggested by his son securing the important appointment of custumar of that burgh in 1449, a position he held up to 1456, when he went to live in Galloway, probably on the death of his father.

The elder John Cairnis of Galloway had issue—

1. JOHN, who succeeded him.
2. DIONYSCIUS or Denis of Gaitgal or Littletoun, Parish of Borg. He held this property by a charter under the Great Seal dated 1467, in which he is mentioned as a brother of John, and a brother-in-law of James McDowall of Spottes[1]. In 1463 this Cairnis was guilty of the slaughter of one Robert Rogers. In the accounts of the Lord High Treasurer of date 1473 this fact is recorded as having occurred ten years previously. Why his punishment was so long deferred is not explained, but in the latter year he was compelled to pay the Treasury £6 13s. 4d. in satisfaction for the offence. We do not know whether Robert Rogers was cheap or dear at the price!

[1] Reg. Mag. Sigilli, vol. II., No. 976.—"Rex confirmavit cartam Jacobi McDowall, domini de Spottis [qua concessit Dionyscio de Carnis fratri suo, ejus benemeritis, auxilio, &c. :—terras de Gaitgil, alias nuncupatas Litiltoun, in parochia de Borg dominio Gallvidie, Senesc. Kirkcudbricht, Visc. Drumfres ;—Tenend dicto Dion. et heredibus ejus masculis de corpore ejus legitime procreatis, quibus deficientibus, Joh. de Carnis de Orchardtoun et heredibus ejus quibuscunque a dicto Jac. McDowall de rege—Apud Drumfres, 18 Jan., 1467.]" The charter following this in the register shows James McDowall to have been married to Margaret, sister of Dionyscius Cairnis. As Litiltoun passed afterwards to John Cairnis of Orchardtoun, it is evident that Dionyscius died without issue.

3. HENRY of Knocklittle. He was a member of the international commission appointed to come to some working arrangement for the settlement of Border disputes. It assembled at Newcastle-on-Tyne in 1451, and consisted of about twenty-four members, half English and half Scots. After mature deliberation a treaty was drawn up and signed by all the members of the commission, Henry describing himself as an Esquire of Scotland[1]. He was succeeded in Knocklittle by his son

   ALEXANDER of Knocklittle and Barnbachill, who was succeeded by his son

   RICHARD of Barnbachill, who had possession in 1512. He died 1532, and was succeeded by his son

   ALEXANDER, who died 1569, and was succeeded by his son

   RICHARD, the last recorded of this family. He sold Barnbachill in 1572 to Lord Herries[2].

4. MARGARET, wife of James McDowall of Spottis. The heir

JOHN CAIRNIS is first mentioned as Custumar of Linlithgow in 1449. He was the third of the name in successive generations to hold this office. His tenure was not marked by any of the exciting events such as are recorded of the time when his father was custumar. The state of the

[1] Rymer's Foedera, 1451.

[2] Among the Herries Charters at Terregles are two documents relating to the purchase of Barnbachill, one an attested copy of the sasine of Alexander to the property in 1532, the other a Crown confirmation of the purchase in 1572.

country under the firm rule of the young King James II. had vastly improved, and the robbery of the customs by the more powerful of the nobles was now a rare event. The chief feature of interest, so far as this history is concerned, in the annual returns rendered by this custumar and that of Edinburgh, is a list of expenses in connection with the siege of Blackness Castle, referred to in a previous chapter.

After the capitulation of James de Crichton a considerable quantity of war materials was left over, and in the Chancellor's accounts we find a payment of £10 made to John Cairnis for his services in removing these to Kirkcudbright for use in the reduction of Threave Castle, for all the services he rendered thereat, and for the dangers he underwent. A payment of £4 is also recorded as having been made at the same time to one Laurence Cairnis, a chaplain. For what special services this payment was made is not recorded. This cleric may have been a younger brother of John, but there is no direct evidence of the fact.

Like his father before him, on resigning the custumarship in 1456, John Cairnis retired to his possessions in Galloway. A most interesting item appears in the Exchequer Rolls of this year, recording that he had sasine of the lands of Irisbuitle by the sealed mandate of the King, who remitted to him two years' Crown charges due on the property, presumably as a further reward for his services at Blackness and Threave. The title to this estate was most unusual, the sealed mandate apparently taking the place of the usual charter under the Great Seal, and in the register no such charter is recorded. There can be little doubt but that Irisbuitle was one of the forfeited estates of the fallen house of Douglas, and as the King himself was present at the siege of Threave Castle, it requires but little stretch of imagination to assume that the Royal favours and rewards were there and then meted out to those who had assisted him in crushing the rebellious Douglas.

As the name Irisbuitle is now unknown as applicable to any lands in Galloway, the importance of this entry in the Exchequer Rolls is not at first apparent. So far as we have searched in the various records, no mention appears for 150 years of Irisbuitle by which it could be identified, but by a marvellous stroke of good luck a clerk in the office of the Retours of Sasine inserts three words which clear up the difficulty. Retour no. 108, Kirkcudbright County, 25th January, 1614, relates that "Sir Alexander Kirkpatrick, of Kirkmichael, Knight, heir of Margaret Cairnis Lady Orchardton, his mother, had sasine of one-third part of the 9 merks land of Orchardtoun, *otherwise called Irisbuitle*, in the Parish of Buittill."

On his newly acquired estate John Cairnis proceeded to erect a residence. That he was a man of original ideas and strong individuality of taste there can be little doubt. The castle which he built was unique in Galloway, and almost so in all Britain. It consisted of a rectangular block measuring about eighty feet by sixty. The height cannot now be estimated, as of this portion of the castle only a fragment of the strong arched basement remains. But from the depth of fallen masonry within the four walls, it can be estimated that the building was of considerable height.

However, the most remarkable feature of the castle was the massive circular peill at the end of the main building, and communicating therewith by an arched doorway on the first floor. This remarkable structure has withstood the ravages of time to a wonderful extent, and while the original woodwork has disappeared, the masonry is almost intact. The basement consists of a vaulted chamber of small dimensions. The walls of the basement are almost eight feet thick. This chamber or dungeon is entered by a doorway communicating with the outside, but the stonework round the doorway being of a much more recent date than the castle itself, indicates that originally the dungeon was entered only by a trapdoor in the vaulted roof which forms the floor of the first storey. The first floor of the peill was the entrance hall of the castle, and round the walls are remains of carving which indicate that it was originally handsomely decorated. The floors above the entrance hall were of timber, and have long since disappeared. Opposite the main entrance, which is approached externally by a flight of steps, is an arched doorway formerly leading into the rectangular dwelling-portion of the castle which has now fallen away. The walls on the first floor measure six feet in thickness, and a side door from the hall leads to a circular stone staircase, built in the thickness of the wall, to the upper floors and the roof, round which was a flagged pathway some eighteen inches wide, surrounded by battlements, still in fair preservation.

An examination of the stonework of the rectangular building and the circular peill respectively, suggests the probability that the former structure is of earlier date than

From a Photo.]

ORCHARDTON CASTLE RUINS, near Castle Douglas.

the latter. It is quite probable that there was a castle on this spot before 1456, but there is no doubt that the circular tower and other improvements were added about this period by John Cairnis, who made this his residence, giving it the name of Orchardtoun, a name by which the lands comprising the estate shortly afterwards came to be known. Orchardtoun is first mentioned as the residence of John Cairnis in the records of 1467. From the meaning of the name, literally "a garden of vegetables," we can infer that the owner was a man of domesticated tastes rather than of warlike proclivities, an inference supported by the remains in the tower of some domestic conveniences usually found only in buildings of very much more modern origin.

The round peill of the Cairnises of Orchardton was an object of renown through Scotland, and is still visited by many tourists and antiquaries. As to its origin, the guide books seem to vie with each other in the absurdity of their theories, one calling it a fine specimen of the Danish Rath, another suggesting that from its lonely and secluded position, it must have been built as a hiding place for outlaws! All seem to unite in overlooking the fact that the tower was merely the stronghold or keep of a larger residence now almost entirely demolished by the ravages of centuries. To the present day a representation of this tower forms the crest of the elder branch of the representatives of the family of Cairnis of Orchardton[1].

Whom John Cairnis married is not recorded; he lived to about 1493, and left issue,

WILLIAM his heir.

[1] See chap. X.

HENRY of Cults, which he held by grant from his brother William, confirmed by charter under the Great Seal, dated 2nd April, 1502, with remainder to his heirs male, failing which, to his brother William and his heirs. As this property reverted to William Cairnis, it is evident that Henry died without male issue.

JAMES of Little Spottes.[1]

MARGARET, married first to James Lindsay of Fairgarth, by whom she had issue Michael Lindsay. She married secondly Kentigern Murray, Laird of Broughton.[2]

The heir, William Cairnis of Orchardton, married in 1499 or 1500 Margaret daughter of Patrick Agnew of Lochnaw, fourth hereditary sheriff of Galloway, by Katherine Gordon of Lochinvar his wife.[3] Her sister Katherine Agnew was the wife of Ninian Adair of Kinhilt, ancestor of the Adairs of Ballymena and Flixton Hall, Suffolk.

William Cairnis appears as witness to several charters of 1516 and 1546. He was among those summoned to Parliament by Royal warrant on several occasions, notably in 1525 and 1527. In the latter year the Barons summoned from Galloway were the Earl of Cassilis, Gordon of Lochinvar, M'Lellan of Bomby, Lord Maxwell, Agnew of Lochnaw (the sheriff), the McDowalls of Garthland and Freuch, M'Culloch of Torhouse, Cairnis of Orchardton, and Gordon of Craiglaw. Each was accompanied to the capital by a

[1] The lease of Little Spottes to James Cairnis, brother german of the Laird of Orchardton, is among the Herries charters at Terregles—date 1529.

[2] Reg. Mag. Sigilli, vol. II., Nos. 1506 and 1524.

[3] Ibid., vol. III., No. 501. "Hereditary Sheriffs of Galloway."—Agnew.

numerous band of armed retainers, including sons, kinsmen, and a selection of their tenantry, the lairds apparently vieing with each other in display.[1]

The swashbuckler style in which these gentlemen habitually paraded the streets, their respective followers armed to the teeth, led to encounters of the most serious nature. In two of the frays which attained most notoriety, the Galloway barons were prominent.

In the first, certain partisans of the Earl of Cassilis killed a Dutch nobleman. Of the cause of the quarrel nothing is known; but the extraordinary number of remissions for his slaughter, amounting to no less than two hundred and seventy, gives a startling idea of the fierceness of these street battles, as the opposing forces may be presumed to have been considerable. As usual some of the Kennedys are found fighting on both sides. The official record is drawn in form of a respite to Gilbert Kennedy, Earl of Cassilis, William Lord Semple, and thirteen others, McDowall of Freuch, Alexander McDowall tutor of Garthland, M'Kie of Myrtoun, and 268 others, of whom 35 are named, for the treasonable slaughter of Cornelius de Machitima, Martin Kennedy, and Gilbert M'Ilraith, at the Tolbooth of Edinburgh during the Session of Parliament.

A few days later Gordon of Lochinvar with his nephew, Agnew of Lochnaw, Sir James Douglas of Drumlanrig, the younger Cairnis of Orchardton, M'Culloch of Torhouse and other kinsmen, when sauntering, well attended, down the High Street, met face to face Sir Thomas M'Lellan of

[1] As the late Sir Andrew Agnew of Lochnaw gives a most interesting account of what follows, I take the liberty of quoting in the narrative largely from his "Hereditary Sheriffs," i. 339 f.—Auth.

Bomby, also with a band of friends and followers. Between Bomby and Lochinvar a blood-feud raged. Both parties must needs keep the crown of the causeway. Neither would give place to allow the other to pass. A desperate struggle ensued, Lochinvar eventually keeping the place of honour, but the Laird of Bomby was left dead at the door of St. Giles's. Much litigation ensued, as was to be expected in those days of weak government. The policy of the courts in such cases was to induce aggressors to make compensation to the aggrieved, which end they sought to achieve by refusing to grant remissions for slaughters till "letters of slains" were procured from the bereaved families. And although it was troublesome to effect the actual arrest of people of position, it was not so difficult to have them formally put to the horn and declared rebels, proclamation being thus made that it was legal for anyone who thought he was strong enough to do it to seize their persons. It was consequently thought desirable by aggressors, however powerful, to obtain remissions.

A good instance of the procedure of the courts is furnished in the present instance. We may take it for granted that the guilty ones concerned in this encounter deemed it wiser to depart to their far away homes without unnecessary delay. They were, however, duly summoned, and failing to appear were declared rebels and outlaws. But they remained at large and at peace in their Galloway homes for eleven years. Romance stepped in to heal the breach, and the young Laird of Bomby fell in love with no other than the daughter of his father's slayer. The old Lochinvar wisely smiled on the suit, and all went well.

The outlawry was recalled and remission granted to James Gordon of Lochinvar, Andrew Agnew of Lochnaw, Sheriff of Wigton, Douglas of Drumlanrig, Cairnis the younger of Orchardton, and others, for art and part of the slaughter of Thomas M'Lellan of Bomby, committed eleven years before in the burgh of Edinburgh (13 Jan., 1538).

And so the hatchet was buried and the wedding feasts were spread. The Laird of Bomby married the daughter of Lochinvar, and Peter, brother of William Cairnis, wedded Margaret M'Lellan.

William the elder of Orchardton, who died in 1555, by his wife Margaret Agnew had a numerous issue, of which are recorded—

1. WILLIAM his heir.
2. JOHN of Cults, eventual head representative in the male line of the family through failure of male issue of his elder brother.
3. PETER of Kipp, Parish of Colvend.
4. HENRY of Torr, Parish of Rerwick.

   } For the families of Kipp and Torr See chapter VIII.

5. VALENTINE. Was a witness to a document in 1573, in which he is mentioned as son of the elder William (document in the Register House).
6. ELIZABETH, wife of John Gordon.
7. ISOBEL, wife of John M'Culloch.
8. JANET, wife of John M'Moran.

The heir, William Cairnis the younger of Orchardton, during his father's lifetime resided in Dalbeattie.[1] On his return from Edinburgh after the slaughter of the Laird of Bomby, he had married Janet, daughter of Thomas Kennedy

[1] Acts and Decreets, Register House, XVIII., 72.

of Knockreoch and Knocknalling.[1] On his marriage his father had settled upon him and his wife the lands of Bargalie.[2] He succeeded his father in Orchardton on the death of the latter in 1555, but only enjoyed his possessions for three years, dying in 1558. He left issue only three daughters, co-heiresses—

1. MARGARET, married 1st, WILLIAM KIRKPATRICK of Kirkmichael, by whom she had issue; 2ndly, JAMES KIRKPATRICK in Barmure, brother of Roger of Closeburn; and, 3rdly, EDWARD MAXWELL of Tynwold.
2. JANET, wife of George Maxwell of Drumcoltran, by whom she had issue, Edward and William, died young; John her heir; Herbert; issue if any unknown.
3. ELIZABETH, proved before the Commissaries at Edinburgh[3] to be the lawful wife of John Kennedy, by whom she had issue, one daughter and heiress Janet.

Of the descendants of William Cairnis, last of the name of Orchardton, we shall treat in chapter VIII. The main family having become extinct in the male line on his death, John Cairnis of Cults, second son of the elder William of Orchardton, became the head of the family. In 1548 his father had conveyed to him the estate of Cults, Parish of Cruggleton, Wigtonshire. In the Great Seal Charter conveying this property, the father is described as William

[1] Contract dated 19th August, 1527; Protocol Book of Gavin Ross, in Register House. The Kennedies of Knocknalling hold this property still.

[2] Reg. Mag. Sigilli, vol. III., No. 501.

[3] See chap. VIII.

Cairnis, senior, Lord of Orchardton. In 1552, on the occasion of his marriage, his father granted to John and his wife Margaret, daughter of Alexander M'Culloch of Killaster, the lands of Glenure or Blairboys, Kirkcudbright, and from this charter we learn the interesting fact that the young laird was a gentleman-in-waiting to Mary Queen of Scots. About this time he built a residence on his Cults property. He died in 1568, leaving issue—

1. PATRICK, born, not earlier than 1555. He died young.
2. JOHN the heir.
3. MALCOLM, who appears to have died without issue.

The children being all under fourteen at the time of their father's death, their grandfather John M'Culloch was appointed their tutor.[1]

The heir, John Cairnes of Cults, succeeded to the property on coming of age, about 1578. He married, evidently very early in life, probably in 1577, Margaret Hamilton, and it is regrettable to record that his life seems to have been one of trouble and misfortunes which eventually overwhelmed his house.

He appears to have had but one son, Alexander, and this son was the source of much trouble to his father. As early as 1595 there appears in the Records of the Privy Council an entry relative to this youth, who could not have been more than eighteen at the time, which shows that he was in his early days of a wild and lawless disposition. At the sitting of the Privy Council in the Autumn of 1595, at the complaint of Sir John Vaus of Barnebarroch, George

[1] Acts and Decreets, XLI., 224.

Murray of Broughton went surety for his young relative that he would not harm the complainant. In the same year it is recorded that, evidently in reprisal for some offence committed upon him, either by Alexander Cairnes or his father, Hugh Gordon of Grange, aided by "his servants "with their accomplices, armed with weapons, came to John "Cairnes' lands of Apibe and there wounded divers of his "servants to the peril of their lives, broke his ploughs and "shamefully and barbarously hocheit his oxen." For which offence they were denounced rebels.

Several records of a nature similar to these appear in the few years following, but in 1602 is an entry showing Alexander Cairnes in a deplorable light. It was complained by John Cairnes of Cults that his son Alexander, "among "his many undewtifull and unneturall behavioures had lately "reft from him ane grey horse worth £100." The persuer appeared by Margaret Hamilton his spouse.

In the same year, accumulating difficulties compelled John Cairnes to sell his ancestral property Cults, with the residence and demesne lands, to Peter McDowall. Thus passed from the Cairnes family, after an ownership of 200 years, one of the first properties they had obtained in Galloway, sacrificed to the youthful and careless extravagance of the heir.

The sale was shortly followed by the death of John Cairnes (1603), he being succeeded by his son and heir Alexander in the remaining lands of Blairboys or Glenure. These he immediately sold to M'Clelland of Auchlane and the Lady Katherine Kennedy his wife, thus alienating from the representative in the male line of the family of Cairnes of Galloway the last acre of their ancient estates.

The next step in Alexander's career is recorded in the Privy Council records of 1606, where it is "complained by "ye Provost and Bailies of Wigton against John Dunbar "of Craloch, Alexander Cairnes formerly of Cults, and two "others, for having on 20th August last committed Ryot "and oppression upon Johnne Stewart, servitor to ye said "Provost; had been put in ward in ye Tolbooth of ye said "Burgh; having there been commanded by ye sd Bailies "to deliver their weapons to ye Jailer, ye not only dis-"obeyit but invaidet and pursewit ym of yr lives with a "drawn sword and would have slain them but for the "providence of God and help of some personnes present. "Ye Lrds of Ye Secret Council, having heard witnesses, "find that ye defenders have committed ane grite insolence "and Ryot, and order them to enter in ward in ye Tolbooth "of Edinburgh."

Let us hope that the degradation of his imprisonment and the common sense born of maturer years induced the head of the family to settle down. At any rate no further escapades are recorded, and in 1609 we find him a member of assize.

Bereft of his estates, and with a desire to start afresh, we can well understand the excitement with which Alexander Cairnes and many in a similar position listened to the schemes then promulgated for the plantation of colonies in Ireland. To the favourites and placehunters at the Court of James VI., not long removed to his new kingdom of England, were offered the tempting estates in Ulster recently robbed from their ancient owners the O'Neills, O'Donells, M'Mahons, O'Cahans, and other Irish chiefs. To the fortunate grantees arose a grand opportunity of providing for their younger sons, nephews, and friends. And the opportunity was largely availed of, as in some cases we find that half or more than half of the able-bodied male population of a district was transferred to settle on the new estates of their patrons in Ulster.

Alexander Cairnes seized the opportunity to make a fresh start, and through the influence of the Galloway lairds who secured grants in Ulster, to most of whom he was related, he secured an appointment in connection with the colonisation of the County of Donegal, whither he proceeded in 1610.

TABLE II.

PEDIGREE OF THE FAMILY OF CAIRNES IN GALLOWAY.

1421.
JOHN DE CAIRNIS, Son of William, the Constable of Edinburgh Castle. Born about 1385. Custumar of Linlithgow, 1406–1422. Scutifer to Earl Douglas. Heir of his uncle Alexander, the Provost of Lincluden Died 1456. See Table I. facing p. 16. = ELIZABETH . . . . . . mentioned in lease of 1421 (at Lochnaw Castle).

JOHN DE CAIRNIS, Custumar of Linlithgow, 1449–1456. The first owner of Orchardton. Born 1423. Died 1493. = . . . MAGEE (?)

DIONICIUS OR DENIS DE CAIRNIS, of Gaitgil or Littletoun. Died without issue, his brother John being his heir.

HENRY DE CAIRNIS, of Knocklitle, was a member of the International Commission on Border Feuds in 1451.

1499.
WILLIAM CAIRNIS OF ORCHARDTON, succeeded in 1493. Was summoned to Parliament on several occasions. Died 1555. = MARGARET, daughter of PATRICK AGNEW, of Lochnaw, 4th Hereditary Sheriff of Galloway.

HENRY CAIRNIS, of Cults, d.s.p.

JAMES CAIRNIS, of Little Spottes. Lease dated 1529 (in the Terregles charter room).

MARGARET CAIRNIS, married, 1st. JAMES LINDSAY, of Fairgarth. 2ndly. KENTIGORN MURRAY, of Broughton. Had issue, MICHAEL LINDSAY, of Fairgarth.

ALEXANDER CAIRNIS, of Knocklitle and Barnbachil.

1527.
WILLIAM CAIRNIS OF ORCHARDTON. Born 1502, was one of those who slew the Laird of Bomby in 1527. Died 1558 = JANET, daughter of Thomas Kennedy, of Knockreoch and Knocknalling.

1555.
JOHN CAIRNIS, of Cults, died May, 1568. = MARGARET M'CULLOCH, daughter of Alex. M'Culloch, of Killaster.

PETER CAIRNIS, of Kipp. For issue see table V. facing p. 208.

HENRY CAIRNIS, of Torr. For issue see table V. facing p. 208.

VALENTINE CAIRNS, witnessed a charter, 1573

GEORGE CAIRNS, of Muretoun.

ELIZABETH, wife of JOHN GORDON.
ISOBEL, wife of JOHN M'CULLOCH.
JANET, wife of JOHN M'MORAN.

RICHARD CAIRNIS, of Barnbachil, in possession 1512. Died 1532.

Children of William Cairnis of Orchardton and Janet Kennedy:

MARGARET = 1st. WM. KIRKPATRICK, of Kirkmichael. = 2ndly. JAMES KIRKPATRICK, of Barmure. = 3rdly. EDWARD MAXWELL, of Tynwald.
- SIR ALEXANDER KIRKPATRICK.
  - (?)

JANET = GEO. MAXWELL, of Drumcoltran.
- See page 180.

ELIZABETH = JOHN KENNEDY.
- JANET.
  - (?)

Children of John Cairnis of Cults and Margaret M'Culloch:

PATRICK, under 14 in 1568, d.s.p.

JOHN CAIRNES, heir of his father in the Cults property. Died 1603. = MARGARET HAMILTON.
- ALEXANDER CAIRNES, founder of the family of Cairnes in Ireland. For descent, See Table III. facing p. 106.

Child of Valentine Cairns:

MALCOLM. Issue, if any, unknown.

Son of Richard Cairnis, of Barnbachil:

ALEXANDER CAIRNIS. Died 1569.
- RICHARD CAIRNS, Sold Barnbachil to Lord Herries, 1572. (Title deeds at Terregles).

CHAPTER V.

The Plantation of Ulster—The Galloway Undertakers in Donegal—Alexander and William Cairnes—John Cairnes, M.P. for Augher—Sir Alexander Cairnes, Bart., M.P., of London and Monaghan—His descendants and heirs, the Westenras, Lords Rossmore—Sir Henry Cairnes, Bart., M.P.—William Cairnes, M.P. for Belfast—Collateral descendants.

FOR several years prior to 1609 the deplorable condition of the remoter districts of Ireland had had the earnest consideration of the English Government. Since the complete overthrow and flight of the rebellious Irish chiefs O'Neill and O'Donnell, and their principal followers, a greater part of Ulster had become practically a wilderness. Its native inhabitants, in many cases without houses, stock, farming implements, or seed to raise crops, had fallen into the condition of savages. Many eked out existence by forming themselves into bands of robbers and making raids on the few towns or villages within their reach, but practically all were in a state of absolute destitution and starvation.

To the advisers of James I. must be given credit for the initiation of a scheme calculated to settle the devastated tracts of country, and at the same time to add to the rather depleted funds in the Exchequer. As a result of their deliberations the scheme known as the Plantation of Ulster was undertaken.

Royal Commissioners were appointed to survey the

country and report. The outcome of their report was the decision to apportion out six of the nine Ulster Counties, Derry, Donegal, Tyrone, Fermanagh, Cavan and Armagh, among persons of sufficient means and influence to be able to undertake the establishment of colonies on their grants, to build castles and bawns thereon for the protection of the settlers and otherwise carry out the scheme of Plantation.

The County Derry was granted to the Council of the City of London, who elected a body of twenty-six of their members to carry out the effective plantation thereof. They were afterwards known as the Irish Society. This body was incorporated by Royal Charter in 1613, and invested with all the towns, castles, lordships, manors, lands and hereditaments, market tolls, &c., given to the Council. The district granted under this charter was incorporated into a distinct county, to be called the County of Londonderry.[1]

The Irish Society, having laid out some £40,000 in their Plantation, decided to divide the county into twelve equal portions, which they sold to twelve of the principal London Companies, viz., the Clothworkers, Drapers, Mercers, Skinners, Fishmongers, Vintners, Goldsmiths, Haberdashers, Ironmongers, Merchant Taylors, Salters and Grocers, retaining for themselves however, overlordship, as well as the city and liberties of Londonderry and the town and liberties of Coleraine.

The remaining five Ulster Counties[2] in the scheme were apportioned to individual undertakers who received

[1] Previously known as the County of Coleraine.

[2] Monaghan was planted chiefly in Elizabeth's time.

grants of nominally 1,000 to 2,000 acres each[1], at a low Crown rent. In many cases one grantee managed to secure several plots, but as a rule these were in different counties, the original idea in so scattering their properties being to prevent any one undertaker becoming too powerful in his district, thus possibly developing into a successor of the once powerful rebels who formerly had given the English so much trouble. There were of course notable exceptions to this rule, as in the case of Hamilton of Strabane and Sir Arthur Chichester, whose grants extended to many thousands of acres, but whose loyalty was considered beyond question.

The partiality of King James for his own countrymen can be traced in the fact that the majority of the favoured grantees of the confiscated lands were Scotchmen, and in many cases a whole district or barony was parcelled out to a number of lairds from some one district in Scotland. An example of this is the case of the eight Galloway lairds to whom were granted the Baronies of Boylagh and Bannagh, in the County Donegal. These were—M'Clellan of Bomby, Murray of Broughton, William Stewart of Garlies, Sir Patrick M'Kee of Larg, Alexander Cunningham of Ponton, James M'Culloch of Drummorell, Alexander Dunbar, and Patrick Vaus of Barnbarroch.

Of these, at least three, M'Clellan, Murray, and M'Culloch were cousins of Alexander Cairnes of Cults,

[1] The original grants of 1609 were of three grades, namely, greater portions of 2,000 acres of profitable land, middle portions of 1,500 acres of profitable land, and small portions of 1,000 acres of profitable land. In addition were included vast tracts not classed as "profitable," so that in many cases a nominal 1,000 acres extended to as much as 6,000 acres. Each 1,000 acres was subject to a crown rent of £5 3s. 4d., or about a halfpenny per acre on an average.

whose unfortunate history has been briefly related in a previous chapter, and it is not difficult to imagine the pleasure it afforded him, bereft of his property, down in his luck, and probably with the desire to make a fresh start, to accept a position under his friends in their new colony in Ireland. In the Irish Plantation Records we find him, in 1611, installed as general agent of the Galloway undertakers in Boylagh and Bannagh, sub-letting tracts of the undertakers' estates to native tenants.

During the years ensuing we find another Scottish laird, John Murray of Cockpool, establishing himself in Donegal as a large landowner, and obtaining one by one the estates of the original undertakers, so that by 1616, when Pynnar's survey took place, he had become possessed of the greater part of the Baronies. In 1624, by Royal Charter, he obtained from King James, of whom he was a prime favourite, the whole of Boylagh and Bannagh, or the Rosses, with the Earldom of Annandale and Governorship of Donegal. Under him Alexander Cairnes continued to act as an agent, or more properly speaking, a middleman. It was customary for the undertakers, especially in the larger estates, to let large tracts of property to middlemen, who sub-let them out in small portions to tenants, often netting a very respectable margin for themselves. From after events, it is quite evident that Alexander accumulated a considerable competence for himself and his heirs by his astute management of his extensive holdings under the Earl. We do not know how long he lived, but in the inquisitions of Donegal he is mentioned in 1632 as sub-letting lands to some mere Irish. In 1620 there was also on the Annandale property a William Cairnes engaged in the same occupation, but who he was we cannot trace; he may have been a younger brother of Alexander, or his cousin, a younger son of the family of Kipp; we find no prior or subsequent mention of him.

Whom Alexander Cairnes married is a matter of some doubt. In a genealogical account of the family written over a hundred years later by Thomas Wotton,[1] the original settler is stated to have been Thomas Cairnes of Orchardton, in Scotland. The house of Orchardton became extinct in the male line by the death of William Cairnes in 1558, so that the existence of a Thomas Cairnes of Orchardton in 1609 is impossible. Further, the conservatism of Scottish families in regard to christian names is well known; in the whole tree of the family of Cairnes in Galloway, in all its branches, since its foundation two hundred years before 1609, there was not a single instance of the christian name Thomas being given. The accounts of Alexander Cairnes in the Scottish records prior to 1609, and in the Irish records, though less ample, subsequent to that date, put it beyond all doubt, if any doubt existed, that Alexander was the name of the founder of the Irish family of Cairnes. Wotton also states that Cairnes married Jane, daughter of John Scott of Colefadd, Esq., of the house of Buccleuch,[2] by Mary Anne Murray, niece of the Earl of Annandale. The facts that in 1631 Alexander's second son David was engaged with his father as an assignee

[1] Wotton's Baronetage and Peerage.

[2] We have in vain searched in Sir Wm. Frazer's most detailed and authentic History of the Buccleuch family for reference to John Scott of Colefadd. No such person and no such place are mentioned.

of the Earl of Annandale in sub-letting land[1], and that his eldest son John was in 1639 elected a member of Parliament for Augher[2], prove that Alexander must have been married at latest in 1610. At that time John Murray, afterwards Earl of Annandale, was a comparatively young man. The suggestion that he could have had a grandniece of marriageable age is absurd. It is to be regretted that the genealogy as set forth in Wotton's Baronetage, notwithstanding its manifest absurdity, has been copied without question or investigation by authors of similar works[3], and inserted in their pages as authentic.

That Alexander Cairnes married a relative of the Earl of Annandale is, however, very probable, as the position he occupied on the Earl's estate warrants the assumption of at least more than ordinary friendship. There were three intermarriages between the families of Cairnes and Murray, namely, the union between the laird of Broughton and Margaret daughter of William Cairnes of Orchardton[4], and that between Lady Blaney and Colonel Murray shortly to be referred to, and the marriage of William Cairnes of Kipp with Marie widow of Edward Murray of Drumschinschell, a cadet of the Cockpool family[5].

[1] Inquisitions of Ulster, Donegal, 1632.

[2] Parliament Rolls, List of Members of the Irish House of Commons.

[3] Sir Bernard Burke in his *Extinct Baronetage* under "Cairnes" and in his *Peerage* under Earl Cairns (1869 Edit. only). Also Shirley in his History of Monaghan, and the Rev. John Graham, probably the most inaccurate author that ever attempted to write history. As an example of the accuracy of Graham's "Ireland Preserved," see page 302 in that work, note "Cairnes family." He gives therein what he is pleased to call a *geological* account of the Cairnes family. The Cairneses have been since the fourteenth century a respectable family of small lairds, but they have never claimed descent from the old red sandstone period!

[4] Referred to in previous chapter.

[5] See Chapter VIII.

Wotton also states that John, eldest son of the first Cairnes of Donegal, married Jane, daughter of James Miller; this is probably correct, as in a footnote he states that this information was authenticated by the eldest son of the marriage, Sir Alexander Cairnes; but owing to the evident inaccuracy of this family historian, one does not like to place too much credence upon his statements, and therefore we do not record this lady's pedigree[1].

Alexander Cairnes of Donoughmore, County Donegal, had three sons living in 1639—John, Robert and David[2]. That the first-named was the eldest son there can be no doubt. Apart from the very usual Scottish custom at the period, of calling the first-born son after his paternal grandfather, we have the fact that in the will of his brother Robert, his name obtains priority. Further, when the three brothers joined in partnership in the purchase of Sir Richard Cope's property in County Tyrone, the purchase was made in John's name only. The point is not without interest, as upon it depends the question whether the Cairneses of Monaghan or the Tyrone family were the senior representatives of the House of Orchardton.

John, whom we must assume to be the eldest, joined with his two brothers, between 1633 and 1639, in the acquisition by lease from Sir William Parsons of the Manor of Cecil,

[1] The curious (or shall we say credulous?) reader may find in Wotton's book the allegation that Miss Miller's mother was the daughter of a sister of Lord Darnley, and therefore cousin of James I., and that Sir Alexander Cairnes was consequently a second cousin of Charles I. The discrepancy in dates might be got over, but the undoubted fact that Lord Darnley had no sister shows that the pedigree elaborated by Wotton and copied by Lodge, Burke and others, is utterly to be discredited.

[2] Will of Robert in Record Office, 1669.

which they seem to have bought out about 1661 from his son Sir Richard, and in 1640 in the purchase from Sir Richard Cope, of the whole Manor of Killyfaddy adjoining, both in the barony of Clogher, Co. Tyrone.

In 1609, at the original Plantation of the confiscated territories of the O'Neills, we find in the Plantation papers the grant of the small portion[1] containing the lands of Ballaclough, Sheancarragh, Tamlaght Ibrony, Kilnekerey, Balltiney, Tullafoile, Mullaneighane, Glan Ighera, Corcullen, Knockmany, Cormore, Cloneblagh, Doongower, Ballaghenew, Cloncoose, Ardnachine and Lislea, in all, sixteen balliboes, to Wm. Parsons[2], to be held in free and common soccage of the Castle in Dublin, with the right to hold a Court Baron, 1,000 acres, with 300 acres in demesne, created into the Manor of Cecil at a Crown rent of £5 3s. 4d.

Parsons eventually endeavoured to alter the name of the Manor to Parsonstown but was not allowed to do so. He failed to comply with some minor requirements of the Plantation scheme, and like most other undertakers, was compelled by Charles I. to surrender his grant, which was renewed to him at a much heavier Crown rent in 1630. He leased his lands to John Cairnes about 1638, but remained as chief landlord for some years, the Cairnes family eventually buying out his interest.

The adjoining portion was granted in 1609 to William Glegg, who does not appear to have taken possession,

[1] 1,000 acres of profitable lands. The actual area was about 6,000 acres.

[2] William Parsons, merchant, of the city of Dublin, said to have been a man of small beginnings, of great ability and boundless ambition. He named the manor Cecil out of compliment to the celebrated minister of that name from whom he had received favours, and probably hoped for more.

selling his interest in the following year to Sir Anthony Cope[1]. The name under which this portion was granted was "the small portions of Derrybard and Killany." The names of the balliboes or the extent of the grant, curious to say, are not stated in the records. No information as to this portion is procurable from Pynnar's Survey, nor in regranting Cope's lands to his heir Sir Richard Cope in 1630, are the balliboes named or the areas given. However, in this charter the lands are first referred to as Killyfaddy and thereby "created into the Manor thereof with powers to create tenures, and hold courts leet and baron, to be held in free and common soccage of the Castle of Dublin."[2]

The first mention of the Cairneses in Co. Tyrone is that in the list of members returned to sit in Parliament, already referred to. The entry is very peculiar. Under the date 27th February, 1639, the writ is returned announcing the election for the borough of Augher of Captain Robert Birone and John Cairnes of Parsonstown[3], Gentleman. This writ is followed on the 7th March, only ten days later, by another recording the election of Captain Robert Birone and Captain William Paisley. The reason of the two writs

[1] It was one of the laws of the Plantation that no undertaker could legally sell a portion before the expiry of five years. This irregularity was used later on to compel Cope to relinquish his grant, which was renewed to him at a higher rent.

[2] The 1609 grant of Derrybard and Killany was much larger than that of 1630. It is called a "small portion," but was really a large portion. Derrybard is a separate estate from Killyfaddy. It was apparently never formally created into a manor. Killaney is the name of one of the townlands in Killyfaddy Manor, as is also Killyfaddy. In several grants and official documents, some of the townlands mentioned in Parson's charter of the manor of Cecil are afterwards included in the names of the townlands in Killyfaddy, so it is now impossible to make out the real original limitations of the three estates.

[3] *i.e.*, Knockmany or Cecil.

we cannot explain, but the first writ is of great interest as showing that at this date Cairnes had acquired the Knockmany property, by lease we assume, as up to 1661, when Richard Parsons was served heir[1], the Parsons were the owners on the Crown rent roll. It was probably after the succession of Richard to the property that Cairnes bought it out.

The next record relating to Cairnes in Tyrone is in a list of holders of Crown lands in the records of the Auditor General's Office. The properties dealt with under this office seem to have been chiefly those in whose title-deeds a flaw had been discovered. In the early years of Charles the First's reign, when he was in straits for money, the happy thought occurred to those in authority that a goodly increase in the Crown rental might be secured by discovering flaws in the titles of the Ulster planters, and compelling them to take out fresh patents at a higher rent. There was no trouble in finding a flaw in the title of Killyfaddy. The original grantee, William Glegg, had transgressed one of the laws of the Plantation by selling his grant inside five years to Cope, and Cope had offended by letting lands to "mere Irish"; so in 1630 he was given the option of forfeiture or a new charter. He chose the latter, paying an increased rent. Again in 1640[2], on his assigning the property to John Cairnes, a new patent was required,

[1] Inquisitions of Ulster, Tyrone, 1661.

[2] Documents in Auditor General's Office records. It is rather curious that this fruitful source of information as to some of the Plantation estates seems to have been overlooked by most writers on the Plantation of Ulster. Of course these records have never been published like Carew's Reports, Pynnar's Survey and the Inquisitions, but they are well worth close examination by anyone studying this subject. The charter of 1640 will be referred to in detail in the next chapter.

the Crown rent being raised from the original £5 3s. 4d. to £22 2s. 2d., at which it remains.

From the will of Robert Cairnes of Killyfaddy, proved in 1669, we learn that the three brothers, John, Robert, and David were in partnership in the purchases of these lands in the Barony of Clogher. John and David were both living in 1669, and as Robert had no issue by his wife Mary Elliot, his interest in the property, subject to an annuity for his widow, reverted to his two surviving brothers. In this will he refers to his brother-in-law James Cairnes of Claremore, husband of his sister Mary. This property is now part of the Manor of Cecil, but we cannot discover the parentage of this James Cairnes. It may be taken for granted he was a cousin. It is quite possible he was a son of that William Cairnes referred to above as being a contemporary of Alexander Cairnes in Donegal, but we cannot tell with any certainty.

We have very scanty information as to John Cairnes of Knockmany after the dates of the records already mentioned[1]. By Robert's death he became joint owner with David of all the Tyrone estate, but from the facts that by the will of David's eldest son William, dated 1685, we find the whole estate in the hands of David's family, and that about the same time we find John's sons established in extensive business transactions as merchants in London, we are led to the conclusion that he sold out his interest in the Tyrone lands to his brother David, who thus became sole proprietor, and with the purchase-money entered into business, being joined therein by his

[1] He is included in the "49 list" of officers who fought in the Irish wars on the Royalist side.

sons as they grew up. Of David's descendants we shall treat in the ensuing chapters.

As stated above, John Cairnes married Jane Miller, and had issue

ALEXANDER. Born 1665, died 1732, of whom later.

WILLIAM, died 1706, s.p.

HENRY, died 1743, s.p.

FRANCES, wife of CAPTAIN JOHN HENDERSON, of whom later.

MARY, wife of COLONEL FRANCIS BOYD of County Donegal.

The first mention we find of William Cairnes is in 1696, when he was struck off the franchise in the City of Dublin by the Lord Mayor Wall, for what reason we know not. He appealed by petition to Parliament against the arbitrary treatment of the Lord Mayor, and was reinstated. He is described in the petition as a merchant of the City of Dublin. We do not know the nature of his business, but he seems to have been a speculator to a large extent in landed estates. It is quite evident that the three brothers inherited a considerable fortune from their father.

William Cairnes settled in Dublin in 1694 or the following year. At that time a great number of landed estates were in the market, principally those reverting to the Crown through the attaintment of adherents of King James. Cairnes, having ample capital at his disposal, made some very judicious purchases of such. The first of these appears to have been the Blaney estate in Monaghan, upon which the mortgagees of the attainted

WILLIAM CAIRNES, M.P.

From the portrait by Mary Beale).

SIR HENRY CAIRNES, Bart., M.P.

Kneller School).

Lord Blaney[1] had foreclosed in 1690, and afterwards sold to Robert Elchin, a Williamite officer. He resold to Cairnes in 1696. Within the few years following, he purchased the estates of Sharavogue and Derrykeele, King's County, and in 1702 paid the Government £3,793 for some extensive tracts of forfeited lands in Roscommon, Wexford, Meath, and Dublin.

In the following year he entered Parliament, being elected both for Limavady and Belfast. He chose to sit for the latter constituency, which he represented until his death in 1706[2]. His portrait, painted in London by Mary Beale, about 1692, is at Rossmore, and is here reproduced. He was buried in St. Michan's Churchyard in Dublin. By his will he left, subject to a life interest to his widow — whose maiden name we do not know, and by whom he had no issue — all his landed estates in the County of Monaghan and elsewhere to his eldest brother Alexander, with reversion to his son and heir William Henry[3]; failing surviving male issue of Alexander, to his brother Henry and his heirs male ; failing whom, to the female heirs of his brothers ; failing whom, to the issue of his sisters ; failing whom, to the daughter of his beloved cousin David Cairnes of Londonderry. In this

[1] A detailed account of the unfortunate history of the Blaney family and their estates is given in Shirley's History of County Monaghan *(q. v.)*. In speaking of the Monaghan estate, however, Shirley states that it was sold to Alexander Cairnes in 1680. This is quite erroneous. Alexander was then only fifteen.

[2] In Reid's History of the Presbyterian Church, vol. ii., p. 515, he is stated to have been one of those who suffered under the infamous Test Act of 1704. That he was then a Presbyterian there is no doubt, but he certainly appears, like his brother Alexander, to have subsequently subscribed to the test.

[3] William Henry Cairnes, only son and heir of Sir Alexander, died in boyhood.

will both Alexander and Henry are described as merchants in the City of London.

Of the younger brother Henry we know comparatively little. He resided in his earlier years in London, where he married Frances daughter of Mr. Gould of London, brother of Sir Nathaniel Gould, whose daughter Elizabeth was the wife of Alexander Cairnes. Henry Cairnes in his later years resided at Donoughmore, County Donegal, the native place of his father. In 1732, on the death of Alexander, he succeeded to the Baronetcy which had been conferred in 1708. He also succeeded his brother as M.P. for Monaghan, and died without issue in 1743. He was buried at Donoughmore. His widow, Frances, Lady Cairnes, died in 1750.

Of ALEXANDER CAIRNES, the head representative of the old house of Orchardton and Cults, we first find documentary evidence in 1688. In that year he appears to have become possessed of deep religious convictions, and a very long-winded document[1] on the state of his immortal soul, written by him in this year, suggests the writer to have been an extreme fanatic. This document commences—

"O most dreadful God, for the passion of Thy Son, "I beseech Thee, accept of Thy poor prodigal son, "prostrating himself at Thy door. I have fallen from Thee, "by mine own iniquity, and am by nature, a son of death, "and a thousand-fold more the childe of hell by my "wicked practises[2] . . &c."

For the eighteen years following 1688, we regret we can

[1] This document in Sir Alexander's own hand was, and we believe is, still preserved by some of the descendants of his sister, Mrs. Henderson.

[2] Unfortunately we have no details of these.

SIR ALEXANDER CAIRNES, Bart., M.P.

Kneller School].

ELIZABETH, LADY CAIRNES,
and her daughter Mary, afterwards Lady Blaney.

Kneller School].

find no very authentic account of Alexander Cairnes' history. In several works it is stated that he entered the army, and highly distinguished himself under Marlborough at the Battle of Blenheim in 1704, and that in this campaign he formed a lasting friendship with that renowned soldier[1].

On the death of his brother William, Alexander succeeded to the extensive estates which the former had acquired in Ireland. From this time we find him taking a prominent part in Irish affairs, both political and connected with his estates. At the election of a Parliamentary representative for Belfast, consequent on the death of his brother, Alexander stood for the borough, but was defeated by his opponent Mr. Ogilvy. Against this return Mr. Cairnes appealed, alleging bribery and corruption. The case was tried before a committee of the House and Mr. Ogilvy's election confirmed.

In 1708, Mr. Cairnes was created a baronet with remainder, failing his male issue, to his brother Henry and his heirs male.

In 1710–1711 Sir Alexander was granted several important forfeited estates in Tipperary, Kilkenny, and Wexford, and in 1712, by the order of Queen Anne, was appointed Keeper of the Phœnix Park. He was elected M.P. for Monaghan in 1713, and continued to represent this constituency for many years. He married about 1702

[1] So far as we can trace, these accounts of Sir Alexander's career as a military man all emanate from the pen of the Rev. John Graham, and like all his statements, are utterly untrustworthy in the absence of other authority. In "Memoirs of John, Duke of Marlborough," compiled by Archdeacon Coxe from the Blenheim MSS. and other sources, it is stated that the friendship between Sir Alexander Cairnes and the Duke only began in 1718, and that they then met for the first time in the house of General Withers at Blackheath.

Elizabeth, daughter of Sir Nathaniel Gould, Knight, of London.

Sir Alexander, though now chiefly resident in Ireland, also kept a London house at Blackheath, and retained an interest in his banking business. He had as one of his partners General Withers, whose residence adjoined Sir Alexander's. It was at the General's that the Cairneses first met the Duke and Duchess of Marlborough who were on a visit there in 1718[1]. The Duchess took a great fancy to Lady Cairnes, who is described as a lady of charming manners and exquisite tact, and the friendship thus commenced lasted during the lifetime of Lady Cairnes, and was continued between her daughter and the four succeeding Duchesses. Sarah Duchess of Marlborough, in the first instance owing to the liking she had taken to Lady Cairnes, brought Miss Cairnes, who in 1718 was about fifteen, to Blenheim to pay long visits, during which she was the playmate and companion of her grandchildren. Her governess there was Madame La Vie[2]. Among the papers at Blenheim are many bearing upon private theatricals and other amusements of the young people, and Miss Cairnes' name appears as an actress in several of them. She was lively and witty, clever as an actress, musical, and even addicted to writing verse. She married in 1724

[1] Lady Blayney's letters to the Duchess of Marlborough, wife of the fourth Duke. These and many earlier letters of Mary Cairnes, Lady Blaney, are among the Blenheim MSS.—Coxe's Life of John, Duke of Marlborough.

[2] One of the three daughters of Henry, Count La Vie, who fled from France about 1690, during a period of religious persecution. It is related that these ladies escaped hidden in barrels, through the aid of a sympathetic sea captain. One of them, Martha, married in 1700 Robert Edwards of Kilcroagh, and was an ancestress of the mother of the late Canon Bagot of Fonstown Glebe, Co. Kildare. Madame La Vie's portrait is among those now at Rossmore.

MARY CAIRNES, LADY BLANEY.

From the Portrait by Robert Edge Pine].

LIEUT.-COLONEL MURRAY, M.P.

Kneller School]

Cadwaller, 7th Lord Blaney, which, as Miss Cairnes was her father's sole heiress, was a marriage calculated to restore to the Blaney family their ancestral estates. There was no issue of the marriage, and Lord Blaney died in 1732. The same year died Sir Alexander Cairnes. His will is short and to the point. He leaves "to his only surviving child Mary, Lady Blaney, absolutely, and entirely free from the control of her husband Lord Blaney," all his estates and property of every sort. Although he lost heavily in the South Sea Bubble, he died a very wealthy man, and shortly after his death his vast landed estates all over Ireland became greatly enhanced in value.

Thus the year 1732 saw Lady Blaney a widow and a wealthy heiress. She was a lady of the most refined tastes and a rather distinguished connoisseur of art. Many exquisite objects of vertu and bric-à-brac of her selection are still to be seen at Rossmore, and, rare when acquired by her, are to-day the subject of ecstatic admiration on the part of connoisseurs of such objects who are privileged to see them. She was a keen admirer and patron of both Chippendale and Sheraton, her contemporaries, and some exquisite specimens of the works of these celebrated artists in furniture of her selection are to be seen at Rossmore[1].

[1] Thomas Chippendale, among his choicest productions, made a suite of dining room furniture, which was purchased by Lady Blaney for Rossmore. This suite was sold by the 2nd Lord Rossmore to Mr. Temple Reilly of Scarva House, Co. Down. Recently the contents of Scarva House came under the relentless hammer of the auctioneer, and this choice lot fell to Mr. Butler of Dublin, at a handsome figure. The present Lord Rossmore, who inherits to a great extent his ancestress's artistic taste, has restored the suite to its old home.

Lady Blaney resided alternately at Monaghan, Dublin, and London, and was a most distinguished personage at the English and Irish Courts during the reigns of the first three Georges. After the death of Lord Blaney, she married secondly, the Right Hon. Colonel John Murray, M.P., but until her death in 1790 was known as Mary Cairnes, Lady Blaney. She had her portrait painted, as a child, with her mother Lady Cairnes, by an unknown artist of the Knoeller School; and at the age of 81, by Robert Edge Pine, both of which portraits are here reproduced.

By her marriage with Colonel Murray, she had issue,

A. FRANCES, who married in 1752, WILLIAM HENRY FORTESCUE, EARL OF CLERMONT, who died without issue in 1806. Lady Clermont, whose portrait is at Rossmore, and is here reproduced, was a great favourite at the English and French Courts. She resided, when not at Ravensdale, chiefly in London, but she frequently visited Paris, where, between 1770 and 1780, she enjoyed the friendship of Queen Marie Antoinette, often staying as one of Her Majesty's private friends at the little Trianon at Versailles. To this bijou residence, Marie Antoinette was wont to retire to rid herself of the stiff formality and etiquette of the court. Here she loved to have round her her own personal friends, with whom she gladly threw off the rigid dignity and reserve she was compelled to assume at court, but which she always disliked. To Lady Clermont she gave many proofs of affection, and some beautiful presents. Among these were

ELIZABETH, FIRST LADY ROSSMORE.

From the portrait by Hogarth].

MAJOR-GENERAL ROBERT CUNNINGHAM,
FIRST LORD ROSSMORE.

From the portrait by Stewart].

a full length portrait of herself, a ring in which was set a lock of her hair, and a gold arrow set with diamonds, with the inscription "Je pique, mais je m'attache." After the Revolution, Lady Clermont presented the portrait to the Duchesse d'Angoulême. The ring and the diamond arrow, she gave to her grand-niece Mrs. Lloyd, through whose daughter the Dowager Lady Rossmore, they have come to the Rossmore family. After her husband's death Lady Clermont lived in London, reaching the venerable age of ninety-six, and dying about 1824[1].

B. ELIZABETH, who married in 1754, the Right Hon. General ROBERT CUNNINGHAM, of County Wicklow, who was Commander of the Forces in Ireland. By the will of Mary Cairnes, Lady Blaney, her estates passed, subject to certain charges, to her daughter Elizabeth and her issue male, failing whom, to her next daughters in seniority, and their heirs male. After Lady Blaney's death General Cunningham was, in right of his wife, in 1796 created Baron Rossmore, of Monaghan, with the special and peculiar remainder as to the title, to the male issue of Lady Rossmore's sister Anne, Mrs. Jones, failing whom, to that of her next sister Harriet, Mrs. Westenra. The first Lord Rossmore died in 1801, the only son of Mrs. Jones having predeceased him, so that the successor in the title

[1] Personal recollections of her grand-niece, Mrs. Lloyd of Farrinrory, narrated by her daughter, the present Dowager Lady Rossmore.

was the eldest son of Harriet, Mrs. Westenra, the fifth, and fourth surviving daughter. The first Lady Rossmore, in her widowhood, lived in a large house in Merrion Square, Dublin. She was one of the most noteworthy ladies in the capital in her time. Her wit, tact and stately presence, combined with her many accomplishments, made her house a miniature court in its way. No Lord Lieutenant in her day, ever came to Dublin, without at once paying this distinguished lady a visit.[1] She lived in Dublin until her death at the age of 91, about the same year as that of her sister Lady Clermont.

c. MARY, died young, unmarried, 1754.

D. ANNE, married in 1764, the Right Hon. THEOPHILUS JONES, by whom she had issue one son living in 1796, and specially mentioned as heir of the Barony of Rossmore in the grant of that peerage. He, however, predeceased the 1st Lord, unmarried.

E. HARRIET, who in 1764, married HENRY, eldest son and heir of Warner Westenra[2], by whom she had issue,

1. WARNER WILLIAM, who, failing issue of the

[1] Personal recollections of her grand-niece, Mrs. Lloyd of Farrinrory, narrated by her daughter, the present Dowager Lady Rossmore.

[2] The founder of this family in Ireland was a cadet of an ancient and noble Dutch family, who settled in Dublin as an extensive merchant towards the end of the sixteenth century. His eldest son, WARNER WESTENRA, by his wife, a Miss Vincent, had issue, Elizabeth, wife of Samuel Digby, Bishop of Elphin, who died 1720, and HENRY, who acquired considerable property in Kildare and Dublin. He married Elizabeth, daughter of Sir Joshua Allan, and had issue an eldest surviving son and heir,

FRANCES, COUNTESS OF CLERMONT.

From a Pastel].

HARRIET MURRAY, Mrs WESTENRA.

Robert Edge Pine].

ANNE MURRAY, Mrs. JONES.

Robert Edge Pine].

WARNER WESTENRA.

Kneller School]

THE LADY HESTER WESTENRA.

Kneller School].

first Lady Rossmore and the surviving issue of Mrs. Jones, succeeded as the 2nd Baron Rossmore, of whom later.

2. HENRY, 8th Dragoon Guards, a Brigadier-General; he married Anne, daughter of Isaac Corry, of Newry, and d.s.p.
3. MARY FRANCES, married 1788, Sir John Craven Carden, Bart., of Templemore, Co. Tipperary, by whom she had issue (see footnote below).
4. HARRIET HESTER, wife of the Hon. Colonel Edward Wingfield, of the Powerscourt family.

WARNER WILLIAM WESTENRA, on the death of the first Lord Rossmore, in 1801, succeeded, in accordance with the terms of remainder in the patent, as heir of his mother, to the Barony. He was born in 1765. As heir of the Westenra family, and, after the death almost at the same time of his aunts, the Ladies Rossmore and Clermont, as heir of Sir Alexander Cairnes, he was one of the wealthiest peers in Ireland. An influential politician, he returned three members to parliament, though his views were not in agreement with those of his father, who was a member at the time of the Union, and voted for the Union.[1] As well as a strong

WARNER, who in 1738 married the Lady Hester, second daughter of Richard, Earl of Cavan. By her he had issue seven children, of whom the eldest was HENRY, who married the fifth daughter, and eventual heiress of Mary Cairnes, Lady Blaney, the sole daughter and heiress of Sir Alexander Cairnes, and was the father of the second Baron Rossmore. He was also father of Mary Frances, wife of Sir John Craven Carden, Bart., of Templemore, County Tipperary, whose daughter Harriet became the wife of Henry Lloyd of Farrinrory, Co. Tipperary, whose daughter by this marriage, Julia Ellen Josephine, married in 1846 Henry Robert, 3rd Baron Rossmore, whom she survived, marrying secondly Major George W. Stackpole, of Edenvale, Co. Clare. The Dowager Lady Rossmore now resides at Ranby Hall, Retford, Notts.

[1] Sir Jonah Barrington's "Rise and Fall of the Irish Nation."

politician, the second Lord Rossmore was a born sportsman, and loved a hard-fought contest for its own sake; and it is possible that the extraordinary zest with which he forced his nominees into parliament at the elections was as much the outcome of his love for a contest as for politics pure and simple. Within recent years died some old residents in Co. Monaghan who remembered a memorable election in 1826, when Lord Rossmore put forward his son Henry Robert, as candidate for the county. The candidate's views being not entirely in accordance with those of the county at large, the result of the election was by no means certain. At a meeting held in Monaghan in support of Mr. Westenra's candidature, there were on the platform the candidate's uncle, Colonel Henry Westenra, his brother John,[1] and himself. The veteran colonel in addressing the meeting, met with a somewhat mixed reception, and at last, an opponent in the crowd cried out "Arrah sure! who is thim Whistlerows, but only a lot o' tay daylers from Holland?" "Yes," promptly replied the colonel: "and there are three tay daylers here well able to give any three of you your tay!" The crowd knew this was no empty threat, and were taken with the ready repartee. It took well, and the candidate got in. During the course of the election Mr. Westenra in some way fell foul of Colonel Madden, of Hilton. The result was a challenge. A duel was arranged, and on the 10th day of July, 1826, the opponents drove to Ardgonnell Bridge, Co. Armagh side, out of the jurisdiction of the Monaghan High Sheriff. Colonel Lucas was second for Mr. Westenra, and Colonel

[1] Grandfather of the Earl of Huntingdon.

Savage for Colonel Madden. At the first fire Mr. Westenra was severely wounded in the ankle, while Colonel Madden had a button shot off his coat.[1] Mr. Westenra recovered, and the bullet being extracted, is still preserved at Rossmore as a memento of this hard-fought election and duel.

The second Lord Rossmore, as we have mentioned, was an ardent lover of sport. He kept his own pack of hounds, and was a keen huntsman. In the then fashionable sport of cock-fighting, he would allow no cock in the county to stand over his. As a politician he had great weight, and long continued to return his nominees to Parliament. He was H.M.L. for County Monaghan. He died in 1842 at the age of 77, having married, firstly, Mary daughter of Charles Walsh, of Walsh Park, County Tipperary, by whom he had issue as follows ; he married secondly, the Lady Augusta Charteris, sister of the 8th Earl of Wemyss.

A. HENRY ROBERT, above named, of whom later.

B. & C. WARNER WILLIAM, CHARLES, who d.s.p.

D. RICHARD, who married in 1822, Henrietta, daughter of Henry Owen Scott, of County Monaghan, and died in 1838, leaving issue three daughters only, who died unmarried.

E. JOHN CRAVEN, of Sharavogue, King's County, married, 1stly, Lady East, widow of Sir Gilbert East, Bart., who d.s.p. He married, 2ndly, Anne, daughter of Louis Charles Daubez, and died,

[1] Extracted from the MS. diary of Colonel Savage of the Ards, in possession of his grandson, Mr. W. R. Young, of Galgorm Castle, Co. Antrim.

leaving issue, one surviving daughter and heiress, MARY ANNE WILMOT, wife of FRANCES POWER PLANTAGENET HASTINGS, 13th Earl of Huntingdon, by whom she had issue,

a. WARNER FRANCIS JOHN PLANTAGENET, b. 1871, the present Earl.

b. OSWALD WILLIAM WESTENRA, b. 1873, who married, 1896, Mary C. C., daughter of D. Fox Tarratt, Esq., of Ellany, Argyll, and has issue.

c. AUBREY CRAVEN THEOPHILUS ROBIN HOOD, b. 1878.

d. CONSTANCE WILMOT ANNE, wife of Major Sir THOS. SABINE PASLEY, Bart., by whom she has issue.

e. ILEENE FRANCES CAIRNES, wife of COLIN GEORGE PELHAM CAMPBELL, of Stonefield, Argyll, by whom she has issue.

f. IERNE LOUISA ARUNDEL, wife of the Hon. JOHN S. TUFTON, heir presumptive of Lord Hothfield, by whom she has issue.

g. ROWENA GRACE, wife of GRAHAM PATERSON, Esq., of Kingsmede, Windsor Forest, by whom she has issue.

h. WILMOT IDA NOREEN, wife of WILLIAM HAMER BASS, Esq., heir presumptive of the Baronetcy at present merged with the title of Lord Burton.

HENRY ROBERT, 3RD BARON ROSSMORE, succeeded to the title on the death of his father in 1842. He had for many years represented Co. Monaghan in Parliament, and was Lord Lieutenant and Custos Rotulorum of the County during the later years of his father's lifetime, retaining this important office until his death in 1860. He did much to improve his estate, and added a magnificent wing to Rossmore Castle. Through his first wife, the only daughter of the 8th Duke of Hamilton, he became possessed of the greater portion of the Island of Arran in Scotland, where he built a residence, and often resided. Both in County Monaghan and in Arran, his memory is held in affectionate respect. Shortly before his death he sold the Arran estate to the Hamilton family, devoting the proceeds of the sale to the extension and improvement of his Monaghan estates. He married firstly, Ann Douglas, daughter of the 8th Duke of Hamilton, who died without issue in 1844. He married secondly, in 1846, his cousin Julia Ellen Josephine, daughter of Henry Lloyd, of Farrinrory, Co. Tipperary, the present Dowager Lady Rossmore, of Ranby Hall, Retford, Notts. Lord Rossmore died in 1860, leaving issue by his second marriage,

A. HENRY CAIRNES, 4TH BARON ROSSMORE, born 1851, who was only nine years of age on his succession to the title. He was educated at Eton, and entered the 1st Life Guards. In 1874 he was thrown from his horse in a steeplechase at Windsor, and received injuries which shortly afterwards proved fatal. He was much liked by the late Queen Victoria, who several times during his last illness called in person to enquire for him. He died at Windsor Cavalry Barracks.

B. DERRICK WARNER WILLIAM, the fifth and present peer.

C. RICHARD HAMILTON, born 1854, d.s.p.

D. PETER CRAVEN, born 1855, married 1895, Innys Maude, daughter of Landsdowne Daubeny, of Norton Malreward, Somerset, and has issue, two daughters.

E. FRANCES KATHLEEN, who married in 1870 Captain Henry Augustus Candy, 9th Lancers, and has issue,

   1. CAIRNES DERRICK CARRINGTON, born 1875.
   2. KATHLEEN FLORENCE MAY, Duchess of Newcastle, married 1899, to the 7th Duke.

F. NORAH JOSEPHINE HARCOURT, married in 1873, Captain Gilbert Sterling, of the Royal Horse Guards, and has issue—

   1. HENRY FRANCIS, born 1874, Captain 2nd Batt. Coldstream Guards.
   2. REGINALD GILBERT, born 1878, Captain 2nd Batt. King's Royal Rifles.
   3. CHARLES RICHARD, born 1882.
   4. WILLIAM GEORGE, born 1887.

DERRICK WARNER WILLIAM, Fifth and present Baron Rossmore, of Rossmore, Co. Monaghan, H.M.L., married in 1882, Mittie, daughter of Richard Christopher Naylor of Hooton Hall, Chester, and has issue—

1. WILLIAM, born 1892.
2. RICHARD, born 1893.
3. MARY.

Lord Rossmore is the direct heir and representative,

through female descent, of Sir Alexander Cairnes, whose brother, Sir Henry Cairnes, was, prior to his death in 1743, the last surviving representative in the male line of the old family of Cairnes of Cults and Orchardton.[1] The Tyrone family became extinct in the male line on the death of Captain William Cairnes, in 1740, although his grand-nephew and heir, John Elliot, by direction of his grand-uncle's will, assumed the surname of Cairnes in addition to his own name Elliot.

Thus can Lord Rossmore claim to be the head representative, though through female descent, of John Carnys, of Cults, scutifer to the Earl Douglas in 1421, grandson of William de Carnys, who was of that ilk early in the fourteenth century.

ROSSMORE CASTLE.—The illustration' of Rossmore Castle here given is of the front view. The portion in the centre is that built originally by Lord Blaney shortly after the year 1620, and rebuilt by his heir Richard Blaney, afterwards 4th Baron, in 1655. Sir Alexander Cairnes added to the building in 1725. The wing to the right and the square tower and magnificent suite of drawing-rooms abutting thereon, to the left, were built by the 3rd Lord Rossmore.

[1] Of course, strictly speaking, on the death of Sir Henry Cairnes in 1743, the headship of the family in the male line reverted to his distant cousin the laird of Kipp. On the death of George, the last Cairns laird of Kipp, in 1804, the nominal headship of the family would have devolved upon some descendant of a younger son of some of the Cairnses of Kipp, but unfortunately the actual descent of all of these is not distinctly traceable. It is very possible that William Cairns of Magheraconluce, County Down, ancestor of the Earls Cairns, was a cadet of this family. The last Cairns of Galloway whose unbroken descent in the male line from William de Carnys of 1360 could be traced was William Cairns of Torr, who died in 1860. (See chap. VIII.)

Archdall in his Monasticon Hibernicum states that Sir Edward, Lord Blaney, built a castle on the site of the Monastery of Monaghan.[1] If this be correct, which we have no reason to doubt, Rossmore is the successor of the Franciscan Monastery founded by Felim MacBrian MacArdgal MacMahon in 1462.[2] On the suppression of the monasteries in 1538, that of Monaghan was not immediately closed, though it seems to have been granted to some English adventurer.[3] Two years later "the Saxonaig destroyed the monastery and beheaded the garrison and some of the Friars."[4] Thus ended the religious establishment of Muinechain, after a duration of 78 years.[5]

In the State Papers are several grants to Sir Edward Blaney of the castle and lands of Monaghan.[6] In 1620, he was created Baron Blaney of Monaghan, and granted the castle of Monaghan[7] which he was to hold as a Royal Fort, with the proviso "that he was to build another castle with

---

[1] P. 585. Archdall had personal knowledge of this district, and as he lived within a hundred years of Lord Blaney's time, this statement is probably correct. The meaning of Corlattan, the "hill of the monuments"—the name of the townland in which the castle is situated—corroborates Archdall's statement, as the Monastery of Muinechain, we learn from the Annals of Ulster and the Four Masters, was a noted place of burial.

[2] Annals of Ulster and of the Four Masters, Anno 1462.

[3] Archdall gives his name as Edward Withe, but we cannot find any reference to this effect in the Records.

[4] Annals of the Four Masters, Anno, 1540. The garrison were possibly followers of the MacMahons who fortified the Monastery against the invaders. The situation, being on a steep hill, would have lent itself admirably to this. However, the Irish word translated "garrison" by O'Donovan may mean "guardian," and refer here to the chief friar. This is the rendering given by Hennessy in the Annals of Lough Cè.

[5] The Monasticon Hibernicum wrongly attributes some very early references to Mucknoe (Castleblaney) in the A.F.M. and A.U. to Monaghan. There is no reference whatever in the Annals to Muinechain prior to 1462.

[6] Calendar of State Papers, 1615-1625, pp. 284, 300, 301.

[7] The Castle, which formerly occupied what is now the courthouse in the town of Monaghan. It is first mentioned (A.F.M.) as MacMahon's Castle in 1492, but it or its predecessor was probably of earlier date.

ROSSMORE CASTLE, Co. Monaghan.

From a Photo. by Philips, Belfast.]

a hundred acres in demesne lands," &c. In compliance with this stipulation, he built a residence at Corlattan, known as "Mount Maria," which may be on the actual foundations of the monastery. Lord Blaney died in 1630, and was succeeded in the title and estates, and in the Governorship of Monaghan Castle, by his son Henry, 2nd Baron.

In the rebellion of 1641, the Irish captured both Monaghan Castle and Mount Maria, as well as Castleblayney—where his lordship and his family were in residence at the time. In this Lord Blaney's depositions taken at Dublin Castle, relating to his sufferings and losses entailed by the sacking of his houses, he refers to "his two houses of Monaghan"—*i.e.*, Mount Maria and Monaghan Castle. Among his goods destroyed or lost were "his plate worth £500, and a library of books estimated at £500."

In the beautiful carved oak panelling in the library at Rossmore, over the mantlepiece, is carved the date 1655, from which it is probable that Richard, the brother and heir of Edward, 3rd Lord Blaney, who became owner of the estate in right of his wife in 1653[1], restored the castle. In 1725 Sir Alexander Cairnes added considerably to it, and over the former principal entrance is carved—

A.C.
MOUNT MARIA,
1725.

[1] The Blaney estate was practically laid waste in the troubles of 1641-1646. Castleblayney and Mount Maria, as well as Monaghan Castle, were pillaged and burned, so that Edward the third Lord was left penniless, and sold the property to Thomas Vincent, a London merchant, in 1653. His brother Richard in the same year married that gentleman's daughter, to whom her father gave the estate as a dowry. Richard Blaney succeeded as 4th Baron on the death of his brother in 1669.

The 2nd Lord Rossmore, in whose time the place was known as "Cortolvin Hills," added to it, and the 3rd Lord built the splendid wing, now the main portion of the castle, and containing the magnificent suite of drawing rooms. The demesne, one of the most beautiful in Ireland, contains many gigantic trees of rare varieties, which, from their age, cannot have been planted later than the days of Mary Cairnes, Lady Blaney, or of her father Sir Alexander.

Reference has been made above to the two sisters of Sir Alexander Cairnes, Frances wife of Captain John Henderson of Donoughmore, County Donegal, and Mary, wife of Colonel Boyd, of County Donegal.

The former had issue—

1. CAIRNES HENDERSON.
2. WILLIAM HENRY HENDERSON, of Donoughmore.
3. JOSEPH HENDERSON.
4. MARGARET, wife of the Rev. Francis Laird, of whom later.
5. AGNES, Mrs. Wrighton.
6. ELIZABETH. Died unmarried, 1717.

CAIRNES HENDERSON, who was mentioned in the will of his uncle William Cairnes as his ultimate heir failing the issue of Lady Blaney, married his first cousin Mary, daughter of Colonel Boyd, and had issue three sons and three daughters, of whom the eldest JOSEPH HENDERSON had an only daughter ELIZABETH, who in 1774 married JAMES SINGER[1], then of the 47th Regiment, and afterwards

[1] Of a family long settled in Co. Down. There are several representatives of the Singers, farmers on the Downshire and Mussendun estates, in the neighbourhood of Annahilt and Dromore.

of the Commissariat Department in Ireland. He died in 1828, leaving issue,

1. PAULUS ÆMILIUS SINGER, born 1775, died 1861, leaving issue.
2. JAMES SINGER, born 1784; a Major 7th R.I. Fusiliers. Killed at Badajoz, 1812.
3. JOSEPH HENDERSON SINGER, born 1786. He entered Trinity College in 1801, where after a distinguished course he graduated B.A., 1806, M.A., 1811. He obtained a fellowship in 1810, B.D. and D.D. in 1825. In 1850 he became Regius Professor of Divinity, and was appointed to the Rectory of Raymochy, in the Diocese of Raphoe, and in 1851 to the Archdeaconry of Raphoe. In the following year he was appointed Bishop of Meath and Privy Councillor. This eminent ecclesiastic was an able and eloquent preacher, and was at the head of the evangelical party in the Irish Church. He strongly opposed the National Board of Education, his attitude on this question having long delayed his preferment. He died in 1866. He had married in 1822 Mary, daughter of the Rev. Henry Crofton, and niece of Sir Hugh Crofton, Bart., of Mohill. He had issue,

   a. JAMES, d.s.p., 1841.
   b. HENRY, an officer in the R.A. Served in the Crimean War, where he was killed, 1854.
   c. JOSEPH HENDERSON, d.s.p., 1851.

d. MORGAN, born 1831. Became a Vice-Admiral, and marrying in 1857 Frances, daughter of General Burn, R.A., died in 1902, leaving issue—

1. MORGAN, Captain R.N. Married Emmie, daughter of General Desborough, R.A., by whom he has issue one daughter.

2. ROBERT, now of the South African Constabulary.

3. CHARLES WILLIAM, Captain R.E. Married and has issue.

4. FRANCES LAWRENCE, and five daughters.

e. PAULUS ÆMILIUS, Clk., d.s.p., 1902.

f. ROBERT BURN, Captain 5th and 28th Regiments. Married Janet, daughter of General Burn, R.A., and died 1878, leaving issue—

1. JOSEPH HENDERSON.

2. ROBERT, d.s.p., and three daughters.

g. FRANCES CROFTON. Married, 1846, the Rev. Ralph Bourne Baker, of Hasfield Court, Gloucester, and dying in 1881, left issue—

1. WILLIAM MEATH BAKER, now of Hasfield Court.

2. MARY FRANCES, wife of the Rev. Alfred Penny.

3. DOROTHEA, wife of Richard B. Townshend.

h. ELIZABETH, wife of Henry Crofton, R.N. Died 1879, leaving issue.

i. MARY, wife of the Rev. William Gabbett, by whom she had issue.

k. SARAH LETITIA, wife of the late Rev. Robert Staveley, B.D., sometime Canon of Christ Church, and Rector of Holy Trinity, Killiney. She died in 1886, leaving issue,

1. ROBERT, R.N. Married, 1887, Helen ffolliot, daughter of the above Morgan Singer, by whom she has issue.

2. JOSEPH HENDERSON SINGER, Clk., d.s.p., 1891.

3. MARGARET FRANCES FFOLLIOT, wife of F. G. Rambaut.

l. HENRIETTA DOROTHEA. Married 1864, the late William Jameson, by whom she has issue—

1. WILLIAM, Lieutenant R.I.R., d.s.p.

2. SINGER, M.D. Married Miss Heron.

3. MORGAN CLAUDE.

4. MARY, wife of Mr. James Heron.

4. MARY ANNE, married 1798, General Sir Henry Sheehy Keating, K.C.B., Governor of Mauritius. She died 1847, leaving issue.

a. JAMES, Colonel in the Army, d.s.p., 1870.

b. BRYAN, d.s.p., 1826.

c. HENRY SINGER. Born 1804; was called to the English Bar in 1832; Q.C., 1849; M.P. for Reading, 1852-1859; Solicitor-General, 1858-59; Judge of the Court of Common Pleas, 1859 to 1875, when he retired from the bench, being created a Privy Councillor, He died 1888, having married in 1843 Gertrude, daughter of Major-General Evans, by whom he had issue—

HENRY, who married Miss Evans, and died leaving issue.

d. ROGER. Born 1818, d.s.p., 1844.

5. JANE, Mrs. Donovan, who died 1848, leaving issue.
6. LOUISA, Mrs. Anderson, who d.s.p., 1854.

A sister of the above-named Cairnes Henderson, Margaret, married in 1715 the Rev. Francis Laird, minister of Donoughmore, County Donegal, to which he had been ordained in 1709. Their son, the Rev. William Laird, lived at Ray, County Donegal, but afterwards came to Belfast. He married about 1740, a daughter of the Rev. David Fairley, and sister of Alderman Fairley, of Londonderry, who was Mayor of that City, 1769-70. By her he had several children, of whom his daughter Elizabeth married the Rev. John Thomson, Minister of Carmoney, Belfast. By him she had issue—

A. CHARLES, who had issue one son and two daughters.

B. WILLIAM, who married Miss Cochrane, of Armagh, and had issue—

1. CHARLES, deceased.
2. WILLIAM, deceased.
3. LUCY, Mrs. Herdman, now of Belfast.

C. ELIZABETH, who in 1799 married William M'Clure, head of the firm William M'Clure & Sons, merchants, of Belfast, by him she had issue,

1. WILLIAM, Minister at Londonderry. Born 1802. He married, but died without issue.

2. THOMAS, born 1806, of Belmont, Belfast. He entered his father's firm in Belfast, eventually becoming sole partner. In 1857 he purchased Lord Ranfurley's estate of Belmont and Strandtown, now included within the city boundaries of Belfast. He was elected M.P. for Belfast in 1868 as a Liberal, but was defeated in the election of 1874, when he was created a baronet by Mr. Gladstone. He represented County Londonderry in Parliament from 1878 to 1885, was High Sheriff of Down, 1864, and Vice Lieutenant of that county from 1872 to 1877. In 1877 Sir Thomas M'Clure married Ellison, daughter of Robert A. M'Fie, of Dreghorn Castle, Midlothian, and d.s.p. Lady M'Clure died January, 1906.

3. ELIZABETH, died unmarried.

D. JANE, who married in 1809, the Rev. Moses Finlay, minister of Donoughmore, County Down, by whom she had issue,

1. CHARLES, born 1811, who had issue.

2. WILLIAM LAIRD, born 1814. He entered into business in the firm of his uncles, C. & W. Thomson, and in 1852, in partnership with his cousin Sir Thomas M'Clure and his brother Charles, founded the firm of M'Clure, Finlay & Co., extensively engaged in the linen trade. On Sir Thomas retiring the firm became Finlay Brothers & Co., and in 1886 was converted into a private limited company, under the title

of the Wolfhill Spinning Co., Limited. Mr. Finlay, who in his day was one of the most eminent citizens of Belfast, married in 1859, Jeanette, daughter of William Stevenson, of Carrickfergus, and, dying in 1900, left issue—

a. FREDERICK W., now of Wolfhill. Born 1861. Married in 1886 Caroline, daughter of Alan Ker, of Birkenhead, by whom he has issue.

b. CLARENCE, and four daughters.

3. HENRY, deceased.
4. ELIZABETH, deceased.

TABLE III.

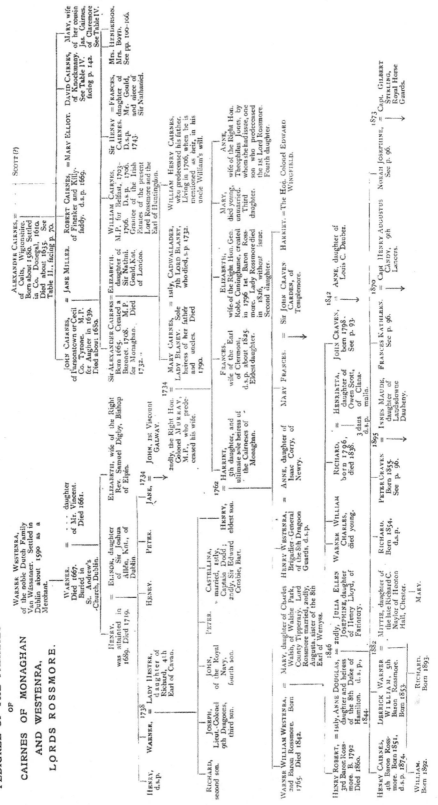

PEDIGREE OF THE FAMILIES OF CAIRNES OF MONAGHAN AND WESTENRA, LORDS ROSSMORE.

WARNER WESTENRA, of the noble Dutch Family Van Wassanaer. Settled in Dublin about 1590 as a Merchant.

WARNER. Died 1667. Buried in St. Andrew's Church, Dublin. = . . . daughter of Mr. Vincent. Died 1661.

HENRY. was attainted in 1689. Died 1719. = ELINOR, daughter of Sir Joshua Allen, Knt., of Dublin.

ELIZABETH, wife of the Right Rev. Samuel Digby, Bishop of Elpin.

HENRY, d.s.p. — WARNER, = (1738) LADY HESTER, daughter of Richard, 4th Earl of Cavan. — HENRY. — PETER. — JANE, = (1734) JOHN, 1st Viscount GALWAY.

RICHARD, second son. — JOSEPH, Lieut.-Colonel 9th Dragoons, third son. — JOHN, of the Royal Navy, fourth son. — PETER. — CASTELLINA, married, 1stly, Captain Dodd; 2ndly, Sir Edward Crosbie, Bart. — HENRY, eldest son. = (1762) HARRIET, 5th daughter, and ultimate sole heiress of the Cairneses of Monaghan.

ALEXANDER CAIRNES, of Cults, Wigtonshire. Born about 1580. Settled in Co. Donegal, 1610. Died about 1635. See Table II., facing p. 70. = . . . SCOTT (?)

JOHN CAIRNES, of Parsonstown or Cecil Co. Tyrone. M.P. for Augher in 1639. Died about 1680. = JANE MILLER. — ROBERT CAIRNES, of Finesker and Killyfaddy. d.s.p. 1669. = MARY ELLIOT. — DAVID CAIRNES, of Knockmany. See Table IV. facing p. 142. — MARY, wife of her cousin Jas. Cairnes, of Claremore See Table IV.

Sir ALEXANDER CAIRNES = ELIZABETH. Born 1665. Created a Baronet. 1708. M.P. for Monaghan. Died 1732. — ELIZABETH, daughter of Sir Nathnl. Gould, Knt. of London. — WILLIAM CAIRNES, M.P. for Belfast, 1703–1706. D.s.p. 1706. Grantee of the Irish Estates of the present Lord Rossmore and the Earl of Huntingdon. — Sir HENRY CAIRNES. D.s.p. 1743. = FRANCES, daughter of Mr. Gould, and niece of Sir Nathaniel. — Mrs. HENDERSON. Mrs. BOYD. See pp. 100–106.

2ndly, the Right Hon. Colonel MURRAY, M.P., who predeceased his wife. = (1734) MARY CAIRNES, LADY BLANEY. Sole heiress of her father and uncles. Died 1790. = 1stly, CADWALLADER, 7th LORD BLANEY, who died, s.p. 1732. — WILLIAM HENRY CAIRNES, who predeceased his father. Living in 1706, when he is mentioned as heir, in his uncle William's will.

FRANCES, wife of the Earl of Clermont, d.s.p. about 1825. Eldest daughter. — ELIZABETH, wife of the Right Hon. Gen. Robt. Cuninghame, created in 1796 1st Baron Rossmore. Lady Rossmore died in 1826, without issue. Second daughter. — MARY, died young, unmarried. Third daughter. — ANNE, wife of the Right Hon. Theophilus Jones, by whom she had issue, one son who predeceased the 1st Lord Rossmore. Fourth daughter.

WARNER WILLIAM WESTENRA, 2nd Baron Rossmore. Born 1765. Died 1842. = MARY, daughter of Charles Walsh, of Walshe Park, County Tipperary. Lord Rossmore married, 2ndly, Augusta, sister of the 8th Earl of Wemyss. — HENRY WESTENRA, Brigadier-General of the 8th Dragoon Guards, d.s.p. = ANNE, daughter of Isaac Corry, of Newry. — MARY FRANCES. = Sir JOHN CRAVEN CARDEN, of Templemore. — HARRIET. = The Hon. Colonel EDWARD WINGFIELD.

HENRY ROBERT, 3rd Baron Rossmore. B. 1792 Died 1860. = 1stly, ANNE DOUGLAS, daughter and heiress of the 8th Duke of Hamilton. d.s.p., 1844. = (1846) 2ndly, JULIA ELLEN JOSEPHINE, daughter of Henry Lloyd, of Farinrory. — WARNER WILLIAM CHARLES, died young. — RICHARD, born 1796, died 1838. = HENRIETTA, daughter of Owen Scott, of Clanamulla. 3 daus d.s.p. — JOHN CRAVEN, born 1798. See p. 93. = (1842) ANNE, daughter of Louis C. Daubez.

HENRY CAIRNES, 4th Baron Rossmore. Born 1851, d.s.p. 1874. — DERRICK WARNER WILLIAM, 5th Baron Rossmore. Born 1853. = (1882) MITTIE, daughter of the late Richard C. Naylor of Hooton Hall, Chester. — RICHARD. Born 1854, d.s.p. — PETER CRAVEN Born 1855. See p. 96. = (1895) INNES MAUDE, daughter of Landsdowne Dauheny. — FRANCES KATHLEEN. See p. 96. = (1870) Capt HENRY AUGUSTUS CANDY, 9th Lancers. — NORAH JOSEPHINE, See p. 96. = (1873) Capt. GILBERT STIRLING, Royal Horse Guards.

WILLIAM. Born 1892. — RICHARD. Born 1893. — MARY.

CHAPTER VI.

The Cairnes Family in County Tyrone, Lords of the Manors of Killyfaddy and Cecil—The Elliots and Elliot-Cairneses—The division of the property—Killyfaddy left by will to Mrs. Seaver, of Heath Hall—Cecil sold to Mr. Gervais—Colonel John Elliot-Cairnes, K.H.—Professor John Elliot-Cairnes—The Family of Stameen, &c.

AS has been related in the last chapter, Alexander Cairnes, formerly of Cults in Wigtonshire, lineal head of the family of Orchardton, came over to the County Donegal between 1609 and 1611 as general agent to the undertakers in the Baronies of Boylagh and Bannagh. He had three sons, John, Robert and David, and one daughter Mary, wife of her cousin James Cairnes of Claremore[1]. The date of Alexander's death is not recorded. He must have died possessed of a considerable fortune, and probably about 1635, as between that year and 1639 we find his eldest son John (who acted for himself and his brothers Robert and David jointly[2]) in possession of the manor of Cecil or Parsonstown; and by indenture dated January, 1640, he purchased from Sir Richard Cope the manor of Killyfaddy. The purchase price of the property, consisting of sixteen townlands, was only £1,350; owing to the terrible state of the country in 1640–42, estates could be got for next to nothing, the only difficulty being to induce anyone to take them. The original title deed

---

[1] Will of Robert in Consistorial Court Records, Raphoe, 1669. We cannot trace the parentage of James Cairnes; that he was a cousin, whether first or more remote, of his wife, cannot be questioned.

[2] Will of Robert Cairnes.

of the Cairneses of Killyfaddy is a most interesting document, and is here reproduced. The names of the townlands included are as follows:—Killyfaddy, Carntalmore, Carntalbeg, Milltown, Aughendrimon, Fogart, Greyroyle, Corboe, Upper Lislea, Lower Lislea, Tulnadowney, Altenorva, Kilnahussogue, Mullans, Dunmore, and Killany, comprising the manor of Killyfaddy[1]. The three brothers, for a time at least, resided on the estate, as we find them in various documents described as John of Parsonstown, Robert of Finesker, and David of Knockmany. The exact positions of the residences cannot now be accurately traced. There do not seem to be any remains existing of a castle or bawn, nor can we find in any of the Plantation papers that such a structure was at any time erected on either of the manors, in conformity with the regulations binding the early undertakers. The stable of the present mansionhouse of Cecil was originally the old family residence, known as Savile Lodge, which was probably built early in the eighteenth century; and it is very likely that the present mansion of Killyfaddy was built on the site of an older residence. It is quite possible that Savile Lodge may have been of earlier date than 1700, and have been the successor of an older residence identical with the Parsonstown mentioned as the designation of John Cairnes in 1639.

Robert Cairnes predeceased his two brothers in 1669. He had married Mary Elliot, who survived him, but by

[1] This portion, together with that next it, was called "The Small Portion of Killany and Derrybard" at the 1609 Plantation. We have no trace as to when Derrybard was separated. The 1630 grant to Cope is of Killyfaddy only, it being formally created thereby into a Manor.

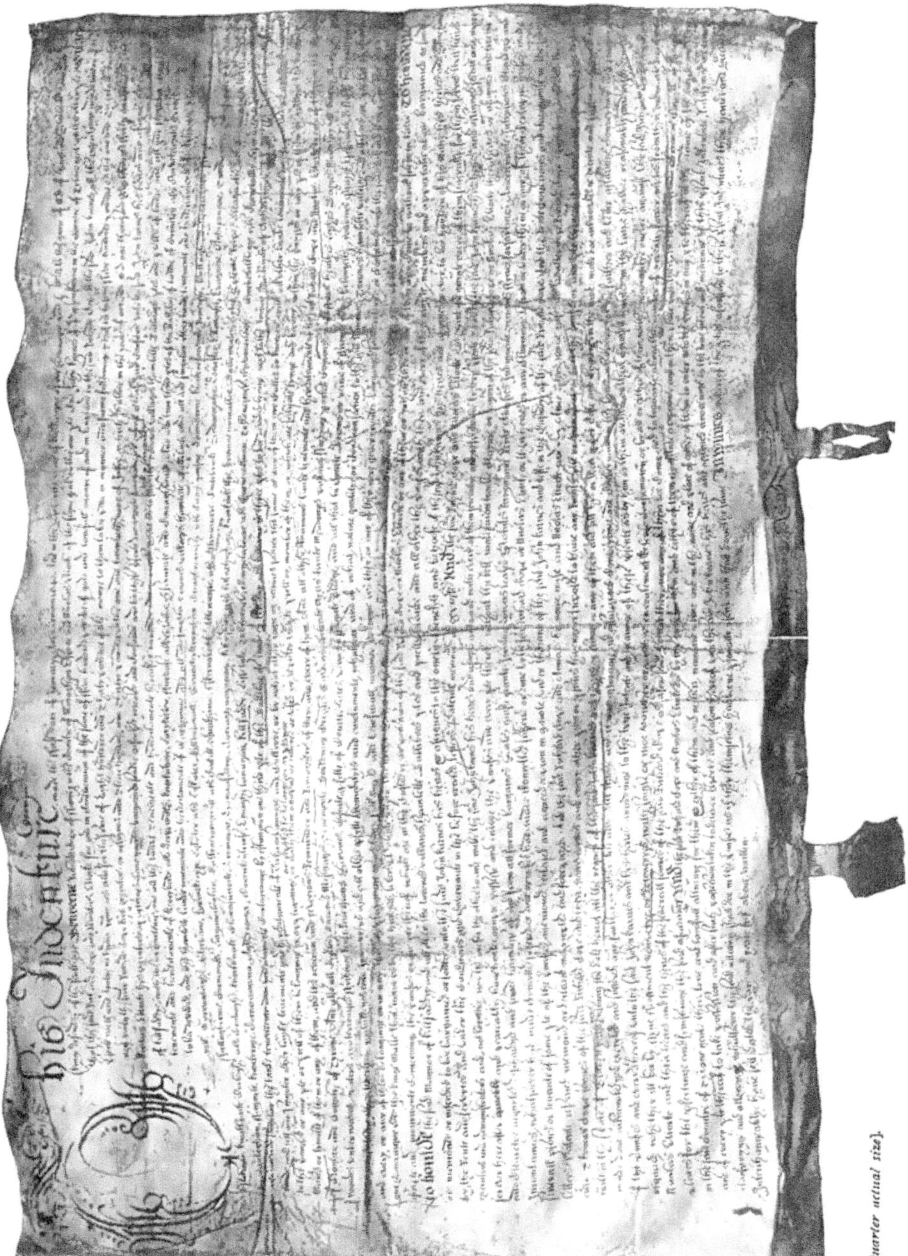

Quarter actual size.

CHARTER FROM SIR RICHARD COPE TO JOHN CAIRNES

OF THE LANDS COMPRISING

THE MANOR OF KILLYFADDY.

1640.

whom he had no issue. Subject to an annuity for his widow, his third share of the property reverted to John and David. The date of death of either John or David cannot be traced. John's interest in the estate passed, by sale we presume, to his brother David. The will of either is not to be found[1], but by 1678 the whole of the two manors seems to have been in possession of David's two sons, William and David, with the exception of the Claremore portion of Cecil, which belonged to James Cairnes, or more probably to his wife, a sister of the three brothers[2].

Whom David married we have not been able to trace. He was survived by

A. WILLIAM, his chief heir. Born about 1640.

B. DAVID. Born 1645, of Knockmany and Londonderry, of whom later. (Chap. VII.).

C. A daughter, married to William Elliot, by whom she had issue,

1. WILLIAM, of Cloneblagh, of whom shortly.
2. MARY, wife of her cousin, Dr. Thomas Cairnes.
3. LETTICE, wife of the Rev. Humphrey Thomson, of Monaghan.

D. MARY, wife of her first cousin James Cairnes, of Claremore (whose father James, above mentioned, died in 1678, leaving also a son John, a merchant

[1] A most exhaustive search in the Records of the Prerogative and Consistorial Courts of Ireland, the Prerogative Court of Canterbury, the Court of the Archdeaconry of London, the Consistorial Court of London, the Courts of the Deans and Chapters of St. Paul's and Westminster, and the Court of Husting has failed to produce the wills either of John or David Cairnes. These documents would doubtless have supplied much interesting matter.

[2] Wills of James Cairnes of Claremore, 1678; William Cairnes of Killyfaddy, 1685; and David Cairnes of Londonderry, 1722, in Public Record Office, Ireland.

in Dublin, who died in 1732 apparently without issue), by whom she had issue,

1. JOHN, a captain in the army. He died 1732, and was buried at Clogher Cathedral, having married Elizabeth Waddell, by whom he had issue one daughter only, Elizabeth, who married John Carlisle. By him she had issue, John, of Claremore, William, James, and Elizabeth. Claremore was sold by the Carlisles to Mr. Gervais about 1805[1].
2. WILLIAM, a merchant in Limerick, where he died without issue and intestate in 1725.
3. SUSANNA, wife of Captain Foster, of County Fermanagh.
4. LETTICE, wife of the Rev. Robert Wilson.
5. MARTHA, Mrs. Jones.

WILLIAM CAIRNES, of Killyfaddy, eldest son of the elder David, inherited from his father the two manors, with the exception of six townlands left to his brother David (and still possessed by his descendant), and the Claremore property[2]. He married Jane Holland, by whom he had a large family, five sons and four daughters surviving him. By his will he left the main portion of the estate to his eldest son, and two townlands to each of his younger sons, with the proviso that should they die without lawful issue, their lands should revert to the eldest son or his

[1] The family vault of the Claremore Cairneses at Clogher Cathedral is marked by several most interesting tombstones, bearing legible inscriptions, with dates from 1678. Several of the Carlisles were also buried here. We regret we have been unable to trace this family since they parted with the property.

[2] All in Cecil Manor.

heirs. All his sons eventually died without issue, and the eldest finally succeeded to the whole property left by his father.

William Cairnes died in 1685, leaving surviving issue,

A. William, his heir, who was born probably about 1664, of whom later.

B. Robert, who was left by his father Greyroyle and Corboe; he left no issue.

C. James was left by his father's will the townlands of Mullans and Kilnecully; he died in 1732, without issue.

D. David, of Tulnedowna and Tibley, died without issue.

E. Thomas, "a doctor of Physick"; was left the townlands of Dunmore and Altanorba. He married his cousin Mary, daughter of William Elliot, and sister of William Elliot, of Cloneblagh, to be referred to shortly. This Thomas Cairnes seems to have been a disreputable person, from the following entry in the will of his uncle David Cairnes, of Londonderry, "and to his (William Elliot's) sister, my niece, that was married to Thomas Cairnes, Doctor of Physick, whom we hear to be now (1721) dead, the same as to her brother now last mentioned, and forty shillings over and above, because of their low condition and poverty, and the very ill and unjust doings and carriage of her husband towards her, which I will here say no more of." He died without legitimate issue.

F. MARY, eventual sole heiress, wife of her first cousin William Elliot above named, by whom she had issue,

1. WILLIAM, of Cloneblagh, who married Elizabeth, daughter of Hugh Montgomery, of Lisduff, County Longford. (See Appendix II.). He predeceased his wife's uncle, Captain William Cairnes, of Killyfaddy, dying in 1729, and was buried in Augher Laugher Churchyard, County Fermanagh. He left issue,

   a. JOHN. Born 1700, ultimate heir of his granduncle, of whom later.

   b. JAMES, who died without issue in 1775.

   c. CATHERINE. Born 1707, wife of Hugh Armstrong, of Dereheley, County Fermanagh, by whom she had issue.

   d. NICHOLINA, wife of John Moore of Rockfield, County Fermanagh, by whom she had issue Elizabeth, wife of John Pockrich of Derrylusk, Co. Monaghan, by whom she had issue an only daughter Nicholina, the sole heiress of her father, who in 1787 married Jonathan Seaver, of Heath Hall, near Newry. We shall refer to this lady later.

Captain William Cairnes of Killyfaddy, who was about eighteen on his father's death in 1682, was in Derry in 1688, and was one of the celebrated band of Thirteen "Apprentice Boys" who, on the approach of the Earl of

Antrim's regiment, rushed to the Ferry Gate and closed it against them. He became a captain in King William's army, and fought under him at the Battle of the Boyne. Through the death, without issue, of all his brothers, he eventually succeeded to the whole of his father's property. He was a man of note in his native county, where he constantly resided after the close of his military career, and where he came to be familiarly known as "The Old Captain." He seems to have been a man of kindly disposition, yet dignified and proud of his ancient and honourable name. He married (his wife's name was Lydia, but her surname is unknown), but had no issue. On his death in 1740 the Cairnes family of Tyrone became extinct in the male line, all his brothers, and the sons of David of Londonderry and James of Claremore having predeceased him. In his will, dated 1739, he refers with regret to this fact, and in making John Elliot, grandson of his sister Mary, his heir, he stipulated that he and his heirs should assume the name and arms of Cairnes; and failing the issue of John Elliot, he appointed his brother James Elliot as eventual heir, he and his heirs being bound by the same condition as to change of surname. He left £300 to his natural daughter Margaret Cairnes, and £20 to William, natural son of his brother Doctor Thomas Cairnes above mentioned, and a bequest to the Presbyterian Church at Clogher. The old Captain died in 1740, and was succeeded by his grand-nephew and heir,

John Elliot, who assumed on his succession the surname and arms of Cairnes. This assumption of surname was not registered in the Office of the Ulster King of

Arms, but it appears that at this date such registration was not essential to the legality of the change of name; and the omission did not affect his right to bear the name and arms, which has since been officially admitted. He married Jane, third daughter and co-heiress of the Rev. Hans Montgomery, of Ballymagown, Co. Down, Vicar of Ballywalter, and curate in charge of Springvale and Grey-abbey (see Appendix III.). This lady had three sisters, Mary, wife of Nicholas Forde of Seaforde, Lucy, wife of Alderman Harman of Drogheda, and Alice, wife of Alan Bellingham of Castlebellingham (of whom later). Their mother was Elizabeth, sister of Henry Townley Balfour, of Townley Hall, Co. Louth.

Of John Elliot Cairnes we have but scanty information. He was of an irascible and uncertain temper, and tyrannical with his children, whom, as they grew up, he constantly threatened to disinherit. In 1774 his four sons and one daughter, fearing that, as he was constantly making new wills intended to carry out these threats, he might die leaving the property to the favourite of the moment, to the entire exclusion of the rest, secretly drew up and duly signed a document agreeing that no matter how their father left the property, "he being of an odd out-of-the-way temper, and subject to strange whims," they would make a fair division thereof among themselves. Their father died in 1778. His last will showed a remarkable preference for his two younger sons, George and James. The eldest son was abroad at the time, serving in the army. The settlement was deferred until his return home in 1779. The will was duly proved, although so complicated in its terms that no one could understand it very clearly.[1] Had the eldest son wished, he could probably have upset the will, and so come in as heir-at-law for the whole estate. However, he did not do so. The only clear items in the document were that the testator left to his second son John Elliot the townland of Kilnahussogue, and the residence and lands of Savile Lodge (the predecessor of the present Cecil Manor House and demesne), with a small annuity payable by the eldest son, and to his daughter Anne Bellingham an annuity of £90 per annum.

The eldest son, Captain William Cairnes, was anxious to realise his portion, which by the family arrangement was to amount to about half the property, he being responsible for the annuities to his brother John and his sister, and for all his father's debts. James was allotted as his portion the house and townland of Killyfaddy, the townlands of Dunmore and Mullans, and the island of Mullinacoagh, or Cuckoo Hill, in Lough Erne (a leasehold property of little value), subject to a small annuity to John, and a head rent to William. George received the townlands of Carntalmore, Carntalbeg, Mullinriegh, and the corn mill of the manor, also subject to an annuity to John, and a head rent to William. Thus of the sixteen townlands comprising the manor, William seems to have got nine, John one (the Savile Lodge property is in Cecil Manor), George three, and James three.

JOHN ELLIOT CAIRNES died in 1778, leaving issue,

A. WILLIAM, a Major in the army. On the completion of the family arrangement just referred to he sold

[1] The opinion of counsel was taken on it, but even counsel could not solve the testator's meaning, and advised a family arrangement.

out his portion of the property to Major-General Edward Maxwell, of the Finnebrogue family, in trust for his nephew William, for a sum of £10,400, out of which he paid his sister, Mrs. Bellingham, £3,000 in discharge of her annuity. He also paid his brother John £600 in discharge of the portion of his annuity payable by him. Major Cairnes died in 1789 at Negapatam, having married, 1stly, his first cousin Elizabeth, daughter of Alan Bellingham, and sister of his brother-in-law Alan Bellingham, by whom he had issue,

1. JOHN WILLIAM, Captain in the 54th Regiment, born 1775. This officer was present at the capture of the Island of St. Vincent, where he was severely wounded, eventually dying, unmarried, at Castlebellingham, where he was buried in 1820.

Major William Cairnes married, 2ndly, in 1784, Jane, daughter of the Rev. Robert Heyland, of Coleraine, and by her had issue,

2. ROBERT MACPHERSON, born 1785; also in the army. He was at the siege of Copenhagen in 1807, the siege of Badajoz in 1811, the siege of Cadiz, the battle of Vittoria, and the siege of Bayonne, where he was severely wounded. In 1815, as Major in the Horse Artillery, he displayed magnificent bravery at Waterloo, where he was killed. There is a monument to his memory in Canterbury Cathedral, and another in the church

near the field of Waterloo. He was unmarried.

3. JAMES WEBBER ELLIOT, Commander R.N. Born 1787. He entered the Navy in 1800, and saw continual active service in the French, Spanish, and American wars, up to 1826, when he was appointed Captain in the Preventive Service at Berwick-on-Tweed. He was unmarried, and died at Newcastle-on-Tyne in 1830.
4. JANE, wife of the Rev. Philip Le Geyt, of Marsden Vicarage, Kent.
5. ELIZABETH, wife of the Rev. Charles Graham, Vicar of Petham, Kent.
6. MARGARET, wife of the Rev. Thomas Bruce, of Wingham, Kent.

B. JOHN ELLIOT, of Savile Lodge and Kilnahussogue, eventual representative of the Tyrone family, of whom later.

C. GEORGE, who, in addition to his own portion of the property, succeeded by will to the portion of his brother James on his death in 1791. He thus became proprietor of almost half the manor, including the residence of Killyfaddy. He married Elizabeth, eldest daughter of Jonathan Seaver of Heath Hall, near Newry. Her brother Jonathan married Nicholina Pockrich mentioned above, who was a first cousin once removed of George Cairnes.[1] By his marriage with Miss Seaver George Cairnes

[1] See above, p. 112.

left no issue, though he had a natural son George Cairnes. He died in 1802, leaving all his estates in Tyrone and Fermanagh to Nicholina Seaver, Joseph Foxall, and the Rev. Joseph Henry, or the survivors of them, as trustees, to pay an annuity of £150 per annum to his wife Elizabeth Cairnes or Seaver, and the following legacies:—£100 to his natural son George, and £50 to his godchild Nicholina Foxall. The residue of his estate he left to his children (if any) by his wife Elizabeth, failing whom to his natural son George for life, with ultimate reversion to his "dear friend" and cousin Nicholina Seaver, of Heath Hall.

How vain were the hopes of the old Captain that his name and race should be continued in Killyfaddy! Through the sale by William, and by the will of George Cairnes, every acre of the family property, with the exception of the portion owned by his brother John, passed to the hands of strangers, after an uninterrupted possession of nearly two centuries. The new owner, Mrs. Seaver, though of Cairnes descent through her mother, let no sentimental ideas restrain her from turning her legacy into cash. The sale of the property was soon effected, and by an arrangement with the trustees and the life tenant, George Cairnes, it was in 1805 sold to the trustees of Mrs. William Maxwell, who thus became owner of the whole manor, with the exception of Kilnahussogue. About the same time, the lands in the Manor of Cecil passed into the hands of the Rev. Francis Gervais. The former now belongs to the descendants of the purchaser, Mr. Ancketill of Killyfaddy, and Mr. R. D.

Percival, of Dillon House, Downpatrick. The Cecil portion, to which Mr. Gervais added by separate purchases Claremore and the residence and demesne of Savile Lodge, are now in the possession of his grandson, Mr. Francis Peter Gervais, D.L., of Cecil. Almost on the site of Savile Lodge Mr. Gervais, about 1810, erected the present mansion of Cecil. The old house was retained to serve as out offices. Being struck by the natural beauty of the surroundings, he spent a great deal of time and money in laying out and replanting the demesne, and to his excellent taste must be ascribed much of the beauty of Cecil to-day. The lands of Cecil Manor consist of seventeen townlands, all purchased by Mr. Gervais from the Seavers, Carlisles, and Cairneses, while the Killyfaddy estate is of almost similar extent.[1]

D. JAMES, the youngest son, was unmarried. He did not reside in Killyfaddy, which he leased to his cousin Mr. Richard Armstrong. A rough statement of his affairs, made out after his death, conveys the impression that he was of a rather extravagant and unbusinesslike nature. He left numerous debts of varying amounts, having apparently negotiated sundry loans from most of his relatives and acquaintances who would respond. Among these may be mentioned Priest M'Cue, £3,200; John Simpson, £160; Richard Armstrong, £300; John

[1] The whole estate owned by the Cairnes family in Tyrone originally consisted of about forty townlands, the rental of which to-day would probably amount to about £6,000 per annum. The six townlands known as the Raveagh Estate, and the townland of Kilnahussogue are all that now remain in the hands of Cairnes descendants, the former belonging to Mr. Hugh Gore, the latter being in joint-ownership of Mrs. Lawlor and her sister Miss Cairnes, and Mr. Alfred Cairnes.

Brown, £480; Alan Bellingham, £50, &c. These sums are mostly made up of bonds and notes of hand for small sums, excepting Priest M'Cue's debt, which was a mortgage.

He died in 1791, leaving Killyfaddy Manor-house and lands, with the lands of Dunmore and Mullans, and the Island in Lough Erne called Mullinacoagh, or Cuckoo Hill, to his brother George; to his "dearly beloved" brother John Elliot, one shilling; to his brother-in-law Alan Bellingham, £5, to buy mourning for him, and a few other small legacies.

E. ANNE, wife of her first cousin, Alan Bellingham, of Castlebellingham. This gentleman's father, also Alan, married in 1738, Alice, daughter of the Rev. Hans Montgomery above mentioned, by whom he had the following issue (he died 1796):—

A. HENRY (born 1739, died 1800), a Colonel in the army, whose issue in the male line became extinct on the death without issue of his grandson William Henry in 1822.

B. ALAN, above mentioned, of whom later.

Γ. O'BRYEN, who married Anne, daughter of Edward, and niece of James Napper Tandy, by whom he had one son, Alan O'Bryen Bellingham of Dunany, who having married 1stly Elizabeth, daughter of James Pratt; 2ndly, Christiana Nicholson; 3rdly, Sophia, daughter of Colonel Rowley Heyland, died without issue in 1859, and two daughters.

ANNE ELLIOT CAIRNES,
Mrs. BELLINGHAM

ALLAN BELLINGHAM
of Castlebellingham.

SIR ALLAN BELLINGHAM, Bart.,
of Castlebellingham
(2nd Bart.)

From a Miniature].

Δ. THOMAS, of the Royal Navy, who d.s.p.

E WILLIAM, eventually the 1st Baronet of the second creation. He represented Reigate in Parliament, and was for some time Private Secretary to William Pitt, to whose warm friendship and patronage he was much indebted. In recognition of his political services, he was in 1796 created a Baronet of the United Kingdom, with special remainder failing his own male issue to the heirs male of his father. He married in 1783 Hester Frances, daughter of the Hon. and Rev. Robert Cholmondeley, by whom (she died 1844) he had no issue. On his death in 1826 the baronetcy descended, according to the terms of the remainder, the male issue of his eldest brother having predeceased him, to the heir of the second brother Alan, husband of the above Anne Cairnes.

Z. ELIZABETH, wife of the above mentioned Major William Cairnes.

H. MARY ANNE, wife of the Rev. William Woolsey of Prior Land, Co. Louth, by whom she had issue. Her daughter Marianne, married William Cairnes of Stameen (of whom later), and her grandson is the present Major-General Woolsey, D.L., of Milestown, Co. Louth.

Θ. ALICE } Both unmarried.
I. LUCY }

ALAN BELLINGHAM and ANNE CAIRNES were

married in 1774, and had issue—(the following is extracted from the Family Bible)—

A. ALAN (the 2nd Baronet), born in Dublin 2nd February, 1776; christened 8th March by Dean Woodward.[1] Sponsors—Alan Bellingham (grandfather), John Elliot Cairnes (maternal grandfather), Mrs. Woodward.

B. JANE, died in infancy.

C. HENRY, born at Castlebellingham 5th July, 1778; christened 10th August by Mr. Ogle. Sponsors—Colonel Henry Bellingham, Mrs. Tenison, and Colonel Hart.

D. ALICE, born in Dublin 18th July, 1779; christened at Castlebellingham 27th August by Mr. Ogle. Sponsors—Mrs. Ogle, Mrs. MacLane, and William Cairnes (uncle). Died in infancy.

E. JOHN, born in Dublin 17th March, 1781; christened 7th April by Dr. Law.[2] Sponsors—Charles Hamilton, John Cairnes (uncle), and Mrs. Harman (grand-aunt). Of whom later.

F. THOMAS, who died in infancy.

G. WILLIAM CAIRNES, born in Dublin 20th April, 1789; christened privately by the Bishop of Cloyne. Sponsors—William Bellingham (uncle), William Cairnes (uncle), and Catherine Cairnes (wife of John Elliot Cairnes of Savile

[1] The Very Rev. Richard Woodward, D.D., Dean of Clogher, and afterwards Bishop of Cloyne.

[2] The Rev. Richard Law, D.D., F.T.C.D., afterwards Bishop of Killala (1787) and of Elphin (1795).

Lodge). Eventually Captain in the 64th Regiment, d.s.p. 1835.

Mrs. Bellingham died after the birth of her son William Cairnes in 1789, and her husband married 2ndly, Mary, daughter of Ralph Smith of Drogheda, by whom he had no issue. He died 1800.

Of the above, the second son Henry became a Major in the army, and having in 1809 married Elizabeth, daughter of Captain William Cruden, R.N., died in 1826, leaving issue,

1. Henrietta Anne, wife of Henry Shebbeare, M.D.
2. Mary, died unmarried.
3. Jane, wife of her cousin William Stewart Bellingham, of whom later.

The third son John married, 1st, Eliza, daughter of William Stewart of Wilmont, Co. Down, and had issue, besides Alan who d.s.p. in 1835, and two daughters unmarried,

1. William Stewart, of Ravensdale, Co. Kildare, and Howth, who married in 1841 his cousin Jane above named, and dying in 1869, left issue,
   - *a.* William, d.s.p. 1875.
   - *b.* Henry, of Tansey House, Sutton, Co. Dublin, who married in 1870, Harriet Eleanor, daughter of Henry Smyth of Stephenstown, Co. Louth, and has issue,

1. WILLIAM GUY HENRY STEWART, born 1873.

2. HENRIETTA FRANCES JANE.

c. JOHN, of Tresserve, Aix en Savoie, who, in 1887, married Alice, daughter of the Hon. Bouverie Francis Primrose, C.B., brother of the late Earl of Rosebery.

d. THOMAS EUDO, who married in 1882, Grace, daughter of the Rev. William Harkness.

e. ARTHUR D'ARCY, who married in 1892, Nannie, daughter of Addison Hone, and died in 1903, leaving issue,

ARTHUR STEWART.

f. O'BRYEN CAIRNES, who married in 1892, Wilhelmina (who d.s.p. 1897), daughter of William Vincent.

g. HESTER FRANCES, wife of Charles Page, of Stanley Mount, Oxton, Cheshire.

h. HENRIETTA ANNE, wife of John H. Ryan, C.E., of Waterloo Road, Dublin, and Co. Tipperary.

j. JANE ALICE, wife of Alfred E. Ruthven. She died in 1894.

John Bellingham married, 2ndly, Katherine Anne, daughter of R. Clarke, and had issue one son, who died in infancy.

2. ANNE, wife of Dr. John Peebles of Dublin, by whom she had issue.
3. FANNY, wife of the Rev. Hyacinth D'Arcy, of Clifden, Co. Galway, who d.s.p.

The eldest son, ALAN, who succeeded as second baronet on the death of his uncle in 1826, married in 1799, Elizabeth, daughter of the Rev. Edward Walls of Boothby Hall, Lincoln, who died 1822, and had issue,

A. ALAN EDWARD, 3rd Baronet.
B. HENRY RICHARD, d.s.p. 1836.
C. O'BRYEN, M.D., married Matilda, daughter of Bryan Molloy of Melicent House, Co. Kildare, and d.s.p. 1857.
D. SYDNEY ROBERT, who resided in Canada, where he married Arabella, daughter of William Holmes, of Quebec, and sister of Mrs. Montgomery Cairnes, of whom later. He d.s.p. 1900.
E. WILLIAM JOHNSTON, Colonel in the army, who in 1852 married Felicia, daughter of the Rev. John Short Hewett, D.D., and dying in 1903 left surviving issue,
    1. SYDNEY EDWIN, born 1853, a Major in the army. He married, 1880, Helen Mary, daughter of A. A. Dunlop, of Sutton, County Dublin, and died 1893, leaving issue,
        a. Alan Mure.
        b. Maude Alice.

2. Alan Hele, d.s.p. 1900.
3. William Edward Patrick.
4. Mary Louisa, wife of Arthur Macan of Drumcashel, Co. Louth.
5. Alice.
6. Dorothea.

F. Mary Anne Jane, wife of the Rev. John Cheales, Vicar of Skendleby, Lincoln, who died 1865. She died 1887, leaving issue. (See Burke's "Landed Gentry").

G. Frances Elizabeth, wife of George Wilson Maddison of Partney, Lincoln, who died 1888. She died 1886, leaving issue. (See Burke's "Landed Gentry").

H. Charlotte Sophia, wife of the Rev. John Alington, Rector of Candlesby and Croxby, Lincoln, who died 1883. She died 1898, leaving issue. (See Burke's "Landed Gentry").

Sir Alan Edward, 3rd Baronet, born 1800, married in 1841 Elizabeth, only child of Henry Clarke of West Skirbeck, Lincoln (who died 1887), and died in 1889, leaving issue,

A. Alan Henry, 4th and present Baronet.

B. William Claypon (The Rev.), M.A., Rector of Kilsaran, County Louth (Castlebellingham), born 1847, married in 1878 Susan Caroline, daughter of the Ven. Ambrose Power, Archdeacon of Lismore (fourth son of Sir John Power, Bart., of Kilfane), and died in 1892, leaving issue,

1. Eudo William Alan of Dunany, County Louth, born 1884.
2. Vera Susan.
3. Alice Marian.
4. Hester Frances Zoe, died 1900.

c. Hester Elizabeth, married 1864, Sir T. P. Butler, Bart., of Ballintemple, County Carlow, and died 1904, leaving issue.

d. Alice Sophia, married 1864, Sir Victor A. Brooke, Bart., who died 1891, leaving issue.

e. Charlotte Mary, married 1872, the Right Hon. Frederick S. Wrench, P.C., Chief Commissioner of the Land Courts in Ireland and of the Estates Commission, by whom she has issue.

f. Frances Anne Jane, who married in 1869, Richard Altamont Smythe of Killiney, and has issue.

g. Agnes Matilda, who married 1875, Montagu Yeats-Brown, C.M.G., late H.B.M. Consul at Boston, and has issue.

Sir Alan Henry Bellingham, 4th and present Baronet, of Bellingham Castle, County Louth, D.L., M.A. (Oxon), formerly Private Chamberlain to H.H. Pope Leo XIII., and Private Chamberlain to the present Pope, was born 1846. He married, firstly, in 1874, the Lady Constance Julia, daughter of the 2nd Earl of Gainsborough, by whom he has issue,

1. Edward Henry Charles Patrick, his heir

presumptive, late of the Lothian Regiment; born 1879.

2. ROGER CHARLES NOEL, Lieutenant R.A.; born 1884.
3. IDA MARY ELIZABETH, a nun of the Sacred Order of the Holy Child.
4. AUGUSTA MARY MONICA, married 6th, July, 1905, John Stuart, 4th Marquis of Bute.

He married, 2ndly, in 1895, the Hon. Lelgarde Harry Florence, younger daughter of Augustus Wykeham Clifton, and Bertha, 23rd Baroness Grey de Ruthyn.

Owing to the failure of the male issue of Major William Cairnes, the lineal headship of the Tyrone family reverted to the family of JOHN ELLIOT CAIRNES of Savile Lodge and Kilnahussogue. This gentleman was married on the 26th September, 1779, by the Rev. Mr. Trail, Rector of Killinchy, at the residence of the bride's father, to Catherine, daughter and eventual co-heiress of John Moore, of Moore Hall, Killinchy, Co. Down. (See Appendix IV.). He died in 1802 at Dungannon, where he had a house, and was buried at Killyman. By his will he left his lands to his children as tenants in common, not joint tenants. He left as his executors Robert Lowry of Pomeroy House, Robert Eccles, and Catherine Cairnes his wife. The two former refused to act in concert with the latter, and renounced the trusteeship, leaving Mrs. Cairnes sole executrix and trustee for the children, then minors. During the absence of her eldest son in Java (about 1810), she sold the residence and demesne of Savile Lodge to Mr. Gervais, who built thereon

JOHN MOORE
of Moore Hall, Killinchy, Co. Down.

From an old Pastel].

Mrs. MOORE
of Moore Hall, Killinchy, Co. Down.

From an old Pastel].

CATHERINE MOORE,
Wife of John Elliot Cairnes of Savile Lodge,
Co. Tyrone.

From an old Pastel.]

GEORGE CAIRNES
of Killyfaddy.

Silhouette.]

the present mansion of Cecil. The sale was absolutely illegal without the separate consent of each of her children. Several of these were minors at the time, and the eldest son was abroad, whence he did not return for many years. Portion of the purchase-money was afterwards devoted to the purchase of his commission, so that on his return he took no steps to recover the property. Mrs. Cairnes was evidently a lady of marked individuality of character, strong in her prejudices, and in her determination to have her own way. The family papers show that she was much given to favouritism among her children, her daughter Anne and her youngest son George, renamed Henry Moore, being her special favourites. For her second son William, she seems to have had a feeling almost amounting to dislike. She left him five shillings in her will, a sum which we are inclined to think was the measure of her affection for him. She resided in Rutland Street, Dublin, after her husband's death. She died in 1838, leaving issue,

A. John Elliot, born 1785. He entered the Louth Militia in 1800, being in 1803 gazetted as Lieutenant in the 56th Regiment, then stationed at Galway. In 1808 he went with his regiment to India. He saw continuous active service in the East, and in 1812 was gazetted to the 69th Regiment, under the command of Colonel Rollo Gillespie, then proceeding to Java. Under this celebrated leader, afterwards Major-General, Cairnes won much distinction in the battle of Cornelis, where, his superior officers having been killed, he was placed in command of three companies of the 14th, 59th, and 69th Regiments. Towards the close of the battle he was dangerously wounded, and his name was returned among the killed in the despatches; owing to this error, it was excluded from the list of recipients of the Java medal. On his return home years afterwards strong representations were made with a view to having the mistake remedied, but the War Office, at that time somewhat fettered by red tapeism, replied in effect that once an officer was killed in their books, he had no business to expect a medal. The Java medals had, as a matter of fact, all been distributed at the time of Cairnes's return home (1817), and a new one could not be struck for one officer. He returned to India in 1813 as Captain and Aide-de-camp to Sir Rollo Gillespie, then appointed Major-General and second in command of the forces in India. He returned home in 1817, and in 1824, having meantime attained his majority, was put in command of the depôt at Hull. In 1827 he was promoted to the rank of Lieutenant-Colonel, and shortly afterwards retired on half-pay. In 1834, in recognition of his military services in Java and elsewhere, William IV. conferred upon him the honour of Knighthood of the Royal Hanoverian Guelphic Order (Military). Colonel Cairnes on retiring from the army lived at Castleroe House, near Coleraine, and afterwards at Portstewart, Co. Derry. He died in 1847, having married on 10th March, 1825, Susanna, daughter of Thomas

LIEUT.-COLONEL JOHN ELLIOT CAIRNES, K.H.

From a Miniature).

SUSANNAH JACKSON, Mrs. CAIRNES.

From a Miniature).

Jackson, of Duddington Hall, Northampton[1] (who died in 1857, from shock on hearing of the death at Delhi of her only son), leaving issue,

1. WILLIAM JOHN DRUE, born at Castleroe, 25th July, 1835; baptised at Macosquin Church. Sponsors—Mr. and Mrs. Drue of Portstewart, Mr. and Mrs. William Cairnes of Stameen, Mr. and Mrs. M'Clure of Londonderry,[2] Miss Galbraith of Dungannon, and William Cairnes of Limavady.[3] He entered the army, joining the Munster Fusiliers as Lieutenant in 1855. He proceeded with his regiment to India on the outbreak of the mutiny, and at the siege of Delhi displayed the bravery and warlike spirit of his family. He was one of the first to pass through the Cashmere Gate, and at the outset of a promising career was killed by a falling beam from the upper structure of the gateway.
2. CATHERINE, born at Hull; baptised in Trinity Church, Hull. Sponsors—Hugh Jackson of Duddington Hall and Wisbeach, D.L.; Mrs. Cairnes, 47 Rutland Street, Dublin; and Mrs. Douglas, of Edinburgh. She married in 1846

[1] The lineal representative in the male line of this ancient family of Duddington is Mr. Graham Jackson, a well-known architect and Royal Academician, of Eagle House, Wimbledon, Surrey.

[2] See p. 104. The Rev William M'Clure was a brother of Sir Thomas M'Clure, M.P.

[3] A descendant of one of the natural sons of the Cairnes family, probably a grandson of the William Cairnes mentioned in the Old Captain's will. Colonel Cairnes always maintained friendship with this gentleman. He died unmarried about 1850.

John Hilliard, third son of Jeremiah Lawlor, of Tralee, and has issue. (See Appendix V.).

3. ANNE, born at Hull; baptised at Trinity Church, Hull. Sponsors—Hugh Jackson of Duddington Hall and Wisbeach, D.L.; Mr. and Mrs. Coulson, Hull; and Mrs. Jackson of Duddington. (Now of 1 Carlisle Terrace, Kingstown).

B. WILLIAM, born 1787. In opposition to the wishes of his mother, who intended him for the army, he decided on a business life, and became an apprentice to his relative Mr. Woolsey at Castle-bellingham Brewery. Eventually he became a partner in the firm, but owing to some difference with his partners he severed his connection with Castlebellingham, and about the year 1825 started on his own account at Drogheda. He soon made the Drogheda Brewery an unqualified success. He is still remembered not only for his great business capacity, but also for the deep interest he took in charity. He married his cousin Marianne, daughter of Rev. William Woolsey, and died at his residence, Stameen, near Drogheda, in 1863, leaving issue,

1. JOHN ELLIOT, sixth child, but eldest surviving son, born at Castlebellingham, 1823. He entered the brewery with his father, but disliking the business, he entered Trinity College, where he graduated, obtaining his M.A. in 1856. He afterwards devoted himself

to the study of Political Economy and Jurisprudence, and was appointed professor of these subjects in the Queen's College, Galway, in 1859. While here he wrote some remarkable books on the slave question in America, which made a great sensation both in England and the States. In 1866 he was appointed Professor of Political Economy in London University, and went to live at Blackheath. While there he enjoyed the friendship, only ended by death, of John Stuart Mill, Henry Fawcett, and other of the greatest thinkers of the day. His works on Political Economy and kindred subjects raised him to the foremost rank of the literary men of his time. He was in 1874 made an honorary LL.D., of Dublin University. He died in 1875, having married Elizabeth Charlotte, daughter of George Henry Minto Alexander, a Judge of the High Court in India, by whom he left issue,

a. WILLIAM ELLIOT, born 1862. He entered the 3rd Dragoon Guards, afterwards transferring to the Royal Irish Fusiliers. He inherited much of his father's literary abilities, and contributed many articles on military subjects to the *Times* and other leading journals. During the Boer war he acted as war correspondent to the *Westminster Gazette*, his articles displaying great brilliancy, and being widely read.

Among his best known books are—"The Coming Waterloo," "Lord Roberts as a Soldier in Peace and War," "An Absent-Minded War," "The Army from Within," "Social Life in the British Army," the last three having been published anonymously. He acted as secretary to the committee appointed by the Government to consider the education and training of officers in the Army, and shortly before his death was appointed secretary to the Military Court of Inquiry into the Remount Department. He married in 1884, Mamie, daughter of the late M. M'Clelland of Glendarragh, County Londonderry, who survives him, and dying in 1902, left issue one daughter Dorothy Elliot.

b. FREDERICK, born 1864, now of Killester House, Raheny, the present lineal head of the Tyrone family of Cairnes. He married in 1899, Lucy Barbara, third daughter of Sir Herbert Croft, Bart., and has issue,

1. JOHN ELLIOT, born 1904.

2. EVELYN LUCY.

3. KATHLEEN ALEXANDER.

c. ANNA ALEXANDER, wife of Major Rowland Brinkman (of the Monk Bretton family[1]),

[1] See Burke's Peerage and Baronetage.

of the Royal Irish Fusiliers, by whom she has issue,

1. Rowland Egerton, born 1894.

2. Denys, born 1896.

3. Doris, died in infancy.

2. William Henry, born in 1827. Entered the army and served in the Crimean war, after which want of health obliged him to retire at the rank of Major. He is well remembered as a first-class all-round sportsman. He married Isabella, daughter of John Jameson, and dying at Pau in 1889, left issue,

a. William Alan, late Major R.E., who saw considerable active service both in the Black Mountain Expedition and in the late South African war. He married Miss Stevenson, and died at Malahide, leaving issue.

b. John Jameson, now resident in U.S.A. He is married and has issue.

c. Hugh Montgomery, of Lissen Hall, Swords, Co. Dublin. He married Althea, daughter of Mr. Haig, of Ramornie, Fifeshire.

d. James Elliot, late Captain Royal Artillery.

3. Thomas Plunket, born 1830, and named after his godfather, the Rev. Thomas Plunket, afterwards Lord Plunket, and Bishop of Tuam. At an early age Thomas Plunket Cairnes entered

the Drogheda Brewery, of which he became owner on the death of his father. He was a man of immense business and financial capacity, and was connected with many public undertakings, amongst others being Governor of the Bank of Ireland and Deputy Chairman of Great Northern Railway (Ireland). But it is as a philanthropist that he will be long remembered; he gave largely not only of his means but also of his time and of his abilities. His services to the Church of Ireland, especially in connection with its finances at the disestablishment, to hospitals and charitable undertakings of all sorts will not easily be forgotten. He married Sophia, daughter of Charles Gaussen, and died at Monkstown Park, Co. Dublin, in April, 1904, leaving issue,

a. WILLIAM PLUNKET, now of Stameen, who married Alice, daughter of the late General Algar, by whom he has issue,

1. THOMAS ALGAR ELLIOT.

2. FRANCIS HERBERT.

3. WILLIAM JAMESON.

b. CHARLES ELLIOT, Clk., who died unmarried in 1895.

c. ALAN THOMAS, who married Julia, daughter of Edward Beans of Moatlands, Paddock Wood, Kent, who predeceased him, and dying in 1902, left issue,

1. WILLIAM EDWARD PLUNKET.

2. VIOLET.

3. AUDREY.

d. ALFRED BELLINGHAM, who married Katherine, daughter of Mr. Winslow of Eccles, near Manchester.

e. EDITH SOPHIA, wife of the Rev. Percy Smith, M.A., Vicar of Dartford, Kent.

f. ALICE, wife of William Carson, by whom she has issue.

g. HELEN, wife of Major Douglas Seckham, by whom she has issue.

h. MABEL LUCY.

4. MARY ANNE, wife of John Robertson, by whom she had issue,

a. WILLIAM, now of Dundrum, Co. Dublin, who married Margaret, daughter of Henry Jameson.

b. ROBERT, who married Miss Belcher, and died leaving issue.

c. ELLEN, widow of the late Rev. Maurice Neligan, D.D.

d. ALBERT, Major R.A., now of Delgany, Co. Wicklow, married, and has issue.

e. ALICE, unmarried.

5. LUCY, now of Glencormac, Bray, widow of the late James Jameson (of the firm of John Jameson & Sons, Distillers), by whom she has issue,

a. WILLIAM, who married Miss Sargeant, and died leaving issue.

b. JAMES ORMSBY, who married Miss Hone, and has issue.

c. ROBERT D'ARCY, now of Delvin Lodge, Balbriggan, who married, firstly, Maud, daughter of Ralph Smith, by whom he has issue, and secondly, Miss Eva Harrison, by whom he has issue.

d. THOMAS M., now of Cottesbrooke Grange, Northampton, who married and has issue.

e. GEORGE, of Rutland Square, Dublin.

f. FRANCIS BELLINGHAM, of Villa Tréve, Pau, who married Miss Cardew.

g. ALICE, wife of R. S. Longworth-Dames, by whom she has issue, one son, who married Miss M'Farland.

6. ANNA, wife of the Rev. John William Hallowell, by whom she had issue,

a. MARY, widow of the late Captain Frederick Hardy, R.N., by whom she has issue,

1. ARTHUR, now of Seafield, Co. Dublin, who married Miss May M'Farland, and has issue.

2. HENRY, married Miss M'Geough Bond, and has issue.

3. ANNA, wife of Henry Fraser.

b. LUCY, wife of Robert Irwin (a grandson of the Rev. Blaney Irwin, of whom later).

7. FRANCES, died unmarried.

8. ELIZABETH, died unmarried.

c. Montgomery, born 1789. Of the 60th Rifles, and afterwards Captain 81st Regiment. He married in 1817, Theresa, daughter of William Holmes, M.D., of Quebec (sister of Mrs. Sydney Bellingham of Castlebellingham, above mentioned), and by her (who died 1888) had issue, six children, of whom only survived

1. William Bellingham, born in Dublin 1832. He emigrated in 1854 to Victoria, Australia, and is now one of the principal merchants of Yarrawonga in that Colony, and a magistrate of both Victoria and N.S. Wales. He married in 1856, Elizabeth, only child of Robert Mathews of Castlemaine, Victoria (formerly of Leicester, England), and has issue,
    - *a.* William, born 1857, d.s.p. 1880.
    - *b.* Montgomery, born 1862, married Alice, daughter of Cuthbert Allison.
    - *c.* Robert Mathews, born 1868, died in infancy.
    - *d.* George Alexander, born 1869.
    - *e.* Henry Moore, born 1871.
    - *f.* Alan Bellingham, born 1880.
    - *g.* Thomas William, born 1884.
    - *h.* Mary Elizabeth, wife of Henry Elvins.
    - *j.* Theresa Holmes, wife of John Maxwell M'Kay.
    - *k.* Anne Irwin, wife of Josias Pitman.
    - *l.* Ellen Laura, wife of Alfred Ewins.
    - *m.* Emily Bellingham, wife of A. W. Steel.

n. Flora Moama.

o. Arabella Bellingham, died in infancy.

p. Elsie May.

D. Alan Bellingham, born 1791, a Lieutenant in the 34th Regiment. Was killed at the battle of Vittoria in 1813. Unmarried.

E. George, so christened, but re-named and always known as Henry Moore, born 1796. This alteration of the name evidently given out of compliment to the child's uncle George, seems to have been either the cause, or more probably in consequence of a dispute between the brothers. That there was a deep-rooted ill-feeling between the brothers is evident from George's will leaving the Tyrone estate to strangers. Henry Moore Cairnes commenced business as a merchant in Dublin, but met with misfortune. He married Emily, daughter of John Claudius Beresford, the last holder of the obsolete but lucrative office of cup taster to the Lord Lieutenant of Ireland, and a cousin of the late Primate Beresford, Archbishop of Armagh. By her he had issue,

1 Claudius Beresford, now Manager of the Bank of New South Wales, at Paramatta, N.S.W., and a magistrate for the Colony. He married and has issue,

a. Charles Beresford, born 1884.

b. Beresford Henry, born 1887.

c. Thomas, died in infancy.

d. Mary.

e. Dora.

2. Elliot Moore, now of Melbourne, F.R.G.S., Vice-President of the Victorian Chamber of Mines, &c. He married, and has issue,

a. Claude.

b. Elliot.

c. George Sydney.

3. Catherine, unmarried.

4. A daughter, Mrs. M'Kenzie, living in Australia.

F. James Elliot, born 1798. Died in infancy.

G. Anne, wife of the Rev. Blaney Irwin, Rector of Larracor (Trim, Co. Meath), by whom she had issue,

1. Robert.
2. John, who had issue.
3. William.
4. Montgomery.
5. Henry.
6. Elizabeth, unmarried.

Of Kilnahussogue, the remnant of the Tyrone property now remaining in the family, it may be of interest to note the sub-division. On the death of John Elliot Cairnes of Savile Lodge in 1802, the property was left equally among his six surviving children. On the death of Alan in 1813, intestate, his sixth portion reverted to his eldest brother Colonel Cairnes, who also purchased the sixth share of his brother Montgomery, thus owning three-sixths. William Cairnes of Stameen inherited one-sixth, and also bought most of his brother Henry's portion. The remaining sixth share belonged to Anne Irwin. This lady by her will divided her portion among several of her children. One of these, Elizabeth Irwin, intended to leave her moiety to a favourite niece, but making her own will, omitted to mention specifically by name which niece she counted the favourite. Each niece claimed to be the heiress, and as there were many, endless confusion occurred; a sort of settlement was come to, but the rent of Kilnahussogue, so far as Elizabeth Irwin's share is concerned, is so sub-divided as to be hardly worth distributing. The proportions distributable are as follows :—

To the two daughters of Colonel Cairnes, Mrs. Lawlor, and Miss Cairnes jointly	$\frac{1}{2}$ the total rent.
To Alfred B. Cairnes, who was bequeathed his grandfather William's portion	$\frac{1}{6}$ of total rent. $\frac{2}{12}$ of another $\frac{1}{6}$th. $\frac{1}{7}$ of remaining $\frac{10}{12}$th of this sixth. $\frac{1}{7}$ of another sixth.
To the descendants of Anne Irwin in various proportions, seven receiving each only $\frac{1}{90}$th of the total rent,	the balance.

As to who, if anyone, can lay claim to the honour of the lordship of the manor of Killyfaddy to-day there may be some doubt. By an arrangement come to in the beginning of the nineteenth century, when the bulk of the manor was sold to the trustees of Mrs. Maxwell, one of the Maxwell family was chosen as the nominal Crown lessee of the manor. His representative is Mr. R. D. Percival of Dillon House, Downpatrick. But as his ancestor's interest was largely that of a mortgagee (the

TABLE IV.

PEDIGREE OF THE FAMILY OF CAIRNES OF KILLYFADDY, SAVILLE LODGE, KNOCKMANY and STAMEEN.

ALEXANDER CAIRNES, formerly of Cults, Wigton, who settled in Co. Donegal in 1610. See Table II. facing p. 70.

JOHN CAIRNES. See Table III. facing p. 106.

ROBERT CAIRNES of Finesker. D.s.p. 1669.

DAVID CAIRNES of Knockmany, eventually Lord of the manors of Killyfaddy and Cecil.

MARY = JAMES CAIRNES of Claremore, D. 1678.

WILLIAM CAIRNES, Heir of his father in the Tyrone Estate, with the exception of the six townlands left to his brother David, and the Claremore Estate. D. 1685. = JANE HOLLAND.

DAVID CAIRNES, the defender of Londonderry. See Chap. VII.

MARGARET wife of WILLIAM ELLIOT, by whom she had issue.

MARY = JAMES CAIRNES of Claremore.

JOHN CAIRNES, merchant in Dublin, who died 1732.

WILLIAM CAIRNES. B. 1664. A Captain in King William's army. One of those who rushed to shut the gates of Derry against Lord Antrim. "The Old Captain." D. 1740. s.p. = LYDIA.

ROBERT, of Greyroyle. D.s.p.

JAMES, of Mullans & Kilnecully. D.s.p. 1732.

DAVID, of Tulnedowna. D.s.p.

THOMAS, a Physician of Dunmore. Dead in 1721. S.p.

MARY ELLIOT.

LETTICE, wife of the Rev. Humphrey Thomson of Monaghan.

MARY = WILLIAM ELLIOT, an officer in King William's army.

WILLIAM ELLIOT, of Cloneblagh, D. 1729 = ELIZABETH, dau. of HUGH MONTGOMERY of Lisduff.

JOHN CAIRNES, of Claremore, a Captain in the army. He married Elizabeth Waddell, and dying in 1732, had issue,

ELIZABETH, sole heiress. = JOHN CARLISLE.

WILLIAM CAIRNES, a merchant in Limerick. D.s.p. 1725.

SUSANNA, wife of Capt. Foster.

LETTICE, wife of the Rev. Robert Wilson.

MARTHA, Mrs. Jones.

JOHN ELLIOT, Born 1700. Ultimate sole heir of the estates of his grand-uncle the Old Captain; on succession thereto in 1740 he assumed, by direction of his grand uncle's will, the arms and surname of CAIRNES. He died in 1778. = (1742) JANE, dau. and co-heiress of the Rev. HANS MONTGOMERY of Ballymagowan, Co. Down; sister of Mrs. Bellingham, Mrs. Forde, and Mrs. Harman.

JAMES ELLIOT, B. 1702. D.s.p. 1775.

CATHERINE, wife of Hugh Armstrong, of Derehely, by whom she had issue.

NICHOLINA, wife of John Moore of Rockfield, by whom she had issue. See p. 112.

JOHN CARLISLE, of Claremore. ?

WILLIAM CARLISLE. ?

JAMES CARLISLE. ?

ELIZABETH.

WILLIAM CAIRNES, B. 1743. A Major in the army. Sold his portion of the estate to the Maxwells. D. 1789. = 1stly, ELIZABETH, dau. of ALAN BELLINGHAM = 2ndly, JANE, dau. of the Rev. ROBT. HEYLAND of Coleraine.

JOHN ELLIOT CAIRNES, of Saville Lodge and Kilnahussogue. D. 1802. = (1779) CATHERINE, dau. of JOHN MOORE, of Moore Hall, Co. Down. D. 1832.

GEORGE CAIRNES, D.s.p. 1802. See p. 117. = ELIZABETH, dau. of JONATHAN SEAVER of Heath Hall.

JAMES CAIRNES, D.s.p. 1791. See p. 119.

ANNE, wife of ALAN BELLINGHAM, of Castlebellingham. See pp. 120-128.

JOHN WM. ELLIOT CAIRNES. B. 1775. An officer in the army. D.s.p. 1820.

ROBT. M'PHERSON CAIRNES. B. 1785. A Major in the army. Killed at Waterloo, 1815. s.p.

JAMES WEBBER ELLIOT CAIRNES. B. 1787. Captain R.N. D.s.p. 1830.

3 daughters, married.

JOHN ELLIOT CAIRNES, B. 1785. A Colonel in the army, and K.H. D. 1847. = SUSANNAH, dau. of THOMAS JACKSON, D.L., of Duddington Hall, Northampton. D. 1857.

WILLIAM, B. 1787, of Stameen. D. 1863 = MARIANNE, dau. of the Rev. WM. WOOLSEY.

MONTGOMERY, Born 1789. See p. 139.

ALAN BELLINGHAM, B. 1791. D. at Vittoria. S.p. 1811.

GEORGE, re-named HENRY MOORE. B. 1796. See p. 140.

JAMES, died in infancy.

ANNE, wife of the Rev. Blaney Irwin. See p. 141.

WM. JOHN DREW CAIRNES, B. 1835. Head of the Tyrone Family. Lieutenant in the Munster Fusiliers. One of the first to enter the Cashmere Gate at the Siege of Delhi, where he was killed, 1857. s.p.

KATHERINE, now of 5 Rossmeen Gardens, Kingstown. = (1840) JOHN HILLIARD LAWLOR. See Appendix V.

ANNIE CAIRNES, now of 1 Carlisle Terrace, Kingstown.

JOHN ELLIOT CAIRNES (Professor). B. 1823 Eventual head of the Tyrone family. D. 1875. = ELIZABETH CHARLOTTE, daughter of S. H. M. ALEXANDER.

WILLIAM HENRY. See p. 134.

THOMAS PLUNKET. See pp. 135-136.

Five daughters. See pp. 137-138.

WILLIAM ELLIOT. B. 1863. Capt. R.I. Fusiliers. D. 1902. See p. 133.

FREDERICK, the present head of the family. See p. 134.

ANNA ALEXANDER. Mrs. Brinkman. See p. 134.

mortgage having been since 1805 largely reduced), and as it was merely as a matter of family convenience he was chosen as the one to pay the Crown rent, it is possible that the late Mr. Fitzammeline Maxwell Ancketill[1] of Killyfaddy had justification for his claim to the somewhat empty honour.

[1] This estimable and venerable gentleman, who was much interested in the production of this book, gave me much valuable information bearing upon the manor of Killyfaddy. His death occurred while the present chapter was being written, and his nephew, after his death, forwarded me a letter to myself but half finished—the completion of which was interrupted by the messenger who will call us all.

CHAPTER VII.

The Cairneses of Knockmany—David Cairnes of Londonderry—His part in the Siege of Londonderry—Recorder and M.P. for the City—Agent for the Irish Society—His death, 1722—His will—His descendants the Edwards family and the Gores of Raveagh—The Earls of Castlestuart.

DAVID CAIRNES the Elder, of Knockmany, County Tyrone, as has been mentioned in previous Chapters, joined with his brothers John and Robert in the purchase of the manors of Killyfaddy and Cecil, in 1640. He left two sons, William (of whose descendants we have treated in Chapter VI.) and David, who was born in November, 1645. To the latter he left the six townlands now known as the Sixtown Estate of Raveagh, and consisting of Finesker, Dovesker, Corkhill, Larganclare, Liscator, and Raveagh, with the corn mill in the last named. Of the early career of David Cairnes we have no information. Some years previous to 1680 he went to reside in Londonderry, where he started in practice as a lawyer; in 1680 he was elected a burgess of the city.[1] He resided alternately at Knockmany and Londonderry.

Since the accession of James II. to the throne, but more particularly since the notorious Tyrconnell had become practically dictator in Ireland, the determination of the King and his evil advisers to exterminate the Protestants in Ireland became daily more evident. Among the early

[1] Ashe's Diary of the Siege—"A bomb fell on (Counsellor) Cairnes' house"—and Municipal Records of Londonderry, 1680.

steps taken towards this end was the disarming of the Protestant militia. Although these had done good service in the suppression of Monmouth's rebellion, and had in many ways proved their loyalty to the King, that rebellion was used as the ostensible reason for the "remodelling of the army in Ireland," as a letter addressed by the King and Council to the Lords Justices in Ireland proves. It declared "That there was reason to believe that Monmouth's rebellion had been of that spreading contagion, that many were infected by it, and that therefore it was not safe for the Kingdom to have the arms of the militia dispersed abroad, but they would be in greater readiness for the militia and their own defence, to have them deposited in several stores in each county."[1] To carry out the scheme, Colonel Richard Talbot was put in full charge of the remodelling of the army, with powers completely independent of the Lord Lieutenant (the Earl of Clarendon), and with the title of Lieutenant-General of the Forces in Ireland. The result of the above letter was the issue of a proclamation, dated 20th June, 1685, stating that, "from private information received," it had come to be known to the authorities, that the arms given out from the stores to the militia or purchased by the counties, or by individual soldiers at their own expense, were not in safe keeping, but "scattered up and down, exposed to the attempts of robbers," and requiring that on or before the 14th of July ensuing all such arms and ammunition should be collected together by the officers and deposited in their own houses or in the nearest place of safety. They were further

[1] Harris, "Life of King William III.," p. 106.

desired to make returns to the Lords Justices of all such stores, with the names of all individuals in their companies who had failed to return their arms by that date, and to make arrangements for the cleaning and keeping in order of such arms as they had received, that they might be ready at any time for the King's use. This plausibly worded proclamation was successful in its object. What had great weight with the Protestants was a speech by the Lord Primate to the Lord Mayor and Aldermen of Dublin counselling loyalty to the throne and obedience to the King's proclamations. The result of this speech was that the militia of Dublin brought in their arms almost to a man, and their example was followed in the country districts. Early in autumn but few arms remained outstanding, and the Government had full returns of the quantity handed in and the names of the few delinquents.

On the 16th of October following was issued a fresh proclamation to all officers, requiring them to deposit the arms and stores so collected in the Government stores, so that by the end of 1685 all were in the hands of the Lieutenant-General.

Talbot (created Earl of Tyrconnell, June, 1685), having thus succeeded in disarming the majority of the Protestants without rousing too strongly their suspicions of his ulterior objects, commenced the real remodelling of the army. One by one the officers were cashiered, each being compelled to hand in his personal accoutrements and horses. These, even if purchased at his private expense, were either paid for at the valuation of the Government valuator (a moiety of their worth), or not paid for at all. The vacancies thus created were filled by Irish Roman Catholics, and by the end of 1687 the remodelling of the army was completed. It was officered almost entirely by Roman Catholics, many of whom were descendants of the old Irish gentry whose ancestors had been driven from their estates during the Elizabethan, Jacobean, and Cromwellian plantations. They were buoyed up with the hope of the restitution of their old family estates, by the promise of Tyrconnell that the Acts of Settlement and Explanation were to be revoked, and by his statement that King James had pledged himself to restore to his faithful Irish Catholic subjects the lands formerly granted to the Protestant settlers. The rank and file of the remodelled army were drawn from the lowest ranks of the native population, and were Roman Catholic almost to a man. The arms so artfully collected from the old militia were freely distributed among the new soldiers, who were encouraged to raid the houses of the Protestants, seize all arms and ammunition, and requisition for the King's use all the serviceable horses to be found in the stables. The so-called searching for arms became a mere pretence to cover the wholesale plunder of the Protestants, whose houses were broken into, their women insulted, and their property ransacked.

In England King James, entirely guided by his confessor, Father Petrie, openly protested his intention to preserve to his loyal subjects in the Three Kingdoms entire freedom of religion, and this benevolent purpose was proclaimed loudly, and apparently with all sincerity, in Ireland by the Lord Lieutenant. Even there, many of the Protestants accepted these assurances, notwithstanding the treatment they were receiving. The King's real intentions with regard to the Protestant landowners in Ireland may be gathered from his statement made to a deputation of the representatives of a number of the old English Roman Catholic families who waited upon him craving his protection and advice. Many of these viewed with dismay the King's incapacity. They foresaw with alarm the inevitable result of his fondly-cherished hope of the ultimate Romanising of England, and rightly judged that his efforts could only end in his downfall and expulsion, and probably their own. This deputation came to him craving permission to sell their estates, and praying him to use his influence with the King of France to enable them to find new homes in that country. His reply was "That he had often thought of them before their desires came before him, and that he had provided a sure sanctuary and retreat for them in Ireland, if his efforts should be blasted in England, which he had made for their security, the success of which he had no reason to despair of." This assurance was accompanied by zealous protestations of his ardent love for the holy Church, for which he was ready to lay down his life.[1] The "sure sanctuary and retreat" for his faithful English co-religionists was of course to be the forfeited estates of the Protestant landowners in Ireland, which the King hoped soon to have in his gift.[2]

The King's intentions soon became whispered in Ireland, and the well-founded uneasiness of the Protestants was

1 Harris, "Life of King William III.," p. 109.

2 See the list of attainders of the Protestant gentry promulgated by the Parliament of King James held in Dublin, 1689. (King, "State of the Protestants in Ireland"). Had these been carried into effect, the old native dispossessed Irish and the English Roman Catholic gentry might have been made pretty comfortable.

added to by the growing arrogance of the Roman Catholics. Tyrconnell, lately promoted to the Lord Lieutenancy in place of Lord Clarendon, in whom the Protestants placed implicit trust, now threw off all semblance of tolerance. The Protestants were openly pillaged on all sides. Appeals for legal redress were futile, as one of the first acts of the new Lord Lieutenant was the dismissal of the judges, in whose place he put minions of his own, mostly unscrupulous adventurers. No Protestant, however just his cause, could obtain a verdict against a Roman Catholic. So unbearable did the state of the former become that several thousand families fled to England, Scotland or the Isle of Man, while, more especially in districts where the Protestants were in a minority, many succumbed to necessity, and became Roman Catholics. Every inducement was held out to this end. Any convert to Roman Catholicism who chose to bring an action against a Protestant was sure to win his case, no matter how glaring the injustice. Robbery and even murder, if only the victims were Protestants, were condoned or unpunished.

Little wonder that the news which arrived in the autumn, that a deliverer was at hand, was received with joy by the Protestants, many of whom remembered the massacre of 1641, and foresaw in the state of the country sure signs of a repetition of that awful time.

William, Prince of Orange, landed in England early in November, 1688. The news soon travelled to Ireland and spread like wildfire to the remotest districts; but along with the joyful intelligence came vague and sinister rumours which spread terror into the minds of the Protestants, a nameless dread, intensified by the goings to and fro of strange priests, and the secret meetings and whisperings of the Roman Catholics. That some great movement was on foot was certain, but none dared give word to the terrible thoughts uppermost in their minds. On all sides the Roman Catholics were secretly arming, even women and children providing themselves with pikes and dirks. Every blacksmith in the Roman Catholic districts was employed in making these. These preparations were traced to an announcement made at Mass in all the Roman Catholic Chapels in the North on a certain Sunday in October by the priests "that they had a great design in hand which would highly concern all the nation, of which they would have particular notice as soon as it was convenient ; that these Masses were being held through all the North in furtherance of this secret intention." They warned their people "that it was their indispensable duty, at the peril of their salvation, to do whatever their priests should direct them, requiring them to furnish themselves meantime with the best weapons procurable." In Londonderry, after the Mass, a friar preaching to the Roman Catholics of the garrison, took as the subject of his discourse, Saul and the Amalekites. He laid stress upon the sin of Saul in sparing even one of those whom God, through His prophet, had doomed to destruction ; that as God had then punished Saul, so now He would utterly destroy all those who failed to carry out His ordinances as proclaimed through His prophets, who were the priests.

King James, on the landing of the Prince of Orange, had hastily sent to Ireland for several regiments quartered there, with orders to Tyrconnell to raise others to take their places with all speed. Lord Mountjoy's well disciplined regiment was then quartered in Londonderry. His Lordship, with several of the officers and some of the men were Protestants, his influence having been sufficient to preserve his regiment alone from Tyrconnell's scheme to exclude Protestants from the army. For this reason the citizens had great confidence in the garrison. They heard with dismay that the regiment was chosen as one of those to be sent to England, and that the Earl of Antrim had been ordered to call out his regiment and proceed to Londonderry.[1]

On the departure of Mountjoy's regiment, the citizens were much perturbed at being without a garrison. Several public meetings of the burgesses and freemen of the city were held, in which David Cairnes took a prominent part. He came to Londonderry from Knockmany, where he resided with his family[2] when not in the city, to assist in

[1] For an account of this nobleman see the Rev. George Hill's "M'Donnells of Antrim," pp. 356–360. The regiment was composed chiefly of recruits from the Earl's Antrim estate. Of the officers, ten are described as "Magdaniels" (*i.e.*, McDonnells) in the "Jacobite Narrative" (p. 40, quoted in Dwyer's Siege of Derry). Besides the Earl, there were really twelve officers of this regiment MacDonnells. The term Magdaniels referred to above must not be taken to infer that the rather celebrated Daniel M'Donnell, an illegitimate son of the 3rd Earl, had ten sons in the regiment. The Earl's son Daniel, proprietor of the Hollow Sword Blade lands, was a captain in this regiment, and was afterwards attainted, his lands reverting to the Crown. On the failure of the Hollow Sword Blade Company, to whom they were granted, they were sold, and now are included in the estates of Mr. Turnley of Drumnasole, Mr. Cuppage, and others.

[2] The year of David Cairnes' first marriage is uncertain, but it probably took place in 1676 or 1677; he had several children prior to 1680. His first wife, through whom he obtained a considerable property in the city, was Margaret (born 1656), daughter of Hugh Edwards, Lord of the Manor of Hastings, Co. Tyrone, which he purchased from Lucy, wife of the Earl of Hastings, and only daughter of Sir John Davis, the original grantee (1609). Hugh Edwards was Mayor of Derry in 1668. He died 1672, and was buried in the Cathedral.

the discussion which arose on the city being left unprotected. He seems to have been well informed as to the movements and intentions of the Roman Catholics, as he strongly advised the citizens to be prepared for the worst, and, being thus left unprotected, to form a garrison themselves ***and watch the gates.*** He saw that a number of the younger men of the city, among whom was his nephew William Cairnes of Killyfaddy,[1] then aged about 25, were prepared for the worst, and leaving his nephew and several of his contemporaries and friends to carry out his suggestions—the wisdom of which was so soon to be proved—he returned to Knockmany.

The mysterious movements of the Roman Catholics throughout the North proceeded apace without their ultimate object being divulged. Day and night the hammers of the country blacksmiths were heard behind closed doors; mysterious messengers, clerical and lay, flitted about from place to place, and several ships arrived at the ports with consignments of firearms which were secretly distributed.

On the 4th of December, 1688, a day ever to be remembered, the Earl of Mount Alexander received the following letter from an anonymous writer in Comber:[2]—

"December 3rd, 1688.

"Good my Lord,

"I have written to let you know that all our Irishmen "through Ireland are sworn that on the ninth day of this

[1] Son of his brother William, who died in 1682. We cannot ascertain what business or profession he followed in Derry, if any. He may have only come there with his uncle on this momentous occasion.

[2] The Rev. George Hill, slow to believe evil of any man if good might be attributed to him, and others, doubt the existence of the planned massacre; but reviewing

"month, being Sunday next, they are all to fall on, to kill "and murder man, wife and child, and to spare no one; "and I do desire your Lordship to take care of your self, "and all others that are adjudged by our men to be heads; "for whoever of them can kill any of you, is to have a "Captain's place. So my desire to your Honour is to look "to yourself, and to give other Noblemen warning, and go "not out at night or day without a good guard with you; "and let no Irishman come near you, whatever he be. "This is all from him who is your friend and father's "friend, and will be, though I dare not be known as yet, "for fear of my life.

"Direct this with care and haste

"To my Lord Montgomery."

About the same day letters of similar import were received by Mr. Brown of Lisburn and Mr. Maitland of Hillsborough. Inquiries made by these three gentlemen, in their several districts, led to confessions from individual Irishmen of the truth of the statements in the letters. Realising the terrible urgency of the case, each of the recipients of the letters had them copied out, and sending the originals with all speed to Dublin, despatched messengers with utmost haste to all the principal gentry throughout Ulster, with instructions to warn all in their districts of the

the preparations that were being made, the secret arming of the Roman Catholics, the deliberate forcible disarming of the Protestants, the withdrawing of the only regiment who could be relied upon to protect them, and finally the sermon of the friar above referred to, the fears of the Protestants, knowing what had occurred in 1641, were evidently well founded. After all, the opinion of the Protestants of the time, formed from what they actually saw around them, must be of greater weight than that formed by the most unbiassed judge of modern times, who has to weigh masses of conflicting and often unreliable evidence.

common danger. On the morning of the 6th of December messengers arrived throughout the country districts in Tyrone and Derry, in the City of Londonderry, and in Enniskillen.

In Londonderry the citizens were in consternation, Alderman Tomkins, among the first to hear the news, proceeded to the house of the Rev. James Gordon, a Presbyterian minister of considerable influence, who counselled the immediate closing of the gates, and manning the walls, and wrote to various friends outside the city to warn them. Mr. Tomkins proceeded thence through the now crowded Diamond towards the house of Alderman Norman, reiterating Mr. Gordon's advice as he proceeded. Mr. Norman, slower to convince, advised a consultation with Dr. Hopkins the Bishop of Derry, and with Mr. Tomkins proceeded to the Bishop's house. The Bishop, having heard the announcement, advised loyalty and absolute faith in the King, and discredited the news. His persuasive eloquence altered the views of the aldermen, who returned to the Diamond and endeavoured to calm the excited populace. For the nonce they partially succeeded, and towards the evening the city resumed something of its usual calm. So passed the 6th of December. On the morning of the 7th began to arrive affrighted Protestants from the surrounding district, warned by the messengers sent out by Mr. Gordon and others, and all bringing in stories corroborating the letters. Soon the Diamond was again filled with an excited crowd. The Bishop, accompanied by Aldermen Norman and Tomkins, and several of the clergy, shortly appeared upon the scene, urging the crowd to refrain from panic, and place utmost reliance upon the wisdom of their lawful King. While the Bishop was thus addressing the multitude, there ran up from the Ferry Gate one with the news that the new garrison, the Earl of Antrim's regiment,[1] had arrived at the Waterside, and that a detachment of it was now crossing the river. The excitement, then somewhat allayed by the Bishop's eloquence, broke out afresh. The citizens beheld in the advancing Irish soldiers men whom they deemed to be their murderers. In the middle of the Bishop's speech, Alexander Irwin, an apprentice boy, and a Presbyterian, interrupted with "My Lord, your doctrine is excellent, but it will keep!" Forthwith he and William Cairnes and eleven others, separated themselves from the crowd, rushed down the hill to the Ferry Gate, of which they seized the keys, and locked it in the face of the first contingent of the new garrison. They then ran round the three other gates, joined by a host of the townsmen, overpowered the turnkeys, and, shutting the gates, left guards to keep them shut.

Let no time ever efface from the memories of Englishmen, citizens of the freest country on which the sun shines, the names of that noble band of thirteen! "There is scarcely a blessing which the British Dominions enjoy to-day—there is scarcely a blessing which England has diffused through the other countries of the world—that was not secured by the Revolution of 1688; and that Revolution

[1] The descriptions handed down of the rank and file of the regiment are not prepossessing. The men are described by M'Kenzie as "rake-hells," and their women, who, expecting plunder, accompanied them in numbers, as "vultures." The men were all six feet or over, Highland and Irish Papists, and with the motley crowd of women, numbered in all over 1,200. Archbishop King describes them as "a pack of ruffians, many of whose captains and officers were well-known to the citizens, having long lain in their jails for thefts and robberies."

was secured by the defence of Londonderry now so unpretentiously begun."[1] The names were:—

William Cairnes.[2]	Samuel Hunt.
Henry Campsie.	Alexander Irwin (the leader).
William Crookshanks.	Robert Morrison.
Alexander Cunningham.	Daniel Sherrard.
John Cunningham.	Robert Sherrard.
Samuel Harvey.	James Stewart.

James Strike.

To these must be added the name of the Rev. James Gordon, Presbyterian minister, to which denomination most, if not all these belonged.

Meanwhile the Bishop, supported by the Church clergy and many of his followers, continued to protest against the conduct of the people, and a "Declaration" was drawn up by a few to be sent through Lord Mountjoy to Tyrconnell. This document was composed in a spirit of apologetic excuse for the misconduct of "a few of the younger and meaner sort"[3] in shutting the gates.

In the afternoon of that memorable day, arrived in Derry from Knockmany, David Cairnes, who was the first gentleman of position in the surrounding counties to reach the city, where he had hastened on receipt of the despatch

[1] Graham—"Ireland Preserved," p. 264. The Rev. John Graham hardly over-estimates the importance of the defence of Londonderry. Had the city fallen into the hands of King James, all resistance in Ireland would have been practically at an end, and his way would have been clear to unite his forces with Claverhouse in Scotland. Had he been able to effect this, it is more than probable things would have ended differently. It is perhaps too much to say that the united armies would have driven King William out of the Kingdom, but the fact remains that the defence of Londonderry was the cause of King James' ultimate defeat.

[2] See above, p. 112.

[3] See Dwyer, "Siege of Derry," p. 43.

from the Earl of Mount Alexander containing a copy ot the famous letter. On his arrival he found the Rev. Mr. Gordon, almost alone among the citizens of prominence, upholding the course taken by the Apprentice Boys. The Bishop and his admirers, comprising most of the better-class members of the Church of Ireland in the city, strongly dissented therefrom, and were busy framing the Declaration. Cairnes at once addressed the citizens in the Diamond, strongly approved of what had been done, and in glowing terms commended the bravery of those who had shut the gates. His influence was soon felt, and the Bishop's party was at once weakened by the loss of Aldermen Norman, Tomkins, and others, who now joined Cairnes in supporting the majority of the citizens. The Bishop fled early next morning to Raphoe, whence he shortly proceeded to England. He resigned the Bishopric and accepted a small living in London, dying in 1690.

On the morning following. Cairnes summoned a meeting of the prominent citizens, and the magazine having been seized, caused an inventory to be made of the arms and ammunition available, and of the provisions to be counted upon in case of a siege. These proved to be but scanty. The meeting drew up a statement and requested Cairnes to proceed to London, and lay it before King William, with an urgent entreaty for speedy assistance. Having a vessel of his own in the Foyle, he consented to act as their agent in negotiating with the Government and the Irish Society, and sailed that night.[1]

[1] For an account of the proceedings in Londonderry from this date see the several Histories of the Siege, among which may be mentioned Dwyer's "Siege of Derry" and Harris's "Life of King William III., Prince of Orange."

Stress of weather long delayed Cairnes in his journey to London, and it was well on in January ere he reached the Capital. On his arrival he lost no time in bringing the critical state of the Protestants of Ulster, and the City of Derry in particular, before the authorities. Most of those who could have hastened assistance were with the army in the North of England. The King's great aim at first was to secure his position in Great Britain, leaving Ireland for settlement later. The influence of the Irish Society, whose interest was so much at stake, and for which Cairnes was law agent in Derry, soon however obtained for him an interview with the King, who ordered prompt measures to be taken for the forwarding of military supplies to the city. Captain James Hamilton was at once despatched with arms and accoutrements for 2,000 men, 480 barrels of powder and £1,000, and the King appointed Colonel Lundy, then looked upon as one of the ablest officers in the army and a staunch supporter of His Majesty, governor of the city, with express instructions to proceed thither, fortify it, and hold it at all risks.[1] Hamilton arrived in Derry on the 10th of March with supplies, and two veteran regiments were ordered to follow.

On the 12th March, having so well achieved his mission, Cairnes left London, bearing a despatch to Lundy from the King desiring him to assure the citizens of his

[1] The instructions to Lundy, dated 22nd February (see Appendix XXV., Harris's "Life of King William III."), were so minute as to the carrying out of Cairnes's recommendations for strengthening the weak parts of the fortifications, that it is little wonder that Cairnes, on arriving in Derry on the 10th of April following, and finding nothing done towards this end, at once detected treachery.

DAVID CAIRNES, M.P.,
Of Londonderry and Knockmany.

From the copy by Catterson Smith, P.R.H.A., of the original painting by Sir Godfrey Kneller].

concern on their behalf and of speedy aid, and containing the following directions to himself:—

"You are with what convenient speed you can, forthwith to repair to London Derry, in the Kingdom of Ireland. At your arrival there, you are to acquaint the Governor and Magistrates of the said city of His Majesty's great care and concern for their security, which he hath shown not only in sending thither at this time, men, arms, and ammunition, but in the further great preparation he is making, as well for the particular defence of that place, as for the safety and protection of that whole kingdom.

"You are particularly to inform yourself of the present condition of London Derry, both as to Men, Arms, and Ammunition; and whether the country thereabouts can be able to furnish provision for a greater force intended to be sent thither, without carrying provisions from England; an exact account whereof you are to bring, yourself, with the best speed you can, or to send it with the first conveniency to me, or to the Committee of Council appointed for Irish affairs.

"You are to get the best information you can, what Force the Enemy has, as well Horse as Foot; in what condition the Troops are, and how armed, and what care is taken for their subsistence, whether by providing Magazines, and Stores, or by trusting on what provisions they shall find when marching.

"You are to enquire what new levies have been made of Horse, Foot, or Dragoon, by those Collonels, who had their Commissions sent them some time since by Captain Leighton, of what Numbers they are, and how disposed of.

"Given at our Court of Whitehall
"this 11th day of March, 1689."

Cairnes arrived in Derry on the 10th of April. He seems to have landed some distance down the Lough, and there to have left his ship, and whence he proceeded by road to the city. On the way he was met by several officers and many citizens who were abandoning the city on the advice of Colonel Lundy, who declared that the city could not withstand a siege. To these Cairnes gave encouragement, and news of the help at hand, inducing the officers to return. They were met by others who also turned, and on their arrival at Derry Cairnes at once sought out the Governor, to whom he handed the King's despatch. He then read his own warrant authorising him to ascertain and report to his Majesty what had been done for the defence of the place, and to what extent it was now prepared to withstand the approaching enemy. On the authority of his warrant he desired the Governor to summon the magistrates and principal citizens, to whom assembled, he that evening read the King's message, telling them of the army already embarked for their assistance. His hearers, hitherto thoroughly disheartened, now became enthusiastic, and at once made arrangements for an organised defence of the walls. Lundy, to allay the suspicions already awakened as to his treachery, ostentatiously encouraged them, and even volunteered himself to lead the regiments in person against the enemy now approaching Strabane ; but by deliberately withdrawing soldiers from the points where they were most needed, he allowed the enemy to cross the fords below Strabane, and drive himself and his men back to the city. On the next day, the 15th, the joyful news was spread that the English regiments mentioned by Cairnes had arrived in the Lough under Colonels Cunningham and Richards. Cairnes, Murray, and Walker now openly upbraided Lundy in the Council with cowardice and mismanagement of the previous day's proceedings, as well as for his deliberate neglect of the fortifications of the city. He replied that no efforts or preparations could possibly have enabled the city to withstand the enemy, 25,000 strong, and armed with heavy siege guns. He recommended surrender on the best terms that could be made, and abruptly dismissed the Council. He secretly conveyed intelligence to the colonels and officers of the English regiments that the defence of the city was now hopeless; that the troops had been defeated by the enemy the previous day at Strabane; that they had not more than two weeks' provisions, and that the Council had decided to surrender. He prevented their having any intercourse with the citizens, who were quite unaware of what he was doing, and on his orders the English ships set sail on the night of the 16th for England.

When the citizens heard of their departure on Lundy's orders, their indignation knew no bounds. Colonel Murray headed an open mutiny, and promptly organising a body of citizens, overpowered the sentries at the gates, which they placed under strong guard. The treachery of Lundy being exposed, he would have been torn to pieces had he been seen. Murray, who had now become the guiding spirit, actuated by charity, and by the fact that Lundy, traitor or no, was Governor by the King's writ, allowed him the option of escape. Of this he gladly availed himself, and fled in the night, disguised as a woodman. The citizens unanimously desired Colonel Murray to accept the Governorship. Being above all a soldier, he felt that he had not the general qualities required for the post, and modestly declined the honour, recommending the citizens to choose his friend Colonel Baker instead. They followed his advice, and Colonel Baker became Governor. He, too, felt himself lacking in some of the varied qualifications required for his position, and begged that the Rev. George Walker might be chosen his assistant,[1] chiefly to superintend the commissariat, a very important department in the management of a besieged city.

Cairnes duly fulfilled his written instructions, and having gained all the information he could with regard to the state of the city, and the possibility of its withstanding a lengthened siege, and having satisfied himself that under the new Governor the best that could be done under the

[1] The above statement that Mr. Walker was at first only appointed assistant to Governor Baker is made after careful consideration of the evidence. That he was eventually Governor of Derry there is no doubt, but that he was duly and properly so chosen, there seems to be no evidence but his own. In his diary of the siege Mr. Walker states that "The Garrison . . . . unanimously resolved to choose Mr. Walker and Major Baker to be their Governours"; McKenzie asserts that the Council assembled and nominated Baker, Mitchelburn, and Richard Johnson; of whom Baker had the majority of votes and was chosen Governor. He asked the Council to allow him "an assistant" (not "an assistant governor") for the stores and provisions, and suggested Mr. Walker, to whose appointment the Council assented. The anonymous author of "Ireland Preserved" (edited in 1840 by the Rev. John Graham), by some supposed to have been Mitchelburn, mentions Walker merely as "commissary of the stores." Mr. Walker's statement is thus diametrically opposed to those of the other authorities cited. In placing his own name before that of Baker, and even in saying that he was appointed joint-governor, Mr. Walker seems to have been guilty of assuming a position to which he had no title.

KEY PLATE TO THE PRINT OF "THE RELIEF OF DERRY."

(Size of Print, exclusive of margin, 33 x 20 inches.)

1. Rev. George Walker, Governor of Derry.
2. Colonel Mitchelburne.
3. Alderman Tomkins.
4. [illegible], afterwards Colonel, Cairnes.
5. Captain William [illegible].
6. [illegible]
7. Alderman [illegible].
8. William Blacker, of Carrickblacker.
9. James [illegible].
10. Augustus [illegible].
11. Mrs. Boyd.
12. Mrs. Ash.
13. Mrs. Browning, wife of the Captain of the Mountjoy.
14. Mrs. [illegible] and Child.
15. "Roaring Meg." (18 Pounder).
16. The Mountjoy, Phoenix, and Dartmouth Frigate.
17. Macnaghten of Benvarden (Child in Arms).
18. Group of Apprentice Boys.
19. James Spaight, with the Crimson Banner.
20. Colonel Murray (wounded during the Siege).
21 & 22. Irish Conscripts [illegible] under the Walls.
23. Captain [illegible], an ancient of Lord [illegible].
24. Tents of the Enemy.
25. Captain Ash.
26. Centre of Butcher's Gate.
27. [illegible]

Published by JAMES MAGILL, 7, Donegall Place, Belfast.

THE RELIEF OF DERRY, 1689.

From the painting by George F. Folingsby.]

circumstances was being done, set sail for England to lay before the King the state of affairs. He arrived some time in May, and reported the treachery of Lundy, and the consequent dire distress and danger of the city. The King was fully alive to the importance of the successful defence of Derry, as it alone barred King James's advance to Scotland and his junction with Viscount Dundee. He immediately despatched Major-General Kirke, with a fleet containing ample provisions, for the relief of the distressed city. Lundy was at once arrested in Scotland, where he had fled from Derry, and lodged in the Tower. His end is uncertain. Kirke arrived in Lough Foyle in the middle of June, and lay inactive for six weeks outside the city, not even making an effort to approach.

Of David Cairnes' movements we have no record for some time[1] after his securing the despatch of supplies to

[1] "Derriana," a lyric poem supposed to have been written by one present at the siege (edited by the Rev. John Graham, 1823), implies that the King on hearing of Kirke's delay in relieving the city, sent Cairnes with orders to Kirke to relieve it at once, and that it was on his arrival with the Royal orders that the relief took place. We cannot find corroboration of this elsewhere. We have endeavoured without success to ascertain whether Cairnes re-entered the city before its relief; it does not seem probable that he did. If not, the well-known picture of the Relief of Derry here reproduced is inaccurate in including him among the besieged. Notwithstanding that it was he who successfully undertook the hazardous journey to England and secured the despatch of, first, the war stores and money by Colonel Hamilton and the regiments under Cunningham and Richards, and secondly, the relief fleet under Kirke, Walker little more than mentions him in his celebrated "Diary of the Siege." A student of Walker's diary, who reads between the lines, and who follows the writer's subsequent actions, cannot fail to notice—First, the writer's self-laudation, cloaked though it is by a parade of modesty. According to him, he, and he only, was the mainstay of the defence; as a warrior of desperate bravery he headed sorties; as a military tactician he, and he alone, devised the most skilful manœuvres; as a minister of the Gospel he, and he only, preached sermons and prayed prayers worthy to be recorded, during the siege (these he had printed and circulated immediately after the relief); in fact according to his diary, it would be hard to believe that ever before or since had the world produced a man of so many parts. Secondly, not a Presbyterian, where it could be avoided, is rewarded with even a word

Derry under Kirke. As Agent for the Irish Society in Derry, he made several journeys between that city and London in 1690-1. While in London he had his portrait painted by Kneller. On his return to Londonderry, his grateful fellow citizens honoured him by electing him member for the city in the new Parliament assembled at Dublin.

of praise. The name of the very minister who first caused the shutting of the gates—the Rev. James Gordon—is entirely omitted, as are those of the other ministers who were present at the siege, and did so much in the defence. Mr. Walker merely refers to them as "seven Nonconforming ministers whose names I cannot learn," a statement very difficult to believe. When afterwards compelled to give them (see Walker's "Vindication" of his account of the siege, and the publisher's preface thereto), he so alters some of the names as to render them unrecognisable; for instance, Mr. M'Kenzie he names "Machiny." Mr. Gilchrist he designates "Kil Christ." Thirdly, immediately after the siege had ended Mr. Walker drew up the address to be sent to King William. This document opened with fulsome and undeserved flattery of Major-General Kirke, who in reality had callously lain no less than six weeks in the lough with his ships laden with provisions, while Derry was starving, and had made no effort to relieve it. M'Kenzie in his "Narrative" says of this address, "Many of those that signed it neither knew of the bearer, nor were well pleased with the great compliment passed upon the Major-General, but were not willing at such a time to make any disturbance by any public opposition to it." It can be readily imagined that at the time signatures were easily procured, though it is notable that many names of those present are conspicuously absent from the address. The compliment to Kirke, however, was appreciated, as the Major-General at once deputed Mr. Walker to go in person to present the address to the King. He let no time elapse, and crossed to Scotland on the 9th August. Everywhere he went on his route, *via* Glasgow to London, he was the first to give his account of the Rev. George Walker's defence of Derry. He was received everywhere as a demi-god. As he approached London, so had his fame preceded him, that he was met at Barnet by a deputation, and followed by crowds, was escorted to the capital. He presented his address to the King, who was duly impressed with the merits and loyalty of the Governor (there were two Governors, Walker and Mitchelburn, but little praise and no reward or recompense was accorded to Mitchelburn, absent invalided through wounds) and citizens of Derry. He presented a petition to the House of Commons, and fervently impressed upon the Government the dire straits in which the loyal citizens of Derry were left by the siege. It must be said to Walker's credit, that he certainly pleaded the cause of the citizens of Derry before the King and Parliament with great ability and fervour. The disgraceful neglect afterwards shown them by the Government cannot in any way be ascribed to the weakness of Walker's pleading on their behalf; yet it is a fact that in his "Diary," which he published immediately on his arrival in London, in his petition to Parliament, and in the loyal address to the King the names of several individuals whose services at Derry

He continued to represent the city until 1704, when he was obliged to resign owing to his refusal to subscribe to the Test Act. In connection with the celebrated lawsuit between the Irish Society and Bishop King, a suit which lasted nearly ten years, and was only settled by a special Act of the British Parliament, Cairnes took a prominent part on behalf of the Society.

He was a man of the highest principle and integrity. He it was who first organised the young men of Derry

were quite as great as his own, were placed in a position of very secondary importance, if even mentioned at all. For instance, the Rev. James Gordon, whose active services at the early stage of the siege were the immediate cause of the shutting of the gates, was one of those whose name even "he cannot learn"; David Cairnes, who first organised the apprentice boys and afterwards did so much towards the relief of the city; Colonel Murray, who headed the insurrection of the garrison on the discovery of Lundy's treachery, and did other incalculable services during the siege; and Mitchelburn, his co-governor, who lost his wife and all his children during the siege, who lost, in the expenses of his own regiment alone, over £9,000 (he was eventually imprisoned for debts incurred at the siege), and was severely wounded. For none of these can we find that he pleaded individually, if he even mentioned them at all. Yet, that his influence at Court could probably have secured for these heroes some recognition, if not ample recompense for their sufferings and losses, is shown by the fact that he secured for himself a reward of £5,000 and the wealthy Bishopric of Derry, and for the widow of Colonel Baker, who first appointed him as head of the commissariat department at the siege, a pension of £300 per annum. Walker's "Diary" was published in London immediately on his arrival, and had an enormous sale in England. When copies reached Derry it produced widespread indignation, which found vent in several pamphlets issued by individuals present at the siege. These pointed out many inaccuracies in the "Diary," and exposed particularly Walker's great unfairness in ignoring so pointedly all mention of the undoubted merits of the Presbyterians, individually, or otherwise, in Derry. So clearly did these various pamphlets expose the "Diary," that Walker was compelled to issue a second work on the siege, explaining and modifying the first, which he called "A Vindication of the True Account of the Siege." However, by the time the pamphlets reached London and the "Vindication" was published, the nine days' wonder had run its course, and popular interest in the subject had waned. For a thousand who read the "Diary," probably not five read the pamphlets or the "Vindication," or if they read the "Vindication" they never saw the pamphlets, so that the account of the siege as contained in the "Diary" became engrafted in the popular mind, and so was handed down to future generations. It thus formed tradition, so strong a factor in history, and so hard to combat in endeavouring to review historic facts without prejudice in later times.

into a band afterwards known to fame as the "Apprentice Boys," who on that memorable occasion, instigated and supported by the Rev. James Gordon, closed the gates, and so saved not only the city, but the State. He was the one who first stood up against the paramount influence of Bishop Hopkins, and championed the action of the men who shut the gates; it was he who hastened to England and secured the despatch of the war stores that saved the city, and the regiments that were dismissed by Lundy; and it was he who again undertook the hazardous journey to England and procured the sending of the fleet of ships laden with provisions under Major General Kirke, which at last brought about the Relief of Derry. All his journeys to England were made in his own ship, and at his own expense. His house at Knockmany, in his absence, was looted, and his house at Derry ruined by a shell, yet he never received one penny of compensation or reward. In 1695 the Mayor and principal burgesses of Derry appeared before the Irish Parliament with a petition praying for relief for the impoverished citizens. A committee of the House heard the petition, examined the bearers thereof, and reported to the House. On 12th December, 1695,[1] the Commons sent the following to the Lord Lieutenant:—

"The Humble Address of the Knights, Citizens, and Burgesses in Parliament assembled—

"May it Please your Excellency—

"The Mayor, Commonality, and Citizens of the City of Londonderry, having by a petition lately preferred unto us, set forth the great losses, disbursements and sufferings

[1] Journal of the Irish House of Commons.

by them sustained in the late Revolution, and the great debts contracted on the publick account by their early securing and fortifying the place, . . .

"We therefore humbly desire that your Excellency would be pleased to lay the Petitioners' case before His Sacred Majesty, and recommend the same in the most effectual manner to his Princely consideration; and that your Excellency would be also pleased to take notice therein of David Cairnes, Esquire, a member of that city, and now one of their representatives in Parliament, in regard ot his early services in first securing the said city against the Irish, and the several hazardous journies made by him in order to the Relief of the same, and his great losses by the siege."

"Ordered that Mr. Vanhomreigh, and such members of the House as please to accompany him, do attend his Excellency the Lord Deputy, with the said address, and humbly present the same to his Lordship as the address of this whole House."

Whether as the result of this petition or not, Cairnes was some ten years later appointed Recorder of Derry.[1] He died in 1722, and was buried in the Cathedral. His monument, broken and almost defaced, was restored some seventy years ago by the Irish Society. To the memory of Walker, Cairnes, Baker, Mitchelburn, and Murray, the citizens of Derry, early in the nineteenth century, erected on a prominent position on the city walls the monument

[1] It cannot be said, in the absence of express evidence, that this appointment was made in recognition of Cairnes's services to the State in 1689-90. In the fifteen years intervening between the siege and his appointment as Recorder he had attained eminence as a lawyer in Derry.

bearing these five names, and known as the "Walker Monument." Cairnes was survived only by daughters. His will, dated 19th October, 1721,[1] a most voluminous document of 74 pages, supplies much information, and we therefore give some extracts from it.

The first four pages are devoted to religious sentiments of a most devout strain. On page 5 he refers to "my two daughters, Jane the eldest, whom I had by my first wife Margaret Edwards, and whom I marryed to Thomas Edwards, Esq., her cozen, and she died in 1716, and he is since lately dead, in April 1721, and Mary the younger, whom I had by my second and last wife Mary Barnes long since deceased and whom I marryed to the Rev. Mr. Richard Choppin, minister in Dublin,[2] and she is yet alive, whose marriage portions, considering my circumstances, were sufficiently ample and large . . . ." Page 6: "and by what great charge trouble and expense I was at in many ways by my son John the Captain, who died unfortunately by a Duell at New Castle in England in March 1719, by his unwary conduct of himself, which I need say no more of." Page 8: "I leave to my nephew[3] Lieut. John Cairnes of Claremore in the County of Tyrone, one moydore in gould, of thirty shillings value, and one mourning gould ring with the first letter of my name and surname, and day and yeare of Death engraven therein,

1 Prerogative Wills, Public Record Office, Ireland.

2 The Rev. Richard Choppin was minister of Wood Street Presbyterian Church from 1704 to 1741.

3 The eldest son of his sister Mary, who married her cousin James Cairnes of Claremore. This John Cairnes, as well as David of Londonderry and William of Killyfaddy were on the long list of Protestant gentry attainted by King James's Parliament in Dublin in 1689.

the ring to be of fourteen shillings vallue, and to his daughter Margarett Cairnes, she being the only grandchild of all my brothers and sisters grandchildren that retains our Surname of Cairnes at this day, I leave two guineas in gould to her as a litle memorial of me. and to my said nephew John, his brother William Cairnes of Limrick, Marchant, I leave the same as to his brother John, not including his daughter aforesaid. and to my nephew William Cairnes[1] of Killyfaddy, Esq., the same. and to my niece Susan, wife of Captain Foster in the County of Monaghan, the same. and to her sister, my niece, married to Mr. Betty, the same. and to her younger sister Lettice, married to the Rev. Robt. Wilson the minister, the same and five pounds over and above, as their condition does much require it, not to mention what I bestowed on her at her marriage. and to my niece Lettice Thomson alias Wrey, married to the Rev. Humphrey Thomson, minister in the County Monaghan, the same as to my nephew John aforesaid and to my nephew William Elliot of Cloneblagh[2] in the County of Tyrone, the same. and to his sister, my niece, that was married to Thomas Cairnes[3] Doctor of Physick, whom we hear to be lately dead, the same as to her brother now last mentioned, and forty shillings over and above, because of her low condition and poverty, and the very ill and unjust doings and carriage of her Husband towards her, which I will here say no more of, and is all

[1] The "Old Captain." See above, pp. 113, 156.

[2] The son of his sister and her husband William Elliot. Cloneblagh was in David Cairnes' estate. This William Elliot married Mary, sister and eventual heiress of the "Old Captain" of Killyfaddy. (See Chap. VI.).

[3] Brother of the "Old Captain." There was no issue of this marriage, though Dr. Cairnes left a natural son William.

I need say. These but small memorials are left these my relatives only to show them I had them in my memory." Page 10: "To the Rev. Mr. Jos. Boise, minister in Dublin, my most esteemed friend, whom I generally hear whilst there, the same memorial of me as to John Cairnes aforesaid. and the same also to my good friend Mistress Margaret Bamber wife to Mr. Bamber in Capel Street Dublin. and I leave a ring, such as aforesaid to Mrs. Rebecca Brooke who resides now at my son-in-law Rev. Mr. Chopin in Dublin. Also I leave and devise to the Rev. Mr. Samuel Ross, minister in Londonderry, whom I usually hear when there, the same. And to the Rev. Mr. Nehemiah Donaldson,[1]

[1] The Rev. Nehemiah Donaldson, formerly of Belfast. He was a member of an ancient and at one time most influential family in the County Antrim, settled in and near Glenarm. They were evidently a cadet family of the great clan Donald, descended from a younger, or probably an illegitimate member of the clan. The Donaldsons' lands were all on the Earl of Antrim's estates, and were very extensive. One of their castles, said to have been the successor of the original castle of the Bissets, at the head of the main street of Glenarm, was standing, a ruin, in the early years of the nineteenth century. Another was in the townland of Bay, about a mile north of Glenarm. The writer once purchased an old book bound in parchment, a black letter copy of the Act of Explanation; the parchment cover turned out to be more interesting than the contents. It proved to be a letter or petition from James, son of John Donaldson of Bay and the adjoining townlands of Parishy and Straidkelly, to the Marquis of Antrim, craving a renewal of favours granted to the petitioner's grandfather by the 1st Earl in 1633. From this document we learn that the Donaldsons held the above lands, as well as those of Moyglinne, Ballybraggy, and Blarbane in this neighbourhood; that they had expended over £500—no small sum in those days—in building the castle of the Bay, and that these were part of the lands granted to Lieutenant Smyth in the Cromwellian settlements. They were restored to the Antrim family by the Act of Explanation, and passed to the M'Naughten family, represented at the time of the sale, we believe, by the infant in arms shown in the well-known picture of the Relief of Derry here reproduced. When the Donaldsons disappeared from these lands, we cannot ascertain. Mr. M'Donnell, husband of the Countess of Antrim, in his efforts to reconsolidate the Glenarm portion of the Antrim estate, exchanged these lands with the M'Naughten family, giving them instead the lands of Ballymagarry, of equal value, near Dundarave.

The Drumnasole property was also part of the Donaldson estate. It was purchased by Mr. Turnley, a successful brewer in Belfast, about 1800. He had previously bought the greater portion of the Hollow Sword-blade lands at Cushendall. He built the present Drumnasole House. It is recorded that Mr. Turnley, when building this house, hearing that minister at or near Castlegore in the County of Tyrone, whom I usually hear whilst there, the same."

Then follow minute instructions to his executors on matters of detail, and he finally appoints as his heir, subject to a life annuity to his daughter Mrs. Choppin, his grandson Cairnes Edwards, youngest son of his deceased daughter Jane, and the heirs male of his body; failing whom, his next brother Thomas Edwards and his heirs male; failing whom, his next brother Edward Edwards and his heirs male; failing whom, the eldest son Hugh Edwards and his heirs male; failing whom, his nephew William Cairnes of Killyfaddy and his heirs male.

Page 29: "To Robert Wallace, the tenant of my mill at

---

one of the employés, a common labourer, was actually a son of the late owner, showed him great kindness and eventually employed him as landsteward.

The principal house of the Antrim Donaldsons seems to have been near Cairncastle. The Rev. Classon Porter relates that the head of the Cairncastle Donaldsons, who were connected by marriage with the Shaws of Ballygelly, at one time made great preparations for the erection of an imposing castle at Ballygilbert, near Cairncastle. He proceeded to excavate the foundations, in which the capacious wine-cellars were to be situated; but from a superabundance of wine (we fear, duty free), or a deficiency of cash, the work was dropped. Within comparatively recent times, the remains of these wine-cellars and foundations remained, but have since disappeared. The Donaldson property at Cairncastle passed by sale to the Agnews of Kilwaughter.

The Donaldson family supplied High Sheriffs for County Antrim in 1633 and 1656, but so far as we can learn are entirely extinct in the male line. So far as we can trace, the only owners of land, descendants of the Donaldsons (in the female line) in the district, are the family of Jordan of Owencloughy.

The Donaldsons also held an influential position in County Armagh, the representative of the family of Bay and Parishy, Randal Donaldson, being described in a lease for three lives, renewable for ever of these lands, dated 1748, as "Esquire, of Castle Dillon, County Armagh." Three Donaldsons are mentioned as the first lives in the lease, namely, the lessee, Lieutenant James Donaldson, R.N., and Captain John Donaldson, of the Royal Fusiliers.

The Donaldsons, like the Cairneses, were rigid Presbyterians, and with the Shaws of Ballygelly were included in the list of discontented Antrim men to be banished to Munster in 1653. The transportation was deferred, and owing to Cromwell's death was not carried out.

Raveagh, being also my relative,[1] I leave as a memorial of me, one pistole in gould and a mourning ring; and to Nicholas Gwynne, innkeeper in Londonderry, being also my relative,[1] the same." The will concludes with a rather interesting expression of the testator's disappointments in life relative to the shameful and callous neglect on the part of King William III. of those brave citizens of Derry whose memorable defence of the city secured him his throne. It reads as follows:—

"I did, indeed, once think and expect, and had much reason for it, to have been, ere this, in a much greater and ampler condition as to my outward state and concerns in the world, and in a capacity to have left my children and offspring, and other friends also, much more than I have here done, and might also soon have obtained it, would I but have bartered my conscience for allurements of that kind, which, I bless God, I never did, nor ever inclined to do[2]; and had matters but any way answered my reasonable expectations from the state and government, for the faithful and important services I did them, and the whole Protestant interest in these kingdoms, both in the first securing of Londonderry in December, 1688, that proved of so very great consequence afterwards to these kingdoms, and the many sore and most dangerous journeys and travels I had both by sea and land, with many signal hazards of my life in the spring and summer then following, for the saving and preserving of that city, being sent and employed by the Honourable Lords of the Privy Council in England at

[1] We have been unable to trace the relationship.

[2] He is here evidently referring to the inducements held out to him in 1704 to subscribe to the Test Act, which he steadfastly refused to do.

that time, who have amply attested it under their hands and public seals, yet extant. All these matters, for which I had many good words and promises of great things I had to be done for me, that never yet had any effect or performance, but put me to much trouble and expense in making several applications on that behalf, without any effect. I may, indeed, truly say, I found but few grateful or suitable returns, either from the state or divers other persons and people, I had laboured and done much for, and to their manifest advantage, which I need here say no more of; but that how I myself and that city of Londonderry, for all its services and sufferings that were of such high consequence to these kingdoms, and so amply confessed by their parliaments, both of England and Ireland, come to be so strangely overlooked and neglected as they have been, reflects not a little shame on the honour of these nations, so that all these assurances which I had should be buried in utter oblivion. And lastly, I do hereby earnestly charge and exhort all my offspring, as if by their parent's last dying words, that they live and walk in the fear and love of God, and in the steadfast observance of His commands, worship and ordinances, while they breathe upon His earth here; that they may be serious and constant in humble prayer to Him, and in reading the Holy Scriptures daily; that God may own and bless them in all that they do or set about—that they carefully and watchfully abstain from and avoid, so far as they reasonably can, the society and intimate converse with all notorious, lewd and dissolute persons and company, being of much contagious and pernicious consequence; that they associate themselves, and converse, as far as they can, with sober, serious, and prudent persons; and crave from such, and expect them, that if they, or any of them, come to dispose of themselves in marriage, they do it with much seriousness and earnest prayer to God, for his direction and blessings therein, and with the advice of their best and most faithful friends, lest they repent it all their lives after, when it is too late."

Besides his estate at Raveagh, David Cairnes had a good deal of house property in the city and suburbs of Derry, which, as he mentions in his will, he obtained on his marriage with his first wife Margaret Edwards. By her he left surviving issue,[1]

JANE, wife of her cousin Thomas Edwards of Castlegore by whom she had issue,

1. HUGH, of Castlegore, born about 1700. Married Anne, daughter of Mr. Mervyn, of Co. Fermanagh. She married secondly James Richardson, of Springtown, who, by permission, assumed her maiden name Mervyn. Hugh Edwards died in 1737, having had issue

   (*a*). OLIVIA, who married in 1754, Richard, Earl of Ross. On his death in 1764, the Countess married 2ndly Captain John Bateman of Co. Westmeath, but left no issue by either marriage.

   (*b*), (*c*), (*d*). Jane, Elizabeth, Arabella.

2. EDWARD, of Loughmuck, a major in the army, of whom later.

[1] His eldest son was killed in a duel in 1719. Several children died young and were buried in St. Michan's Church in Dublin, close to Cairnes' lodgings in Capel Street. Of the descendants of Mrs. Choppin, his daughter by his second wife, if any, we cannot find trace.

3. THOMAS, married in 1743 Elizabeth, daughter of William Thwaites of Dublin. On his brother Cairnes Edwards' death in 1747 he succeeded under David Cairnes' will to his estates. He had issue, besides two daughters who died unmarried,

    ESTHER, wife of James Brabazon of Mornington, Co. Meath, a member of the Earl of Meath's family. She was sole heiress of her father and succeeded to David Cairnes' estate, which she left, under romantic circumstances to be referred to shortly, to her relative Hugh Gore Edwards. She died without issue.

4. CAIRNES, heir of his grandfather David Cairnes. He died unmarried in 1747.
5. MARGARET, third child, who married in 1722 Robert Stuart, eldest son of Andrew Stuart of Stuart Hall, Co. Tyrone. By him she had issue,
    (*a*). ANDREW THOMAS, born 1723, who succeeded as 6th Lord Castlestuart.[1] (See Peerage).
    (*b*). CAIRNES, youngest child, born about 1738 died unmarried in 1752.
    (*c*). JANE, died unmarried 1804.

[1] This family of Stuart are the representatives of the ancient family of Ochiltree. The last Stuart Lord Ochiltree, by Royal permission, surrendered the lands and the barony to King James I, receiving the extensive estates in Co. Tyrone now held by his descendant the present Lord Castlestuart. The Earls of Castlestuart claim (rightly, we believe) to be the head representatives in the pure male line of the Royal house of Stuart.

(*d*). HARRIET. For her marriage and issue see Burke under Sir James Hamilton, Bart.

(*e*) ELEANOR, married in 1758, Peter, son of the Rev. Abel Pelisiere, of Laragh Bryan, Parish of Maynooth.

6. MARY, married 1stly Hugh Liston, by whom she had issue. She married 2ndly, Dalway, 2nd son of the above named Andrew Stuart of Stuart Hall, by whom she had issue.

On the death of the above-named Elizabeth Brabazon of Mornington, David Cairnes' estate reverted to Hugh Gore Edwards, grandson of Edward Edwards mentioned in David Cairnes' will as third in remainder.

EDWARD EDWARDS, married about 1735, in the billiard room at Castlegore, Isabella, daughter of James Hamilton of Strabane, of the Abercorn family, and by her had an only son.

EDWARD CAIRNES EDWARDS, born 1742. He became a Lieut.-Colonel in the 32nd Regiment, and married Ann, daughter of Sir L. Mannix, Knight, of Glanmire, Co. Cork, by whom he had an only son.

HUGH GORE EDWARDS, born 1789. He entered the army, and about 1810, when a lieutenant, started on a sea voyage. The vessel encountered terrific weather in the Irish Sea, and became a wreck off the coast of Meath, at the mouth of the Boyne. The survivors in their distress sought refuge in the nearest houses, and by the merest chance, Edwards sought hospitality for the night at Mornington House, close by. The story goes that when admitted, his hostess Mrs. Brabazon above-named, at once recognised him from his features to be an Edwards. Enquiries confirmed her suspicions, and the lady, having no children of her own, called the household together and in presence of all declared the shipwrecked soldier her heir.[1] He duly succeeded to David Cairnes' Raveagh estate. He was presented with the freedom of the city of Cork in 1815. He married Elizabeth,[2] daughter of the Rev. Alexander George Stuart, and was survived by daughters only. He died in 1870 and was succeeded by his grandson Hugh, eldest son of his daughter Elizabeth, by Robert, fourth son of the Hon. and Very Rev. George Gore, Dean of Killala. This gentleman died recently and was succeeded by his son Hugh the present owner of Raveagh, and representative in the female line of the defender of Derry.

[1] This family tradition is doubtless founded upon fact, but a reference to the terms of David Cairnes' will discloses the fact that Mrs. Brabazon had no right to the Raveagh estate. It was strictly limited to the male heirs of the sons of Jane Edwards, and on the death of Mrs. Brabazon's father without male issue, it passed by right not to Mrs. Brabazon, but to young Edwards' father, who was abroad, and probably ignorant of the terms of his ancestor's will.

[2] This lady's eldest sister Frances married Mr. James R. White of Whitehall, County Antrim, and was the mother of Field-Marshal Sir George Stuart White, K.C.B., D.L.

CHAPTER VIII.

The Descendants of Cairnes of Orchardton, Kirkpatricks, Maxwells and Kennedys—Sir Robert Maxwell of Orchardton—The Cairnses of Kipp, Barnbarroch, Torr and Girstingwood.

AS has been related in a former chapter William Cairnes the elder of Orchardton left a numerous family, at least six sons and three daughters, as follows: William his heir, John of Cults, ancestor of the Irish Cairneses, Peter of Kipp, Henry of Torr, George of Muretoun, Valentine, Elizabeth wife of John Gordon, Isobel wife of John M'Culloch, and Janet wife of John M'Moran.

William the elder of Orchardton died in 1555, and was succeeded in the estate by his eldest son William the younger, who during his father's lifetime had resided with his wife Janet, a daughter of Thomas Kennedy[1] of Knocknalling, at Dalbeattie. He only enjoyed his estates three years, dying in 1558,[2] and leaving issue three daughters only, coheiresses, between whom the Orchardton property was equally divided. The eldest daughter Margaret had a remarkable career. She married three times, and some entries in the records of the Privy Council serve to show

---

[1] Kennedy of Knocknalling and Knockcreoch. This family, who are still in possession of these estates, have held them in uninterrupted succession for more than 400 years. The founder of this branch of the family of Kennedy of Cassilis was Thomas Kennedy, whose charter was dated 1476. He appears to have been a second son of Cassilis from the crescent as a mark of difference on his shield.

[2] His widow married secondly David Gordon. Acts and Decreets xx. 179, Register House, Edinburgh.

that her life passed by no means void of adventure. Her first husband was William Kirkpatrick of Kirkmichael, her second James Kirkpatrick[1] in Barmure, a brother of Roger of Closeburn; and her third Edward Maxwell of Tynwald. By her first husband she had a son and heir Sir Alexander Kirkpatrick, Knight, who eventually succeeded as heir of his mother's third portion of Orchardton. The dates of her marriages are not known, but by 1591 she had married her third husband, a marriage evidently most distasteful to her son Sir Alexander Kirkpatrick, who fearing his mother might leave her estate to her husband, seized her person and locked her up. Her husband appeared before the Privy Council to demand redress, and the Lords heard "Ye complaint by Margaret "Cairnis Lady Orchardtoun and Edward Maxwell of Tin-"well her spouse for his interest as follows—In ye time "of ye lait troubles fallen oute betuix ye Lord Maxwell "and ye Laird of Johnstoune her houses of Dargavell "having been burnt, her goods spuilyied and herself "cheisset fra her awne leving, her son Alexander Kirk-"patrick of Kirkmichael had desired her to take shelter "with him quhile she micht peaciblie enjoy her awne "leving; accordingly upon his promise for his dutifull

[1] These Kirkpatricks are now extinct in Galloway where they once possessed so much influence. Kirkpatrick of Kirkmichael was a descendant of him who "made siccar" of the death of the Red Comyn. Several cadets of the family settled in Ireland in the 17th and 18th centuries. One was an officer in one of the ships that relieved Derry after the siege. Others settled in Dublin and Belfast, one of the latter being a merchant in York Street in that city. His daughter was the mother of the Empress Eugenie, and other representatives in the male line are the Rev. Alexander Kirkpatrick, formerly Rector of Craigs, Mr. George Kirkpatrick of Hazelbank, Craigs, Co. Antrim, and the Rev. Canon Alexander Francis Kirkpatrick, Regius Professor of Hebrew at Cambridge.

"behavour towards her, she come to him lippynning for "na thing les than he suld have onywayes misbehavit "himself to her, but efter she had remayned a certain "space with him he begouth be policie and craft to intyse "her to have renunceit her hail leving in his favour; and "finding her na ways correspondent to his desire on that "point, he committed her to warde within ane of his "chalmers, quharin maist unnaturallie and unthankfullie he "deteins her, suffering nane to have access to her; within "the whilke he intendis to keip and detene her quhile he "compall her to renunce her said leving and accept sic "unworthie portioun thair of for her sustentation as he "pleissis to bestow upon hir."

On hearing this complaint, the Lords of the Council commanded Sir Alexander to bring his mother in person before the King, of which command the offender took no notice. How the difficulty was settled is not known, but as Sir Alexander shortly afterwards appears as heir of his mother's portion of Orchardton, it is probable the lady rather conveniently died about this time. Sir Alexander sold his portion of the property, which included Orchardton Castle, in 1616[1] to Robert Maxwell, son of Sir Robert Maxwell of Spottes, Knight, brother of Lord Maxwell. Of the eventual history of Sir Alexander or his descendants, if any, we have no record.

Janet, the second daughter and coheiress of Orchardton, had by her husband George Maxwell, of Drumcoltran, four sons, Edward, the heir, John, George, and Herbert, and a daughter Catherine, who married Bartholomew M'Cartney

[1] Reg. Mag. Sigilli, 2nd January, 1616.

of Auchinleck, by whom she had issue an only son George. (See below p. 186, note.) She married secondly Sir William Sinclair. Edward inherited his mother's property, which he also sold to his relative Sir Robert Maxwell of Spottes about 1640.[1]

Elizabeth, the third daughter, had issue a daughter Janet, by John Kennedy,[2] whom she afterwards married. On her death in 1569 her sister Janet claimed to be her heiress on the ground of the alleged illegitimacy of the daughter. The claim was heard before the Commissaries of Edinburgh in 1570, and the following is an abridgement of their decreet:—

"Anent the actioun and caus purseuit befoir the saidis "commissaris be Jonet Carnis nevoy (*i.e.*, granddaughter) "and air to umquhil William Carnis of Orchartoun, and "George Maxwell hir spous for his interes, aganis Jonet "Kennedy, and Johne Kennedy in Air hir allegit fader for "his interes gif he ony hes. Brieves had been purchased "at the instance of Jonet Kennedy alleged daughter to "umquhil Elizabeth Carnis sister german to said Jonet "Carnis, for serving her heir to her mother; which Jonet

[1] The Drumcoltran Maxwells were cadets of the family of the Lords Maxwell. In the Terregles charter-room are many documents relative to this family, all earlier in date than 1640. The tracing of the descendants of George Maxwell and Janet Cairnes is rendered impossible from the enormous number of Maxwells appearing in the records without the least indication as to the families to which they belonged. The smaller lairds were seldom able to make any provision for their younger sons, who usually became ecclesiastics, lawyers, merchants or farmers. Once parted from their lands, at a period prior to the systematic keeping of parish registers, individuals lose their identity to the would-be genealogist. We regret we have been unable to trace the descendants of any of the heiresses of Orchardton, with the exception of those of Catherine M'Cartney above named, beyond the first generation.

[2] Described in the Commissaries' Decreet as resident in Ayr. He was a brother of David Kennedy of Knockdaw. Contract in Register House, Edinburgh, dated 1573.

"Carnis opposed on the ground that Jonet Kennedy was "illegitimate. The case being remitted to the Commissaries "for decision, Jonet Carnis alleged that Jonet Kennedy "wes gotten and borne in nature manefast and detestabill "fornicatioun, na lauchfull mareage evir being contractit "or solempnizat" between her father and mother. To which it was answered that Elizabeth Carnis "schortlie "eftir the tyme of hir (Jonet's) birth, viz., betuix the feist "of Mydsumer and Lambes in anno 1560 wes lauchfulle "contret with hir said father per verba de presenti be "Schir Thomas Ecklis then vicar pensionar and curat of "the kirk of Colmonell and now reder at the samyn kirk, "the said Jonet then being present at the completing of "the said mareage recognoscit and put be hir said parentis "under the cair claith[1] in wirificatioun that hir saidis "parentis maid hir participiant of the said mareage as use "wes of befoir, as thair barne than being present and

[1] The cair cloth was used in the marriage ceremony from the earliest times. It was held over the bride and groom during part of the service. Its origin is probably pagan. Martène [De Antiquis Ecclesiae Ritibus. Lib. i. p. 2, c. ix., art. iii., § 9] says: "Dum cantaretur benedictio, velum purpureum in signum pudoris super sponsum et sponsam expandebatur ut docent nostri libri rituales innuitque S. Ambrosius in pluribus locis . . . Similiter et Syricius papa." Saint Ambrose flourished in the fourth, and Siricius in the fifth century. It became the custom to include the children, if any, born prior to the marriage, under the cair cloth with the parents, not as absolutely necessary to their legitimation, but as a public acknowledgment that the child or children were theirs. In England, probably as early as the eleventh century, legitimation of offspring *per subsequens matrimonium* had ceased, though the use of the cair cloth in marriage obtained for several centuries later, being only formally abolished in 1549. Not so, however, in France and Scotland, where legitimation *per subsequens matrimonium* still is law. As recently as about a hundred years ago the cair cloth was occasionally used in France, but it appears to have fallen out of general use in Scotland much earlier. See Transactions of the St. Paul's Ecclesiological Society, Vol. III., p. 170, and Maskell's Ritualea (2nd Edit. Vol. I., pp. 88, 89), references which I owe to the kindness of the Bishop of Edinburgh and the Rev. E. S. Dewick.

"exhibitit be thame for that effect, and scho is lauch-"full dochter to tham." Which allegation the Commissaries found proved, and therefore declared the child legitimate.

The child Janet Kennedy having by this decision of the Commissioners been proved heiress of her mother, she inherited the third portion of Orchardton. She (or her representative) appears to have sold the property to Robert Maxwell of Spottes about the year 1600, as shortly after that date he was designated "of Orchardton." By his subsequent purchases of the two other thirds of the estate he reconsolidated the property, which remained in possession of his direct descendants until the financial ruin of the last Baronet Sir Robert, through the failure of the Ayr (or Douglas and Heron) Bank, in which he was heavily involved. He was probably the last resident occupier of old Orchardton Castle. In the days of his prosperity, about 1760, he built a new residence on the estate, about two miles from the old, which is now known as Orchardton. It was formerly called Glenshinnoch. He died in poverty in 1786 without issue.[1]

Many of the local lairds were connected with this bank, and all who were were ruined. Among the estates sold in consequence of the failure was that of Orchardton, which in 1785 was purchased by James Douglas,[2] a brother of

[1] The romantic history in detail of the Maxwells of Orchardton would be out of place in this work, as it must be borne in mind that although the mother of the last baronet was a Cairns of Barnbarroch, they were not the same as the original Maxwells of Orchardton of Cairnes descent. For an account of Mary Cairns of Barnbarroch and her husband Mungo Maxwell of Glenshinnoch and their son the last baronet, see below under Cairns of Barnbarroch.

[2] The first Sir Robt. Maxwell who bought out the three Cairnes heiresses of Orchardton seems to have obtained crown charter for Kirkpatrick's portion only, the transfer of the other two thirds not appearing in the register of the Great Seal. As has

Sir William Douglas, Bart., of Castle Douglas. The new owner of the estate added to Sir Robert Maxwell's house at Glenshinnoch, to which further additions were made by his great-grandson the present W. D. Robinson-Douglas, D.L., of Orchardton.

The two brothers of William the younger of Orchardton next in seniority to John of Cults[1] were Peter and Henry. Which was the elder is uncertain. Henry seems to have obtained a larger estate than Peter, but from the fact that in the Register of the Great Seal recording the charters to the two brothers, Peter's charter is inserted immediately before Henry's, it is probable that Peter was the elder of the two and therefore the third son.

The first mention of Peter Cairns appears to be in the Register of the Great Seal (1553), in the record of a charter confirming the grant from his father, William Cairns the elder of Orchardton, of the lands of Auchinskeauch, parish of Colvend, to Peter Cairns and Margaret M'Clelland his spouse. Under the date 1575 appears a rather confused entry of a grant to Robert Herries of Mabie, of the lands of Auchinskeauch and Auchinschene,

---

been explained in Chapter IV., the original grant to John de Carnys in 1456 was not by charter in the ordinary form. It is therefore improbable that the Maxwells held any legal title deeds of the estate; and when the property came to be mortgaged and finally sold on the owner's money troubles arising, he seems to have had legal difficulties to contend with owing to the absence of title deeds. To set matters right he obtained in 1762 a Crown charter of the whole property. This was probably the time when Sir Robert first entered into business. Twenty years later, in 1782, the crash came, when he made over his interest to his trustees. This was followed in 1785 by the sale to James Douglas. The charter of 1762 is therefore the oldest title deed of Orchardton extant.

[1] For an account of John Cairnes of Cults and his descendants see above, pp. 67-167.

they having lapsed to the King owing to the discovery of an alleged irregularity in the transfer from William Cairns "to Archibald Cairns in Tor or Peter Cairns about forty (sic) years before." This grant, however, was ineffective, probably because Peter Cairns being in possession, defied the efforts of Herries to oust him, and we find in 1687 on the death of his great grandson David, Auchinskeauch was among the lands which reverted to his heir William.[1]

Prior to the Reformation, Peter Cairns held from the Abbot of Dundrennan, as a tenant, the Kipp estate, and on the dissolution of the religious fraternities, he received from Queen Mary a Royal charter of these lands, from which he and his descendants henceforth took their designation.

Of Peter Cairns little is known. The *Scottish Journal of Antiquities* records a local Galloway tradition, quoted by Dr. Trotter in his *East Galloway Sketches*, referring to Sir Peter Cairns.[2] Little credence can be attached to such vague traditions, however strong the probability that they are founded on fact. The story is as follows:—"When riding with his troop of horsemen to drive back English invaders, Sir Peter came upon a well known imbecile who had fallen asleep on the roadside with a pot of honey or butter beside him. He had written on the dusty ground:—

> Here am I, great John A Boe,
> Who killed a hundred at a blow.

[1] Retours of Sasine, Kirkcudbright, 1687.

[2] The use of the prefix "Sir" must not be taken in its modern sense. A graduate of a university and a knight were so styled with equal freedom. This will explain the reference to "Schir Thomas Ecklis" in the evidence relative to the legitimacy case referred to a few pages back. Peter Cairns was not a knight, nor is it probable he had any claim to the title "Sir."

referring to the flies he had destroyed when settling on his market produce. 'If you can kill a hundred at a blow,' said Sir Peter Cairns, 'you are the very man for us,' and immediately John A Boe (who was nearly seven feet high) was mounted on the biggest horse in the troop, and a flag produced with the words he had written in the dust roughly printed on it.

"He was dreadfully afraid, and seized hold of a gallows tree which stood on the roadside to stay his progress, but it came out of the ground in his hands; compelled to proceed with the pole in his hands, he bore it aloft, riding into the midst of the English and laying about him, repeating his doggerel rhyme, the invaders became terrified and fled."[1]

Peter Cairns of Kipp died prior to 1593, and was succeeded by his son and heir Archibald, who died in that year without issue. The estate passed to his next brother Hugh. Isobel, a daughter of Peter Cairns, married John M'Cartney of Leathes, parish of Buittle, in 1585.[2] There

[1] It is to be regretted that Dr. Trotter, in his most interesting book *East Galloway Sketches*, sometimes mixes up without discrimination, fact, fiction, and the wildest fancy. On the same page on which he records this extract from the *Scottish Journal of Antiquities* he states, "Orchardton Tower, it is said, was. so early as the fourteenth century, the "residence of Sir Adam Cairns, who married a daughter of the Earl of Douglas." The State records mention no such person as Sir Adam Cairns. A marriage alliance between a comparatively small Scottish Laird and a daughter of the house of Douglas, practically a Royal Family, is highly improbable, and needs better proof than "*it is said.*"

[2] In the Register of Deeds, Stewartry of Kirkcudbright, there is an obligation, dated 26th June, 1585, by which "Peter Cairns of Kip as principal and John Lewres in Auchencairn "as cautioner bind themselves to content and pay to Johnne M'Cartney of Lethes alias "callit Wattis' Johnne each year for four consecutive years, four bolls meill and twa bolls of "beir, greit messor, together with fifty merks monie and that as complait payment of twa "hundred and fifty merks—the tocher which Peter Cairns was to have given with his "daughter Issobell Cairns." The family of M'Cartney first appear, so far as we have traced in the Scottish Records, almost simultaneously, about 1540, at Dunbar, Haddington-

was also a son George Cairns, whose issue, if any, is unknown.

Hugh Cairns was succeeded in the property by David. We have no doubt he was his son. In a list of those who refused to sign the Covenant in 1640 his name is included.[1]

shire, and in Galloway. The first recorded of the Galloway M'Cartneys is James, who attested a charter of lands near Dumfries in 1542, from Matthew to Herbert Gladstone. He was a notary public. In 1558 he was granted a charter by Archibald Wod of Wattistoun of the lands of Arbrog, in Wigtonshire. Under the dates 1586 and 1588, we find him and John M'Cartney in Arbrog. The latter received a charter of Leathes from the Commendator of the Abbey of Sweetheart in 1584, and married Isobel Cairns of Kipp the following year. In 1587 he alienated the property by charter to Walter M'Cartney, evidently his brother or a son by a former marriage, and Janet his wife. The M'Cartneys of Leathes eventually parted with the property, and we are now unable to trace their representatives. James received a charter under the Great Seal, of Arbrog, or Arbor, in 1598, his son James, a doctor of physic, being co-grantee therein. In this charter the name of the father of the elder James is stated to have been Adam M'Cartney. Another branch of these M'Cartneys was the family of Auchinleck. In 1590, Adam and Patrick, probably cousins, held each one half of the lands of Auchinleck, under John Stuart, who held under the Abbey of Dundrennan. Adam's father, Richard, was living in 1583. He also held the lands of Fagra from the Abbey. Adam had a son John, who married Katherine Whitehead. Patrick M'Cartney had a son Bartholomew, who married a daughter of John Stuart, and in 1593 received a charter from Stuart of half the lands of Auchinleck. He got a Great Seal charter in 1607. His eldest son was Bartholomew. He married Catherine, daughter of George Maxwell of Drumcoltran by his wife Janet Cairnes, the co-heiress of Orchardton; by her he had an only son George. Bartholomew predeceased his father, and his son George was served heir of his grandfather in 1626. In 1649 he settled in Belfast, still retaining the half of Auchinleck. He was an active man of business, and in Belfast engaged in considerable mercantile enterprises. He became one of the most prominent citizens, and eventually sovereign. In 1688, while holding this high office, he proclaimed King William and Queen Mary. He acquired extensive estates in County Antrim, of which he served as High Sheriff, and did much to benefit the town of his adoption, providing it with a plentiful water supply, then a most unusual luxury. Quite recently a quantity of the water pipes laid down by George M'Cartney were dug up in making some excavations. They were made of oak staves hooped together by iron bands, and when dug up were still in excellent preservation, although 250 years old. His great-grandson was the celebrated Earl M'Cartney. The representatives of the family in Ulster now are the M'Cartneys of Lissanoure (Loughguile) and the M'Cartney Filgates of Co. Louth. The old M'Cartney estate of Auchinleck passed from the family, a niece of Earl M'Cartney who inherited it having sold it to one James Henry for £2,200. Another distinguished cadet of this family was the late Sir Halliday M'Cartney, K.C.M.G., who was born at Auchinleck in 1833, and whose sudden death occurred in his native place as this note was in type.

[1] Minute Book of the Covenanters' War Committee. Register House, Edinburgh.

He was then in possession of Kipp. His son and heir William had sasine in 1655.[1] The latter married Marie Maxwell, widow of Edward Murray of Drumstinchell, and had an eldest son and heir David, who succeeded in 1687. His son William was in possession in 1698, and in 1699 put James M'Clellan of Haslefield and Agnes Knaberry his wife to the horn for failure to pay a bond for 500 merks.[2] William and his second son David were joint tenants of the lands of Cloneyeard, and in 1706 were put to the horn for alleged non-payment of the tack duties. They, however, got a suspension of the letters of horning.[3] In 1703 William gave a bond for 1,000 merks to Janet Crosbie, heiress of Andrew Crosbie in Muill of Barnbarroch, and on attempting to sell Kipp in 1706, this lady obtained an inhibition preventing the sale till her bond was satisfied.[4] This record is of interest, as the Crosbies of a later generation obtained the property, apparently as foreclosing mortgagors, and it would thus seem as if the financial obligation of the Cairns family of Kipp to the Crosbies, which culminated in the transfer of the estate, were of very old standing. William Cairns was dead in 1711, and was succeeded by his eldest son George. He also left a second son David of Barnbarroch, who by some means got possession of certain bonds of their father. He instituted proceedings against George in 1711 to recover from him as heir of his father the amount of the bonds, and obtained a decree. He is referred to in the proceedings as portioner of Barn-

1 Retours of Sasine, Kirkcudbrightshire.
2 Hornings and Inhibitions, Kirkcudbrightshire, Vol. IV.
3 Ibid. Vol. VIII., p. 59.
4 Ibid. Vol. IX., p. 12.

GEORGE CAIRNS, Laird of Kipp.

From an old print after Reid of Kirkennan].

barroch.[1] George Cairns married Marie Maxwell, and by her had an only daughter Margaret. Apparently as a marriage portion, he gave her in 1720 a bond for 2,200 marks. In 1723, hearing that her father was negotiating for the sale of Kipp, she took proceedings against him and obtained a decree inhibiting him from carrying out either sale or wadset until her bond was satisfied.[2] It is probable that this lady married, but if so the name of her husband cannot be determined. There is no evidence that she had issue. In 1752 George,[3] son of David of Barnbarroch, succeeded as eventual heir of his grandfather William.[4]

George Cairns, the last laird of Kipp of his name, was well known for his eccentric personality and his caustic and witty sayings, many of which are still handed down in the district. He succeeded to the estate apparently encumbered with debts accumulated by his ancestors, and we fear he was not of a sufficiently thrifty nature to release it.

The late Archbishop Strain, who in his early years had

1 Hornings and Inhibitions, Kirkcudbrightshire, Vol. X., p. 67.

2 Ibid. Vol. X., p. 249.

3 Chancery Precept in favour of George Cairns, as eventual heir of his grandfather William Cairns of Kipp. This document is the oldest extant document among the Kipp title deeds, the original of the Great Seal Charter of 1565, like that of Torr, being lost.

4 In the records cited in the foregoing footnotes, it so happens that only two sons of William Cairns of Kipp, who died in 1711, are referred to. It is more than probable he had others. Our searches only covered *The Acts and Decreets*, *The Hornings and Inhibitions* (*Kirkcudbrightshire and Dumfries*), *The Commissary Court Processes*, and *The Dumfries Sasines, Minute Book, 1701—1711*. These documents are all in the Register House in Edinburgh, and are indexed. We have been unable to go through the local registers at Kirkcudbright and Dumfries, which are difficult of access, and more difficult still to search; nor have we gone through the Books of Council and Session in the Register House. It is probable, had one time and opportunity to make these searches, that much additional information would be forthcoming. In the ensuing chapter we shall refer briefly to William Cairns of Magheraconluce, who arrived in Ireland after the rising of 1715. He was certainly a contemporary of George and David above mentioned, sons of William, and it may be conjectured he was a younger brother.

been Roman Catholic curate at Dalbeattie, and who was a friend of Dean Ramsay, supplied him with an amusing anecdote, of which George Cairns of Kipp was the hero. This anecdote appears in the Dean's well-known book, although the author suppresses the names, probably out of respect to the feelings of the relatives of the laird. George Cairns and his wife, it appears, were dining with their kinsman Edward Cairns of Torr, when, according to the custom of the time, the diners imbibed pretty freely. In the small hours of the morning, Kipp was assisted into his saddle, with his good lady on a pillion behind. At low tide there is a short cut from Torr to Kipp at Kipford, which George took, and proceeded to his home. On dismounting, it suddenly occurred to him that his wife was not with him, but he clearly remembered she had been behind him on the horse when they left Torr. A search was at once instituted, and the search party arrived just in time to find her lying on the sand at Kipford, where she had fallen off the horse. She was good humouredly remonstrating with the incoming tide, which was already trickling into her mouth, in these words, "No anither drap thank'ee—neither het nor cauld."[1]

Whom George Cairns married is not recorded, and we have been unable to trace with certainty a single representative of the Kipp Cairnses living to-day. His will, if he left one, is not in the Scottish records, and we

[1] The story as still told in Galloway adds another incident. It is said that the search party, at a loss to know how to convey the lady home, borrowed a barn door, on which they carefully placed her; and that, when stretched thereon, she opened one eye and seeing the moon remarked, "Pit oot that licht, George, and gie me mair o' the blankets—it's awfu' cauld."

do not know who was his heir. He sold[1] his estate about the year 1783 to a Mr. Crosbie, merchant in Liverpool, in possession of whose family it remained until sold in 1869 to the present proprietor, Mr. Archibald Chalmers.

George Cairns's portrait was painted by Reid of Kirkennan, but where the painting is we know not: from it a rather curious engraving was taken, which is here re-produced. He died in 1804.

We have referred above to David Cairns of Barnbarroch, a younger son of the William Cairns of Kipp who died in 1711. We have no record of him of later date than the lawsuit with his brother already mentioned. He left issue,

GEORGE CAIRNS, referred to above, who succeeded as heir of his grandfather to the Kipp property.

ROBERT CAIRNS, who inherited Barnbarroch. Born 1695.

MARY. Born 1708. She married in 1727 Mungo Maxwell of Glenshinnoch, by whom she had issue the above-mentioned

ROBERT MAXWELL, who succeeded to the baronetcy of the Orchardton Maxwells as seventh and last Baronet, of whom later.

Mungo Maxwell died in 1740, and his widow married secondly Henry Moor, a tenant-farmer at Glenshinnoch, who deserted her, and by whom she does not seem to have had issue.

Robert Cairns of Barnbarroch died in 1771, when his son and heir David, a writer in Kirkcudbright, had sasine.

[1] Sold, or was sold out by the mortgagor. We have not minute details.

David died in 1785. His son and heir Robert Cairns succeeded to the property. He became a merchant in Glasgow, but after some years got into financial difficulties. He was sequestrated in 1814, and in the following year Barnbarroch was sold to Robert Threshie. We regret that we have been unable to record any later descendants of the Cairns family of Barnbarroch.

Of the Torr family, the first mention is of Henry Cairnis in 1537, when he witnessed a charter at Dundrennan. He is here designated as "in" Torr, not "of" Torr, showing that he then only held the lands as a tenant. He is similarly designated in a charter of 1543, and his son Archibald "in" Torr in the charter to Peter Cairns of Auchinskeauch in 1553. In 1559 Adam, perpetual commendator of the Abbey of Dundrennan, granted a lease of the Lands of Torr, Tail of Forest, and portion of Auchencairn to Henry Cairns and Archibald his son and heir. On the same day he gave a similar lease to Peter Cairns and Archibald his son and heir, of the lands of Kipp and the other portion of Auchencairn, with the fishing of the river Urr. After the Reformation both leases were altered to Crown charters under the Great Seal (1565).

It will thus be seen that at this period the Cairnes family in Galloway were large and important landed proprietors, the following being the names of the various properties recorded as belonging to the family in 1565:—Orchardton, Littletoun, Cults, Blairboys, the four mark lands of Dalbeattie, Bargalie, Glenure, Kipp, Auchenskeauch, Auchenskene, Auchencairn, Auchengule, Torr, Tail of Forest, Barnbachill, and the fishing of the river Urr. There were probably other lands not recorded.

Henry Cairns of Torr was succeeded by his son Archibald, who, dying without issue, was succeeded by his brother Henry, who died in 1601. In this year his son Robert had sasine. He was a thrifty man, and paid off a wadset on the estate in 1604. The parchment discharge of this wadset is among the family papers.[1] He was also in a position to assist his cousin of Kipp with a loan in 1627. He died in 1647. The only son whose name is recorded was his eldest son and heir Edward, though most probably he had others.

Edward Cairns of Torr was an ardent Roundhead,

1 It may be of interest to record the list of title deeds under which the Torr estate was held. They were produced as evidence by Robert Cairns in a lawsuit instituted by John Murray of Dundrennan against holders of the abbey lands of Dundrennan in 1610. These deeds were—*a.* A tack dated 20th December, 1555, by Adam, Commendator of Dundrennan, to Archibald Cairns, Henry Cairns his son, and Henry Cairns, son to the said Henry, of the four mark land of Auchencairn and the twenty shilling land of Torr, &c. *b.* Charter dated 14th July, 1559, by the same to Henry Cairns in liferent and Archibald his son and his heirs and assigns of the same lands and the five shilling lands of Tail of Forest. *c.* Instrument of Sasine, past upon the precept dated at Terregles, 14th January, 1579, by Adam, to Henry Cairns, brother-german to the deceased Archibald Cairns of Torr in the above lands. *d.* Tack by Adam, Commendator of Dundrennan, dated 10th June, 1559, to Archibald Cairns and Henry his son of the lands of Forrest. *e.* Confirmatory Charter dated 29th May, 1565, under the Great Seal, by Mary Queen of Scots, of the lands granted in the charter by the said Commendator. *f.* Charter by Edward, Commendator of Dundrennan, to Archibald Cairns and his heirs and assigns of the lands called St. Michael's Close, and the pasturage in Mewlaw Green. Dated 16th August, 1544. *g.* A Charter from John, Archbishop of St. Andrews, and under the Pope's Seal, confirming the last, dated 4th June, 1550. (Acts and Decreets, Register House, Vol. 255). It will be noted that the genealogical information in these deeds is somewhat confusing, if not actually contradictory. In the text above we have chronicled the pedigree as clearly as we can make it out with the assistance of extracts from the Register of the Great Seal. With regard to these interesting old parchments produced at the trial in 1610, at least some of them were extant at the date of the sale of Torr in 1867. As they were then not essential to the validity of title of the vendors, they were not handed over to the purchaser, Mr. Ovens, but such as were forthcoming were given as heirlooms to the eldest daughter of Benjamin Cairns, to whom we shall refer later. This lady, we regret to say, died while this book was being written, and her husband cannot now recollect where these documents connected with the sale were put. Of the ancient parchments relating to the Torr estate, the only one now forthcoming is the release of the wadset by the above Robert, dated 1604.

and fought in the Cromwellian army; for this he was fined £240 after the Restoration (1662). He married in 1647, Margaret, daughter of the Rev. David Leitch, minister of Rerwick. By the marriage settlement, the estate of Torr was settled upon the survivor of them, with succession to the eldest son of the marriage, and his heirs male. His eldest son David, predeceasing his father, left two sons, John and David. Edward gave evidence of his intention, if possible, to break the terms of the settlement by making his second son, Edward Cairns of Girstingwood. his heir, and by granting wadsets on the property to his daughters. In 1706 his elder grandson John brought an action for an injunction against his grandfather to restrain him from incumbering the estate and to compel him to infeft him as his heir apparent, to the exclusion of Edward of Girstingwood. He obtained a decree of inhibition and a full discharge of all the wadsets and charges on the property contracted by his grandfather.[1] Edward Cairns died at an advanced age in 1714, having had issue,

A. DAVID, who married Margaret, daughter of John Halthorne of Cairnfield. He predeceased his father in 1694, being survived by his widow, who died in 1718, and two sons,

1. JOHN, eventual heir of Torr, of whom later.
2. DAVID. He resided during his mother's lifetime at Hardhills, part of the Torr property, which his elder brother, on his father's death in 1714, allowed his mother rent free for her life. On this lady's death

[1] Inhibitions, Kirkcudbrightshire, Vol. VIII., p. 20.

in 1718, David asserted that his mother had been actual owner under a formal transfer, and that his mother had transferred the property to him. John was compelled to enter into a lawsuit with his brother for ejectment, which, after a lengthy trial, he procured.[1] David retaliated by bringing a lawsuit against John, as heir of his father, for £1,400, which he alleged to be due to him as legatee of his mother. The claim was frivolous, and was made up of various items, including the funeral expenses and mourning for their father, whose death had occurred twenty-six years before![2] We have no further record of David, nor can we discover whether he left issue.

B. EDWARD of Girstingwood. During his father's lifetime he became a merchant in England, and seems to have amassed some money. In 1703 he became owner of the Girstingwood estate,[3] where he resided. He seems to have been his father's favourite from the facts disclosed at the lawsuit by his nephew John against his father, above related. We have record of his marriage to Janet, daughter of Archibald Cutler of Orroland, in 1710, and of his death early in 1711. He left at least two children, so that it seems evident

1 Acts and Decreets, July 28th, 1719.

2 Inhibitions, Kirkcudbrightshire, Vol. X., p. 219.

3 Sasines, Dumfries, Minute Book, 1701–1721.

that they were the issue of an earlier marriage. He left issue,

EDWARD CAIRNS[1] of Girstingwood, his heir.

MARGARET.

Edward Cairns the younger succeeded to the Girstingwood estate in 1726. He married in 1757 Catherine, daughter of Thomas Kirkpatrick of Raeberry,[2] but died in the following year, leaving issue an only child Agnes, who was served heir to Girstingwood on coming of age in 1778. In the sasine she is not mentioned as being married, so that we may assume that her marriage took place after that date. She married William Hamilton, M.D., of Craighlaw, Wigtonshire.[3] About 1790, she and her husband sold the Girstingwood estate to Thomas Cairns,[4] a wealthy merchant in London, who about the same time purchased the Dun-

1 In the records of the Commissary Court Processes, 1711, we find that Edward Cairns died in March, 1711. A reference also occurs to his marriage contract with Janet Cutler, dated September, 1710. From this it would seem that Edward and Margaret were children by a former marriage, or, which is improbable, that they were born prior to the marriage ceremony. Edward the younger was only served heir of Girstingwood to his father in 1726. If this may be taken as an indication that he came of age in that year, it would show that his birth took place in 1705; but as Janet Cutler, the widow, had sasine on the death of her husband in 1711, in life rent, it seems more probable that the sasine of 1726 indicates the date of the death of the widow and not the coming of age of the heir. The widow married secondly Samuel Ewart in Kirkcudbright in 1712.

2 This family of Kirkpatrick were cadets of the Kirkpatricks of Closeburn, though we have not the exact relationship. It is quite possible they were descendants of Margaret Cairnes of Orchardton mentioned above, by either of her marriages. The widow of Edward Cairns married secondly William Colthart of Bluehill, near Auchencairn. Her sister was the wife of Roger Cutler of Orroland; and another sister was Mrs. Fergusson of Craigdarroch. Orroland seems to have at a later date passed to the Fergusson family through the marriage of the heiress of Orroland to a Fergusson of Craigdarroch.

3 See Burke, *Landed Gentry*, Hamilton of Craiglaw.

4 A native of Galloway. It is not improbable that he was a cadet of the Torr Family, but as we have no direct evidence, we are unable to record his descent. See following chapter.

drennan Abbey estate. By her marriage with Doctor Hamilton, Agnes Cairns had issue,

1. WILLIAM CHARLES HAMILTON of Craighlaw. Born 1794. He married, in 1825, Anne, daughter of the Rev. Anthony Stewart, D.D., of Kirkcowan. He was a Deputy Lieutenant for Ayrshire, and as a captain in the army fought at Waterloo. He left issue, besides two daughters, his heir,

   WILLIAM CHARLES STEWART HAMILTON of Craighlaw, D.L. Born 1831. He married Margaret Anne Mary, only daughter of Thomas Jones of Hinton Charterhouse, near Bath. He died 1876, leaving issue,

   WILLIAM MALCOLM FLEMING HAMILTON, D.L., late captain Highland Light Infantry, now of Craighlaw.

   MAUDE FLEMING.

   BLANCHE MAUD FLEMING, wife of Major A. F. Evans-Lombe, by whom she has issue,

2. CATHERINE, who, in 1815, married William Cochrane of Ladyland, Ayrshire, by whom she had issue a daughter and heiress,

   AGNES, who, in 1841, married William Charles Richard, second son of Robert Patrick of Trearne and Hassilhead, who on his marriage with Miss Cochrane assumed the name of Cochrane in addition to his own surname Patrick.[1]

[1] See Burke, *Landed Gentry*, under Patrick of Waterside and Ladyland, also under Patrick of Trearne and Hassilhead.

In addition to the above David Cairns and Edward Cairns of Girstingwood, Edward Cairns of Torr had issue,

c. Helen, wife of John Thomson, merchant in Kirkcudbright.

d. Grisel, wife of John Clarke, surgeon in Kirkcudbright.

e. Elizabeth, wife of John Reid, physician in Dumfries. She married secondly James Lindsay, merchant in Edinburgh.

John Cairns succeeded to Torr on the death of his grandfather in 1714. On his succession, he added to and renovated the old Torr House. The date of the original piell of Torr is lost in obscurity. It seems to have been one of the ordinary square towers of which many were erected during the fifteenth and sixteenth centuries. The nature of John Cairns's renovation cannot now be ascertained, as barely a trace of the building remains. He probably added a modern wing to the tower. Over the entrance door he inserted a carved stone measuring about four feet by one, with the raised inscription :—

I + C + 1714

This stone was recently removed from the debris of old Torr House by Mr. Ovens, who, to preserve it, built it into the wall of the barn at Hardhills, where it still remains.

Besides his younger brother David, John had a sister Margaret, married to the Rev. Alexander Telfair, minister of Rerwick. He married in 1715 Anna, daughter of the

Rev. William Tod, minister of Buittle,[1] said to be a sister of one Patrick Todd, a medical practitioner in Donaghadee, County Down.[2]

In 1743 John Cairns apprenticed a younger son Alexander to George Bell, merchant and shipowner of Dumfries. He ran away from his ship, the "Unity of Dumfries," and his father, having been cautioner for him, was called upon to pay the surety money. He refused, and was put to the horn and ordered to be imprisoned in the Tolbooth in Edinburgh.[3] He probably did not undergo incarceration, as his death occurred about this time, early in 1745. His widow survived him. He had issue, besides Alexander, and probably other sons, his heir WILLIAM CAIRNS. Born in 1716.

The latter provided an elaborate funeral for the deceased laird, keeping a careful note (which is still preserved) of the costs incurred. He immediately applied to the Court of Session for an order that these should be payable out of the personal effects of the deceased, to which the Court agreed, ordering, however, a detailed inventory and valuation of these. The valuator's attempt to minimise the value of the personal effects, as shown by the following items taken from the inventory, is inimitable. The list includes:—

"To an old kitchen table - -	1s.
"To an old bedstead - - -	1s. 4d.
"To an old chist - - - -	2s.
"To an old crook, a small chair, and an old saddle - - -	4s. 3d.

[1] Inhibitions, Kirkcudbrightshire. Vol. X., p. 218.

[2] Trotter, *East Galloway Sketches*.

[3] Ibid.

"To 3 old cars and 2 old harrows 1s.
"To 2 old bedsteads - - - 3s.
"To an old coarse big coat and inner coat, half worn - - 10s.
"To two old crooked and glandered horses at £1 3s. 4d. each - £2 6s. 8d. &c."

The total amount assessed as the value of the whole personal estate of the laird of Torr, including furniture, live stock, implements, and farm stock, came to £15 5s. 3d., which about balanced the cost of the funeral!

The new laird of Torr on succeeding thereto at once sold the Auchencairn portion of the estate to John Culton, the purchase price being sixteen years' purchase of the value of the rent as stated by the vendor. Shortly afterwards Culton found the rents received to be less than stated by the laird of Torr, and sued him for a return of part of the purchase money. The case was referred to arbitration, with the result that Cairns got off with the payment of £10 to Culton. About this time the laird also had a dispute with Thomson of Forest, relating to the boundary line between Forest and Tail of Forest, part of the Torr estate. The award of the arbitrators again appears to have been against the laird of Torr, who seems to have been somewhat litigious and grasping. He started in business in Birmingham,[1] and the firm appears to have prospered, and eventually to have had a branch in New

[1] Dr. Trotter says he was a button maker, and that he was once Mayor of Birmingham. Both statements are quite inaccurate. Prior to the incorporation of Birmingham the official duties corresponding to those of a Mayor were performed by honorary officials known as High and Low Bailiffs. These were elected annually, the positions being counted of considerable honour and importance. The charter of the city of Birmingham only dates from 1836, and it had no Mayors prior to that date.

EDWARD CAIRNS of Torr
and Shireland Hall, Birmingham.

From a Miniature by Keid of Kirkennan).

ANNE HUMPHREYS,
Wife of Edward Cairns of Torr.

Silhouette).

York. He married about 1740 Isobel Ewart, and had issue,

A. EDWARD, his heir.

B. JANET, wife of William Nicol, of whom later.

C. MARY, wife of Joseph Frears of Birmingham.

D. SARAH.

A short time prior to his death, which occurred about 1783, William Cairns built a new residence at Bankend, about a mile from the old Torr House, and now known as Torr. Old Torr quickly became a ruin, the stones being carted away by the neighbouring farmers for building purposes. The new Torr was added to by Edward Cairns, who also laid out the beautiful grounds surrounding it, and planted the fine orchard round Torr Cottage, which he built for his sister Mrs. Nicol, about 1798.

Edward Cairns of Torr and Shireland Hall continued, apparently with success, the business established by his father. He became head of the firm of Cairns, Frears, Carmichael and Halliday, of Birmingham and Wall Street, New York. He made Shireland Hall his principal residence during his early years, paying occasional visits to Torr. He married in 1775, Ann, daughter of Abel Humphreys, a merchant in Kidderminster, and had issue,

A. EDWARD, d.s.p. in Cuba, during his father's lifetime.

B. WILLIAM, the heir, resided chiefly in New York, where he married, his wife and only daughter, Virginia, predeceasing him. He died 1860. He was the last Cairns of Torr in the male line, the last clearly traceable representative of pure unbroken male descent of William de Carnys of that ilk, who flourished over five centuries before. On his death the Torr property passed to the representatives of his next brother, five daughters, co-heiresses, of whom but one survives, Mrs. Brinsley.

C. BENJAMIN, born 1794. He married, in 1825, Ann Hawksley, a Sheffield lady (who died 1849), and dying in 1859, a year before his elder brother William, left issue, five daughters, co-heiresses of Torr—

1. ANNE HUMPHREYS, born 1826, wife of Thomas Ramsay Grimes. She d.s.p. 1904.
2. MARY, wife of Thomas Gilman. She died in 1891, leaving issue,
   a. MARY LOUISA, unmarried.
   b. FANNY, who married Henry Terry, chief officer in the merchant service, who died in 1889, leaving issue,
      1. HAROLD CAIRNS, Born 1885.
      2. PATIENCE MARY.
3. ELIZA JANE, wife of John Hickman, whose only child, Eliza Jane, predeceased her in 1894. She died 1904.
4. EMILY REBECCA, who married the late Joseph Brinsley of Birmingham, by whom she has no issue. She now resides in Birmingham.
5. LOUISA, wife of William B. Row, who d.s.p. 1897.

D. ANNE ISOBELLA, of whom later. She married James Chapman, a merchant in Liverpool, and left issue,

1. JAMES, d.s.p.

2. WILLIAM, d.s.p.
3. ISOBELLA, wife of Robert Stiven, writer to the Signet, of Glasgow, by whom she left issue,
   a. JAMES EDWARD, died young.
   b. ROBERT GEORGE, who married Janet Hunter,[1] and died leaving issue one daughter only.
   c. THOMAS FREELAND, d.s.p.
   d. ARTHUR WILLIAM, now a merchant in Singapore.
   e. AMY ISOBELLA, wife of James Ramsey Parsons,[2] banker in London, by whom she has issue,
      1. JAMES RAMSEY.
      2. JOHN CAIRNS.
   f. JESSIE, died unmarried.
   g. MARY. } Now residing at Hillhead, Glasgow.
   h. EDITH BARBOUR. } Now residing at Hillhead, Glasgow.
4. MARY JANE, who died unmarried in 1893.

E. MARY, wife of Mr. Halliday of New York, whose only surviving child is EDWARD CAIRNS HALLIDAY, now of Boston.

F. JESSIE, wife of Mr. Henderson of New York. } Descendants unknown to the Author.
G. SARAH, wife of Mr. Wightman of New York. } Descendants unknown to the Author.

---

[1] Sister of Major-General Sir Archibald Hunter, K.C.B.

[2] Grandson of G. S. Parsons, at one time a midshipman under Nelson on the "Foudroyant," and author of "Nelsonian Reminiscences." He was a nephew of Sir William Herschell, and first cousin of the celebrated Sir John Herschell, Bart., by whom, having been left an orphan in his early infancy, he was brought up.

H. REBECCA, wife of Mr. Wingate, merchant in Liverpool,[1] d.s.p.

I. ELIZA, died unmarried in New York.

On the death without surviving issue of William Cairns of Torr in 1860, this ancient family became, so far as we can ascertain, extinct in the male line. His next brother Benjamin had predeceased him in 1859, leaving daughters only, who thus became co-heiresses. As no proprietor of Torr had been resident on the property since the death of Edward Cairns in 1819, the next owner living in New York, it had terribly depreciated in value, being subdivided into numerous small holdings, and no improvements of any kind having been made. This joint ownership promised no improvement in matters, and the ladies decided to sell the estate, and so realise their shares before they had further decreased in value. The sale took place in 1867,[2] the purchaser being Mr. Ovens, a prosperous merchant of Galashiels and Leith. His son Mr. Walter Ovens entered into residence at Torr, and as the leases of the small tenants expired, took over the entire management of the estate himself. The Ovenses, father and son, effected vast improvements, and the whole estate is now one large farm, worked upon the most expert and up-to-date system of culture. From the condition almost of a wilderness, the property has become one of the best cultivated tracts of land in the South of Scotland.

But we must revert to the family of William Cairns of

[1] Uncle of the Rev. Alexander M'Laren, D.D., of Manchester.

[2] It is interesting to note that Sir Hugh M'Calmont Cairns, just at this time raised to the peerage, had under contemplation the purchase of this old family property, and had some correspondence with the vendors on the subject.

TABLE V.

PEDIGREE OF THE FAMILIES OF CAIRNS OF KIPP, TORR, GIRSTINGWOOD, &c.

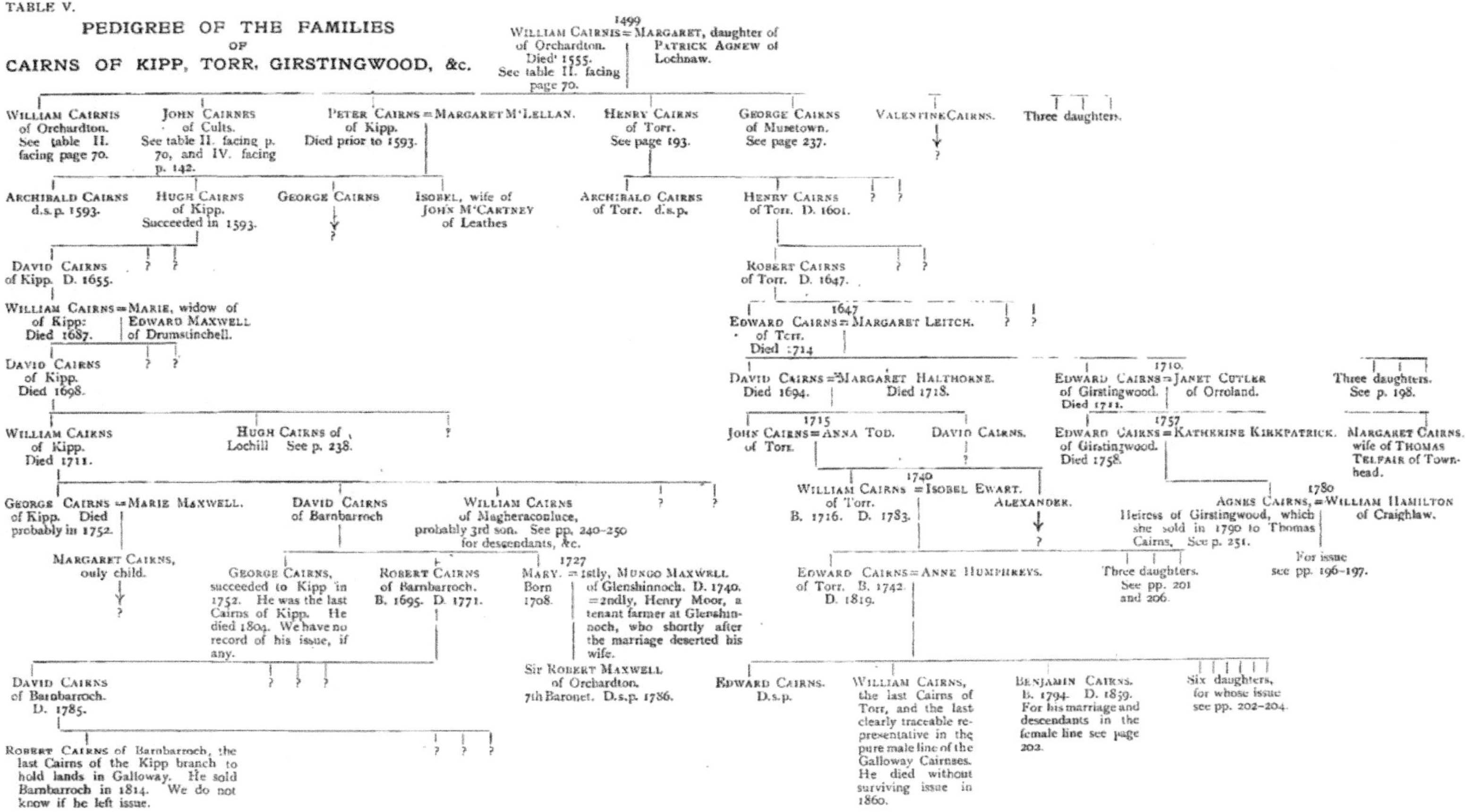

1499
William Cairnis = Margaret, daughter of Patrick Agnew of Lochnaw.
of Orchardton. Died 1555. See table II. facing page 70.
William Cairnis of Orchardton. See table II. facing page 70.
John Cairnes of Cults. See table II. facing p. 70, and IV. facing p. 142.
Peter Cairns = Margaret M'Lellan.
of Kipp. Died prior to 1593.
Henry Cairns of Torr. See page 193.
George Cairns of Munetown. See page 237.
Valentine Cairns.
?
Three daughters.
Archibald Cairns d.s.p. 1593.
Hugh Cairns of Kipp. Succeeded in 1593.
George Cairns
?
Isobel, wife of John M'Cartney of Leathes
Archibald Cairns of Torr. d.s.p.
Henry Cairns of Torr. D. 1601.
? ?
David Cairns of Kipp. D. 1655.
? ?
Robert Cairns of Torr. D. 1647.
? ?
William Cairns = Marie, widow of Edward Maxwell of Drumstinchell.
of Kipp. Died 1687.
1647
Edward Cairns = Margaret Leitch.
of Torr. Died 1714
? ?
David Cairns of Kipp. Died 1698.
? ?
David Cairns = Margaret Halthorne.
Died 1694. Died 1718.
1710.
Edward Cairns = Janet Cutler of Orroland.
of Girstingwood. Died 1711.
Three daughters. See p. 198.
William Cairns of Kipp. Died 1711.
Hugh Cairns of Lochill See p. 238.
?
1715
John Cairns = Anna Tod.
of Torr.
David Cairns.
?
1757
Edward Cairns = Katherine Kirkpatrick.
of Girstingwood. Died 1758.
Margaret Cairns, wife of Thomas Telfair of Townhead.
George Cairns = Marie Maxwell.
of Kipp. Died probably in 1752.
David Cairns of Barnbarroch
William Cairns of Magheraconluce, probably 3rd son. See pp. 240–250 for descendants, &c.
? ?
1740
William Cairns = Isobel Ewart.
of Torr. B. 1716. D. 1783.
Alexander.
?
1780
Agnes Cairns, = William Hamilton of Craighlaw.
Heiress of Girstingwood, which she sold in 1790 to Thomas Cairns. See p. 251.
For issue see pp. 196–197.
Margaret Cairns, only child.
?
George Cairns, succeeded to Kipp in 1752. He was the last Cairns of Kipp. He died 1804. We have no record of his issue, if any.
Robert Cairns of Barnbarroch. B. 1695. D. 1771.
1727
Mary. = 1stly, Mungo Maxwell of Glenshinnoch. D. 1740. = 2ndly, Henry Moor, a tenant farmer at Glenshinnoch, who shortly after the marriage deserted his wife.
Born 1708.
Edward Cairns = Anne Humphreys.
of Torr. B. 1742. D. 1819.
Three daughters. See pp. 201 and 206.
David Cairns of Barnbarroch. D. 1785.
? ? ?
Sir Robert Maxwell of Orchardton. 7th Baronet. D.s.p. 1786.
Edward Cairns. D.s.p.
William Cairns, the last Cairns of Torr, and the last clearly traceable representative in the pure male line of the Galloway Cairnses. He died without surviving issue in 1860.
Benjamin Cairns. B. 1794. D. 1859. For his marriage and descendants in the female line see page 202.
Six daughters, for whose issue see pp. 202–204.
Robert Cairns of Barnbarroch, the last Cairns of the Kipp branch to hold lands in Galloway. He sold Barnbarroch in 1814. We do not know if he left issue.
? ? ?

Torr, who died about 1783, as we have mentioned. His only son Edward carried on the business in Birmingham for many years, residing at Shireland Hall, near that town. In 1806 he was elected Low Bailiff, and as such took a leading part in the movement for the erection of the Nelson statue in Birmingham, which was unveiled in 1806. On his sons reaching manhood, he transferred the business into their hands and retired to live at Torr, where he became a typical squire of a hundred years ago.

He is said to have been a tall, handsome and dignified man, courteous and considerate to all. It is also related that he was in the habit of going down regularly on the arrival of the newspaper, to the cross at Auchencairn, where he read aloud to the villagers all the news of the day, explaining and often exaggerating the extent of the victories over the French. While Edward Cairns has not been actually accused of being a smuggler, he has been credited with at least acquiescing in smuggling carried on by others on his property, and at Craigraw on Torr point many a contraband cargo was landed, much to the annoyance of the laird of Orchardton, who was a bitter opponent of the illicit traffic. The latter, to put it down at Craigraw, eventually purchased this tract of the Torr property from Cairns.

He kept on most friendly terms with the villagers of Auchencairn, but had no great love for those of Buittle and Dundrennan. On Auchencairn fair day he used to superintend the festivities of the fair, to keep his favoured villagers from being contaminated by the "dirtery of Buittle and the dregs of Dundrennan." On one occasion some of the so-called "dirtery" heard of the laird's uncomplimentary description of them, and forthwith attacked him, necessitating his headlong flight for refuge to the village inn, where he was besieged, the "dirtery" nailing up the doors. The Auchencairn folk, however, soon hearing of the laird's difficulty, came to his rescue. They got round to the back of the house and, making a hole in the thatched roof, pulled him out. With him at their head, the "dirtery" were soon put to flight, many being ducked in the mill stream, and few getting back to Buittle without some signs of the fray.

Edward Cairns showed much brotherly kindness to his widowed sister Mrs. Nicol, building Torr Cottage for her in 1798. He died in 1819, and was buried in Rerwick churchyard.

Edward's sister Janet was married to William Nicol about 1775. He was of humble birth, but having in his early youth displayed a taste for learning he was educated for the ministry. It does not appear that he was ever ordained, but his education brought out his great abilities, and he eventually became one of the foremost classical scholars in Scotland. In 1774 he was chosen by competition, out of a large number of applicants, classical master of Edinburgh High School by the City Corporation. It is not as a scholar, however, that his name is known to fame, but as the closest of Robert Burns's friends. This friendship began during one of the poet's visits to Edinburgh, when, unable to obtain his usual lodgings, he put up at the house of Mr. and Mrs. Nicol. The friendship thus begun lasted during the lifetime of the poet. It was in company with Nicol and Allan Masterton

JANET CAIRNS. Mrs. NICOL.

From a miniature by Reid of Kirkennan).

WILLIE NICOL.

From a miniature by Reid of Kirkennan).

(another of the masters at the High School) that Burns made his celebrated Highland tour. During one of their numerous orgies Burns wrote the famous drinking song in which Willie Nicol is handed down to posterity as an adept in the art of brewing punch:—

> O Willie brewed a peck o' maut,
> And Rab and Allan cam' to pree;
> Three blither hearts that lee-lang nicht
> Ye wadna find in Christandee.
>
> . . . .
>
> It is the moon, I ken her horn,
> That's blinkin' in the lift sae hie;
> She shines sae bright to wile us hame,
> But, by ma sooth, she'll wait a wee!
> We are na fou', we're nae that fou',
> But just a drappie in our e'e;
> The cock may craw, the day may daw,
> But aye we'll taste the barley bree.

It is regrettable that no trait in Nicol's character as handed down to us is worthy of admiration. He was irascible in the extreme, violent on the slightest provocation and addicted to drink. His letters show him to be void of religion, and one to Burns of 10th February, 1793, is chiefly devoted to scoffing at his wife's efforts to instruct his children in Scripture.

His violence and ill-temper rendered him unpopular with his pupils, and on one occasion he was the victim of a practical joke at the hands of Sir Walter Scott, who was then a pupil at the High School. On another occasion he assaulted the Head Master in the street, and finally in 1795 he was dismissed for drunkenness. He died two years later.

Burns wrote several sonnets and poems in the Nicols'

house, and the manuscripts of these were in possession of Mrs. Nicol. It is said that some time before her death she lent them to a schoolmaster in Auchencairn to copy. She died before he returned them, and he afterwards denied having received them. The ultimate history of these MSS is obscure; but they probably have been published.

Among the efforts to increase the public fund being raised for Burns's widow was a "Grand Ball with music" in Glasgow. Some papers connected therewith were among Mrs. Nicol's papers, and a ticket for the ball is here reproduced, we believe for the first time.

Mrs. Nicol died in March, 1827, aged 84.[1] She was the last Cairns resident at Torr.

In 1829 Mrs. Chapman, Edward Cairns's eldest daughter, then living in Liverpool, paid a visit to Torr, and wrote a brief diary of the visit, which, as it contains some rather interesting chat about the residents of the district, may be thought worthy of being printed here. It reads:—

"Left home on Tuesday, the 1st of September, 1829, with Miss Douglas of New York, and after staying with some friends on our journey, on Wednesday, the 16th, crossed over in Mr. Greave's boat to Annan, reaching Castle Douglas the same evening, where we slept, arriving at Torr[2] next morning in time for breakfast. Walked over to Orchardton after breakfast and saw Mrs. Maxwell.[3]

1 "The Castle Douglas Miscellany," 26th March, 1827. This negatives the statement that Nicol ran away with her from a ladies' school, as she must have been nearly 27 when he married her.

2 Torr was at this time let to Mrs. Douglas, widow of James Douglas of Orchardton.

3 Colonel Maxwell's wife was the daughter of James Douglas of Orchardton. The Orchardton property, on the death of James Douglas's only son without issue, was divided between his three daughters Mrs. Maxwell, Mrs. Robinson, and Mrs. Maitland of Gelston Castle, and now belongs to the grandson of the second daughter, Mr. W. D. Robinson Douglas.

Grand Ball,

Accompanied with Music,

At 7 Evening,

On Saturday, May 28,

In Mrs M'Graw's, 93 High Street,

For the benefit of Widow Burns.

Tickets, 6d. Each.

Printed at Poet's Box, 80 London-street, Glasgow

Dined at Orchardton, where I met Colonel Maxwell for the first time. We also met Mrs. Hamilton, sister of Mrs. Gordon of Balcary, Mr. and Mrs. Hugh Thompson, Miss M'Culloch, Miss Blair and another lady; besides these there were Miss Douglas, Mrs. John Maxwell, Mrs. Douglas and myself. Next morning, the 18th, Mrs. Maxwell took Miss Douglas and myself to call at Netherlaw. We met Mr. and Mrs. Abercromby on the road going to Orroland; they returned with us; this was the first time I had seen Mr. Abercromby. We then returned to Torr, where the Maxwells dined with us. Next morning I took a ramble by myself to visit poor aunt Nicol's cottage, the tenants and Old Torr. Found Mrs. Abercromby waiting for me when I returned. On Sunday we went to church and saw my father's and aunt's grave, after which we dined at Orchardton. Monday, Mrs. Maitland called. Colonel and Mrs. Maxwell dined with us at Torr. Tuesday, the Orchardton and Torr parties went to dine at Netherlaw, where we met Mr. and Mrs. Bell of the Isle of Wight, Mrs. Tannock and Mr. John Maxwell; stayed all night at Netherlaw; went in the morning to call with Mrs. Abercromby at Orroland, where I saw for the first time dear Mrs. Fergusson. On Friday there was a party for dinner at Netherlaw, consisting of Dundrennan and his son and daughter, the Gelston Castle family, Mr. and Mrs. Fergusson, Mrs. Tuland, and others. Stayed the next night with Mrs. Fergusson at Orroland, and the following day dined with her at Gelston Castle, where we met the Barcaple and Orchardton people, Miss Blair and John Maxwell. On Tuesday we went to Orchardton to stay, but on Wednesday the Orchardton party came over to dine with us at Torr. On Friday there was a party for dinner at Orchardton, Mr. and Mrs. Fergusson, Major Culton,[1] Mr. James Walsh and others. We spent another week in the neighbourhood, and on Tuesday, the 6th of October, Colonel Maxwell drove us into Dumfries in his open carriage on our return journey, and I left dear old Galloway I dare say for ever. We stayed that night with Mrs. Kennedy at Dumfries, leaving next day for Annan, where I had to wait until Saturday for the packet. I arrived home on Sunday morning, the 11th October."[2]

We have referred above to Sir Robert Maxwell the seventh baronet, of Orchardton, son of Mungo Maxwell and Mary Cairns of Barnbarroch. His grandfather, also Sir Robert, the fourth baronet, married firstly in 1680, Barbara, daughter of George Maxwell of Munches, by whom he had issue, besides several children who died young, George, born 1682. Sir Robert married secondly in 1697, Anna, daughter of John Lindsay of Wauchope, who survived him, dying in 1739. By her he had issue two sons, Mungo, born 1700, and Robert of Blackbillie, born 1705. By the terms of his marriage settlement with his second wife, the fourth baronet was obliged to settle all property he acquired after this marriage (1697) on the issue thereof, to the exclusion of the issue of his first marriage. As he was at the time only heir presumptive

1 Major Culton, son of John Culton, who bought Auchincairn estate from Edward Cairns.

2 I am indebted to Mrs. Brinsley of Birmingham, a daughter of Benjamin Cairns, and Miss Stiven of Glasgow, granddaughter of Mrs. Chapman, and therefore great-grand-daughter of Edward Cairns, for the portraits of the Torr family and for the documents referred to above. The portrait of Willie Nicol belongs to the Earl of Rosebery, who kindly allowed me to reproduce it for the first time in this work.

of his first cousin Sir George, third baronet, this settlement carried with it all the landed property which eventually passed to Sir Robert on the death of Sir George in 1719. In 1727 he executed a trust deed settling all his estates on the eldest son, then unborn, of his son by his second marriage, Mungo Maxwell, to the entire exclusion of his eldest son George, the heir to the baronetcy. By this trust deed "Popish" heirs were carefully excluded, Sir Robert having conformed to the Scottish Church in November, 1723. On his death in 1729, the friends of the family succeeded in getting the two half-brothers, George and Mungo, to agree to a division of the estate, setting aside both their father's marriage settlement of 1697 and the trust deed of 1727. By this agreement George, who became fifth baronet, was to obtain two-thirds of the estate, including Orchardton Castle and the old family property of Spottes, and was to take over the heavy debts with which the property was encumbered. Mungo got Glenshinnoch, Potterland, Balcary, and other lands, amounting to one-third of the estate, free of debt. Sir George obtained a Great Seal charter in 1740 of the estate in favour of his son and heir Thomas, as nearest Protestant heir male. Sir George died in 1746, and was succeeded by his son Sir Thomas Maxwell as sixth baronet, of whom later.

Mungo Maxwell, the eldest son of the second marriage of Sir Robert the fourth baronet, was born in May, 1700. He was baptised a Presbyterian, and in his earlier years, up to about 1715, was educated as such, attending instruction in the catechism at school, and the services at the

Established Church. He was, however, as a child, much with Sir George Maxwell the third baronet and his wife the dowager Lady Montague,[1] devout Roman Catholics, and was sent by them to Douai College in 1716.[2] He returned thence a strong and most consistent Roman Catholic, and although his father is said to have used every influence to persuade him, he never swerved in his faith, being very regular all his life in all the observances of his church, and in intimate correspondence with the clergy of the Roman Catholic communion. By the arrangement of 1729, Glenshinnoch and the lands attached were handed over to him. The great lawsuit in which his son Robert engaged against Sir Thomas, son of Sir George, for possession of Orchardton was decided in favour of Robert, because Mungo as a Papist could not succeed, and therefore could not alter his father's dispositions of 1727, and also because the agreement come to between George and Mungo considered only their own interests, to the prejudice of Mungo's son Robert, who, although unborn at the time of the trust deed, was thereby made the heir.

Mungo Maxwell married in 1727, Mary, daughter of David Cairns of Barnbarroch. She was educated as a Presbyterian, but on her marriage conformed to the Roman Catholic faith, which she afterwards renounced on her second marriage. Mungo died (apparently drowned in the Urr) in 1740, leaving issue by Mary Cairns, besides five daughters, Anne, Barbara, Henrietta, Elizabeth and Agnes, an only

[1] A daughter of the Marquis of Powis, and sister of the Ladies Nithsdale and Kenmure.

[2] The entry in the College Register at Douai is: "1716, Decem. 24, Mungo Maxwell. Abiit Londinum, Maio 1720."

son Robert, born 1728. All the children were baptised by a Roman Catholic priest, and Robert and Anne confirmed by a Roman Catholic Bishop. Robert received his early education at the hands of the priest who was private chaplain at Munches, and at the age of eleven was sent to Douai College.[1] Shortly after his arrival there his father died, and during the four or five years he remained at Douai no letters or other communications were sent to him by his mother, nor was anything paid for his education. In fact, his existence was entirely ignored by all his relatives. After four years, during which he repeatedly begged to be set to some business, and had no answer to his letters, he ran away from the College. Being caught, he was imprisoned for two months and then sent back to a very strict custody at College. Four months later he again ran away, absolutely penniless, and enlisted as a private soldier (in one account he is styled a cadet) in Brigadier Ruth's Regiment in the French Army, in which he fought at Dettingen and Fontenoy. He remained thus "in meserable state" till 1745, when Lord John Drummond[2] raised a regiment in France to aid the Stewart cause, and made him an ensign in it. All this time no reply had been sent to his urgent appeals for money and help to his mother and other friends. He came with Drummond to Scotland, fought at Culloden, was taken prisoner, and kept in Dumfries jail

[1] The College Register states: "10 Oct. 1739 Venit e Scotia Robertus Maxwell, 10 annorum, filius Dom. Quintigerni (*sic*) Maxwell de Glenshannuch et Domae. Maria Kerner (*sic*—may be Kernes): 3 Martii 1744 militiam amplexus est. Deficit a fide in Scotia propter hæreditatem. Jam est eques auratus de Orcherston."

[2] Lord John Drummond arrived in Scotland from France 22 Nov. 1745, with 800 men, including the Royal Scots Regiment.

for ten months. The durance was not apparently very "vile," for we hear that all his friends could, and did, come to see him, and on one occasion at least it was a cheery meeting; "a son of the Lady Barncleugh's being prisoner at the same time, his sisters and some other young ladies used to go to the prison; and one day Lady Barncleugh gave an entertainment in the said prison at which the pursuer's (Robert Maxwell) mother was present, and in the afternoon had music and dancing." His mother frequently visited him while he was there and Sir Thomas seems to have been attentive. He was next moved to Berwick jail for seven months, and then sent in a cartel ship back to France. In June 1749 he got leave and came to Scotland for a few months, and in 1750 apparently took formal possession of Glenshinnoch, which had been his for ten years, though he had never received any rent, being always assured that his mother's and sisters' aliment and the heavy burdens on it absorbed everything. In January, 1750, he returned to France till the summer of 1753, when Maxwell of Munches requested him to come over and sell Glenshinnoch. About this time a friend from Scotland had told him a little about his rights and that he could claim all the estate of Orchardton, which his cousin Sir Thomas was rapidly squandering. So in December, 1753, it would seem, he arrived at the door of Orchardton, told Sir Thomas that everything was his, and demanded immediate possession; this very summary notice to quit was not well received by Lady Maxwell, who ordered him off with a very plain expression of her opinion of his conduct. He then began to take legal advice, and as a preliminary step he quitted the French service and renounced his religious faith, taking the formula in October, 1754. He seems to have lived when in Galloway chiefly with Patrick Heron, then an old man of nearly 80 years, who was at that time living in Kelton, where his wife, the widow of Thomas Maxwell, son of Hugh Maxwell of Cuil, youngest son of Sir Robert, had inherited some property, and was assiduous in his new profession of faith. The great lawsuit began on 24th February, 1756, and, with the appeal, continued till 8th August, 1771. Sir Robert, as he became in 1761, was victorious all along the line; he continued in comfortable possession for some years, and built a new mansion house at Glenshinnoch, which he called Orchardton, and made very many improvements. Then came the Ayr Bank catastrophe, in which he was deeply involved, and which ruined him. Orchardton was sold in 1785 to James Douglas. Sir Robert's romantic career was the foundation of Sir Walter Scott's novel "Guy Mannering." He married Margaret Maclellan, eldest daughter of Robert Maclellan of Barscobe (who had been "out" in the '15 and was taken prisoner at Preston). The annuity which for some years was chargeable on Orchardton for her was the very last connection the Maxwells had with their old property. Sir Robert died suddenly 21st September, 1786.

On his death the baronetcy became dormant, but not extinct. The fourth baronet had a third son already mentioned, Robert Maxwell of Blackbillie. He was born in 1705, and married Elizabeth, daughter of Robert Maxwell of Hazelfield, by whom he had male issue, Robert, William and Mungo. The eldest son Robert married about

1754, Elizabeth Henry, and had two sons William, born 1755, and Robert. Both appear to have been living at the death of the seventh baronet, but the impoverished circumstances of this branch of the family at the time, possibly want of knowledge, and the admitted fact that both brothers had fallen to humble positions in life, combined to prevent William, *de jure* the eighth baronet, from assuming the title. As recently as 1806 it was known that several years previously he had enlisted in the 4th Royal Artillery, but his whereabouts, or that of his brother, were then unknown. If the representative in pure male line of this William Maxwell could prove his identity, the dormant title might yet be revived. Failing the existence of such, then that of his brother Robert could claim; failing whom, the heir male of William or Mungo, second and third sons of Robert of Blackbillie.[1]

[1] I am indebted to Mr. Robinson Douglas of Orchardton for the facts related in the above history of the last Maxwell baronets of Orchardton. He has in his possession, among other interesting documents, the decreet of the judges in the lawsuit by Robert Maxwell against Sir Thomas, a manuscript of many hundred folios, containing a vast amount of family history. The above facts, which in many respects differ from the published account of the family, are extracted from this decreet.

CHAPTER IX.

Other families of Cairns—Pilmuir and Mayshiell—Principal Cairns, D.D.—The Cairnses in Fife—Various branches of the Cairns family in Galloway—Cairnses in County Down—Earl Cairns—Cairns of Dundrennan—The Maitlands.

IT will have been noted by those who have read the foregoing chapters that the parent family of Carnys of that ilk, after its estates had passed to the Crichton family through female descent, separated into two main branches. These may for want of a better description be called the Western and Eastern Cairneses.[1] The former, including the families of Cults and Orchardton, Monaghan, Tyrone, Kipp and Torr, held their estates as direct feoffees of the Crown. For this reason we have been able to trace clearly from the State Records the various descents of the heads of the families, so long as they held their estates, for the past 600 years. Unfortunately this is not the case with the Eastern Cairnses. With the exception of the family of Craghouse and Cramonde in the fifteenth century, we cannot discover that any of these ever held land as direct Crown feoffees. Thus in endeavouring to

[1] The spelling of the name in the following pages is a source of some difficulty. The Eastern branch of the family in modern times spell the name invariably "Cairns"; in early records, however, the name appears either "Carnys" or "Cairnis." The modern Galloway families, like the Eastern branches, spelled the name "Cairns," but the Irish family representing Orchardton and Cults have for at least two centuries consistently spelt the name "Cairnes." In conformity with the custom which seems to control some names derived from localities, it would seem as if "Cairnis" should be the correct spelling of the name (compare for example the derivation of the name Inglis); but, curious to say, we cannot find any modern "Cairnis." The nearest approach seems to be the name Cairnes. In these pages we have endeavoured to spell the name as used by the family referred to at the period with which we happen at the moment to deal.

trace their descent, those most fruitful sources of information, the Register of the Great Seal and the Retours of Sasine of land, are of little avail. However, from these records and others, such as those of the Privy Council, we can form a general idea as to the localities into which the Eastern Cairnses gradually spread.

Prior to the latter part of the fourteenth century we have no data to go upon. In the early chapters of this work we have treated with the history of four sons of William Carnys of that ilk. He probably had other sons of whom we cannot find record. Of these four sons we have traced the descent of John, son of the third son William. He was the direct ancestor of the Western Cairneses. The Eastern Cairnses apparently sprang from the remaining issue of John and William, and probably also from brothers (if any) of the William of Carnys and Whitburn, with whom our story commences. The references to them in the early records are, at best, fragmentary and disconnected.

Speaking generally, about the year 1400, any available records tend to show that the name was confined to the districts adjoining Carnys, Whitburn and Edinburgh. During the two centuries following, the Eastern Cairnses seem to have spread northward into Fifeshire, and eastward into Haddington and Berwick and the adjoining portions of the counties of Roxburgh and Selkirk. We find in the Register of the Great Seal references to the family of Carnis of Craghouse and Cramonde,[1] who held those lands from the Crown. In 1450 the lands were held by John, and in 1461 by his heir Richard. In this year he and his son and heir

1 Mid-Lothian.

sold certain lands to William Roule of Cramonde, and in 1465 other lands to James Howisoun and Thomas Turing, a citizen of Leith. Richard's son and heir James succeeded him; he married Elizabeth Malisoune. In 1495 Mariot Carnys, probably their daughter and heiress, succeeded as heiress of Craghouse and Cramonde. She probably married, the estates thus passing to another name.

Of the ultimate history of this branch of the Cairnses we have no information. Nor can we trace the connection between this family and the Cairnses of that ilk; but it is worthy of note that in the charter of 1427 it is mentioned that on the death of Stephen Crichton, referred to in Chapter I, his son George Crichton, heir of the Cairnes estates, was possessor of lands in the Barony of Cramonde.

Another branch of the Cairnses held lands under the Wauchopes of Niddrymerschal. We find by a charter of 1502 that one John Cairnis occupied the lands adjoining those of Pilmuir which he held from Wauchope. This Pilmuir must not be confused with the Pilmuir in East Lothian, where another and important family of Cairnes was established at an early date. They held Pilmuir and adjoining lands, in the Barony of Bolton, under the Earls of Lauderdale, and the lands of Mayshiell, in the parish of Whittinghame, under the Earls of Kellie. Unfortunately for our purpose, these estates being held from the Crown by the Earls, the names of the large landholders thereon do not appear on the Register of the Great Seal, their patents being granted not direct from the Crown, but by the tenants in chief. We have thus been unable to discover the approximate date at which these Cairnses became established either at Pilmuir or Mayshiell. William Cairns or Cairnes, the builder of the present Pilmuir House, inserted above the door of the tower a carved armorial stone dated 1624; this stone will be fully described and illustrated in the next chapter. Its date establishes the age of Pilmuir House, but there is preserved at Kirklands a much older Cairns armorial stone, also described in the next chapter. It bears the initials J. C., but no date. It seems evident that this stone occupied a similar position in the family residence which was the predecessor of Pilmuir House.[1] There can be little doubt this J. Cairns, whose surname is established by the arms inscribed with the initials, was an ancestor of William Cairns, the builder of Pilmuir; but we cannot identify him with any certainty. He may have been John Cairnis, whose seal dated 1462 is described in the next chapter. He was a bailie of Edinburgh, and from the mullet in chief in his seal probably was a descendant of William the constable of Edinburgh Castle, third son of William de Carnys of that ilk.

William Cairns, the builder of Pilmuir,[2] was born in 1565. He married Agnes Broun or Brown, whose arms

1 It was a very general custom in Scotland from an early period for the builder of a house to place in a conspicuous position therein a stone bearing his initials and those of his wife's maiden name, with the family arms, if any were customarily borne. The date was usually included, but unfortunately was not in this case.

2 Pilmuir House remains to-day almost exactly as in William Cairns' time, and is one of the quaintest and most charming examples, in a diminutive scale, of the old Scottish Baronial residences of about the date 1600. It might almost be described as a reproduction of the castle of the Shaws of Ballygelly, Co. Antrim, built almost exactly at the same time. The principal rooms are wainscotted with oak to the ceilings, one of which is richly decorated with ornamental plaster work, in which the cinquefoil, the crest of the Pilmuir family, is conspicuous. I am indebted to the present occupier, Mr. Gray, for the photograph here reproduced of the front view of Pilmuir. At the back is an orchard of nearly

PILMUIR HOUSE. East Lothian.

From a Photo.]

he impaled. As his son Richard appears in the list of Laureations in the University of Edinburgh in 1638, we may assume the marriage to have taken place about the year 1620. He died in 1653.[1] By Agnes Broun he had issue,

A. RICHARD, evidently the eldest son, as he succeeded his father in the estates. He was educated at Edinburgh University. His name appears several times between 1670 and 1684 in the Kirk Session book of Bolton parish. Several of his signatures are preserved, showing that he spelled his name either Cairns or Cairnes. In his testament dative his wife's name is stated to have been Janet Denistoun.[2] She survived him, but there was no issue of the marriage. By a deed dated 1659, he formally adopted his niece Sibilla Borthwick, daughter of his sister Sibilla who had been committed to his care after the death of her mother. A sum

four acres, enclosed by a massive wall. In the orchard is a great stone dove-cote, of venerable age. In ancient Scotland no laird was permitted to keep more doves, or properly speaking, pigeons, than could feed on his own estate; hence the size of the old dove-cotes indicates in some degree the extent of the estate. The size of the Pilmuir dove-cote shows that its builder possessed a considerable property. A remarkable feature about Pilmuir is the fact that its builder must have been an artistic genius, because if viewed from a certain spot in the orchard, close to the dove-cote, every bit of the house is in peculiarly artistic perspective; to attain this, the windows have all actually been graduated in size to fit the view, and the dormer windows and roof sloped to correspond. One can understand a house making a pretty picture, but surely this example of a house being constructed to fit an artistic fancy, and actually built to fit an imaginary picture is unique.

1 He was buried at Bolton, where there is a large "through" stone to his memory. It is at the east end of the Blantyre vault. The inscription, now almost illegible, read "Heir Lyes ye Body of William Cairns of Pilmoor who depairted this lyfe ye XX day of May 1653 aet. 88 years." Round the margin of the stone was inscribed "Ye feir of ye Lord is ye beginning of wisdome and ye way to all happiness. Whosoever walketh therein sal obtaine lyfe everlasting."

2 The Edinburgh register of marriages supplies the date of this marriage as 7th February, 1641.

of £2,000 Scots was settled upon her, to be set aside as a marriage portion when she should require it. At the same time he made an arrangement for the succession of the male heirs of his sister to all his landed property, providing however, that he should retain a life interest, and that should he eventually have issue, the arrangement was to be void. Thus his younger brother William was excluded from all share in the estate. On his death in 1685, his nephew William Borthwick established his claim as a creditor for the total amount of the personal estate, to the exclusion of the brother and widow of the deceased.

B. WILLIAM, indentured a writer to the Signet under Hew Rose in 1636. The meagre information at our disposal seems to indicate that his career was unfortunate. He never qualified as a writer, and as we have seen, he was disinherited by his brother in 1659; in the same year he married Euphemia or Isobel Thomson, which marriage may have been the cause of his brother's displeasure. By this wife he had issue. We cannot discover the names of his children, or whether any of them survived him; but the burial register of Greyfriars Church in Edinburgh records deaths of his children in 1663, 1664, and 1665, and of his wife in June of the latter year. Less than two months later he appears in the marriage register again, his second wife being Catherine Lambe. In 1667 he was appointed to the somewhat humble office of

Messenger of Arms.[1] He married thirdly in 1677,[2] but we have no record whether he had any surviving issue. He was living in 1685.

c. SIBILLA, wife of ALEXANDER BORTHWICK in Johnstonburn, and afterwards in Gilchriston and Saltcoats (Haddington). She died in 1650, leaving with other issue,

1. WILLIAM BORTHWICK of Pilmuir and Mayshiell, chirurgeon in Edinburgh. He was surgeon to the Earl of Mar's Regiment, 31 January 1684, and Surgeon-Major of the Forces in Scotland, 1686.[3] He married 1stly, in 1666, Marion, daughter of James Borthwick of Stow, who died 1676, and by whom he had female issue only surviving. He married 2ndly, Marjorie, niece of Sir Thomas Stewart of Grantully, by whom he had issue,

a. HENRY BORTHWICK, captain in the army, *de jure* 13th LORD BORTHWICK. He was mortally wounded at Ramillies on 23rd May, 1706, but survived to the 27th. He left issue, minors, of whom HENRY afterwards became 15th LORD BORTHWICK, whose mother and tutorix, Mary Pringle, in July, 1707, sold Pilmuir (but not Mayshiell) to the Borthwicks of Falahill.

1 Register of Appointments of Messengers at Arms, MS. in the Court of the Lord Lyon.

2 Edinburgh Register of Marriages.

3 Laing Charters, 2822, 2840.

The male issue of Alexander Borthwick and Sibilla Cairns became extinct with the fifteenth Lord, the Barony of Borthwick descending to another branch of the Borthwick family.[1]

We have been unable to ascertain whether the Cairnses occupied the lands of Mayshiell prior to those of Pilmuir, but from the old armorial stone now at Kirklands, but formerly at Pilmuir, it seems evident that their principal residence was at the latter place from a very early period. We have no evidence that they had at any time a residence at Mayshiell, but early in the eighteenth century a family of Cairns was established on certain lands near Mayshiell, namely, Byrecleuch, Parish of Longformacus. We have not succeeded in finding positive evidence that these were of the same family as the owners of Mayshiell, but it is very possible that they were. The first record we have of the Cairnses of Byrecleuch is in the Kirk Records of Cranshaws; here we find in 1738 the marriage recorded of James Cairns to Jean Wood. He was a son of Thomas[2] Cairns in Byrecleuch. A certain amount of romance is attached to this marriage, which was a runaway match, and was the subject of discussion before the Kirk Session, and finds mention as such in the Session Minutes. James Cairns succeeded his father as tenant in Byrecleuch. He

1 For a full and detailed account of the Borthwick family and Peerage, see "The Scots Peerage," Vol. II., 94, 1905, article by William Macmath, to whom I am indebted for part of my information regarding the family at Pilmuir.

2 The Christian name Thomas, practically unknown in ancient times among the Western Cairneses, is not unknown in such records as are extant relative to the East Lothian Cairnses. As early as 1556, we find in the Register of Deeds a Borthwick contract attested by among others, James Borthwick, Sir Thomas Cairns, and James Borthwick. (See above, p. 185, Note 2).

had one brother John, farmer in Ellemford, who was married, but left no male issue. In the distressing times which followed the insurrection of 1745, the Cairnses like hundreds of others, suffered severe misfortunes. James Cairns, who at one time was an extensive sheep farmer, and held an additional farm at Cranshaws, eventually was reduced to poverty. He left one son Thomas and nine daughters. His son, a victim to circumstances over which he had no control, was obliged to relinquish the farms. He married Janet Geggie, and dying in 1799, left issue,

A. JAMES CAIRNS, who on his father's death moved with his widowed mother and her family to Ayton Hill. He entered the army, and fought throughout the Peninsular War, gaining a medal with no less than twelve clasps. He was in one of his many engagements severely wounded, and lay long in hospital, eventually marrying the nurse, a Portuguese, to whose kindness to him was probably due his recovery. By her he had two sons, who died without male issue, and three daughters.

B. JOHN CAIRNS, who continued for some time to live at Ayton Hill, afterwards removing to Oldcambus, and finally to Dunglass. He married in 1814, Alison, only daughter of John Murray of Ayton, and dying in 1841, left issue,

1. THOMAS, born 1816; married in 1845 Margaret Anderson, and died, s.p. 1856.
2. JOHN, born 1818. At a very early age he displayed a great taste and aptitude for learning. He entered Edinburgh University in 1834,

where he had a distinguished career, taking out his M.A. in 1841, securing first place in Classics, Mathematics, and Philosophy. The degrees of LL.D. and D.D. were subsequently conferred upon him. During his University days he was a prominent member of the Metaphysical and Diagnostic Societies, and here developed that prowess in debate which, with his numerous other qualities, afterwards raised him to such prominence in the Scottish ecclesiastical world. On leaving the University, he spent some time on the Continent, studying at Berlin under Schelling and Neander, and was ordained to the ministry of the Secession Church in 1845, his first and only cure being the Golden Square church in Berwick. Under him the congregation prospered exceedingly, removing in 1859 to the new, spacious and handsome Gothic church known as Wallace Green, in charge of which he remained until 1876. He then removed to Edinburgh to take up his duties as professor in the United Presbyterian College, of which he was elected Principal in 1879. Principal Cairns, was the author of many widely-read and erudite works on Theology. He was an ardent advocate of the union of the churches, and although he did not live to see it, his vast influence and energy helped in no small degree to bring about the union of the United Presbyterian and the Free Church of Scotland. He died unmarried in 1892.[1]

3. JAMES, born 1821, d.s.p. 1845.
4. WILLIAM, born 1823. Became a schoolmaster, and a writer of some note. Among his literary undertakings was the colossal work of indexing the twenty-five volumes of the Encyclopædia Britannica. (A. & C. Black.) He died, s.p.
5. DAVID, born 1825. He was for many years minister of Stitchel, near Kelso, and now resides at 20, Braidburn Crescent, Edinburgh. He married in 1856, Elizabeth, daughter of the Rev David Smith, D.D., and has issue,
    - *a.* JOHN (the Rev., M.A.), born 1857, minister in Dumfries.
    - *b.* DAVID SMITH (the Rev., M.A.), minister at Ayton. Married in 1901, Helen, daughter of H. H. Craw, and has issue,
        - *1.* DAVID, born 1904.
        - *2.* ALISON.
    - *c.* WILLIAM THOMAS (the Rev., M.A.), minister at Abernethy, Perthshire. Married in 1897, Christina, daughter of the Rev. James Cumming.
    - *d.* JESSIE.
6. JEAN, died unmarried, 1875.
7. JANET, twin sister of William.

[1] For a full account of the life of Principal Cairns, see *Life and Letters of John Cairns, D.D., LL.D.*, by Professor M'Ewan, and *Principal Cairns*, Famous Scots Series, by the Rev. John Cairns, M.A.

8. Agnes, married in 1854 the Rev. James C. Meiklejohn, and d.s.p. 1887.

In the Chartulary of St. Andrews we find references to two Cairnses of an early date. The first of these is Thomas de Karnys, whose name appears in a document of 1395, where he is mentioned as a clerk and notary public. In another document, dated 1406, he is styled "venerabilis vir Magister Thomas de Karnys, rector Ecclesiae de Setoun.[1]" He is also mentioned in documents of 1410 and 1411. We have not met with his name elsewhere, nor have we any further information concerning him. As he is described as "venerabilis vir" in 1406, we assume that he was a contemporary of Duncan, John, William and Alexander, referred to in the early pages of this work; very possibly he was a brother. In the same Chartulary, under the date 1406, is mentioned a William de Karnys, notary public. William de Karnys, the Vicar of Glammys, is referred to as such, as early as 1438. It may be that the vicar was the same William de Karnys, notary public, referred to in the Chartulary.

Isolated references to Cairnses in the Kirk Session Book and the Guild Rolls of Berwick show that some families of the name had settled in the town and neighbourhood of Berwick in the seventeenth century. They were probably descendants of the Cairnses who appear to have settled in East Lothian and North Berwickshire in the fifteenth century, though all trace of their actual descent is lost. Several families of these Cairnses still remain in the district.

[1] In the Lothians. Prior to the foundation of the See of Edinburgh, Seton was in the diocese of St. Andrews.

It will not be out of place to record here the gallant conduct of a representative of the Berwick Cairnses in the Boer war. When all England was stirred with the news of the disasters which overwhelmed our forces in the early stages of the war, George and James Cairns, of Alnwick, proceeded to South Africa at their own expense, and enlisted as volunteers in the 2nd Brabant Horse. They were present in several of the severest actions in which the 2nd Brabants were engaged, George having his horse shot under him, and being twice struck by bullets, though not wounded. After the capture of Bethlehem from De Wette, a company was sent out on patrol duty. It consisted of an officer and fifteen men. They suddenly found themselves ambushed, and the trooper who rode beside Cairns was shot in the breast. The officer ordered a hasty retreat, and he and twelve troopers galloped back to Bethlehem. Cairns refused to leave his wounded and helpless comrade, whom he endeavoured to lift on to his horse. This he was unable to do. He was quickly surrounded and called upon to surrender. He promptly refused, and emptied his magazine rifle on the enemy, now close upon him. Drawing his revolver with the determination to fight to the last, he was killed by a bullet fired at close quarters, and fell beside his comrade for whose life he gave his own. The latter became a prisoner, and through care and skilful treatment recovered.[1]

We find various references to the name Cairns in the old records relating to Edinburgh and Leith, and during

1 This account of the bravery and heroic death of George Cairns was supplied by his wounded comrade, Trooper Wright, after his release.

the sixteenth century we find that they had spread to several districts in Fife. In 1525, Henry Cairns, indweller in Leith, was summoned before the Privy Council to answer a charge of heresy. For the same offence he was again summoned before the Council, and his goods seized and confiscated. The names of his children are recorded as Charles, James, Robert, George, John, Andrew, Archibald, Helen, Margaret, Elizabeth, Isobel, and Agnes.

In 1560 one John Cairns appears as reader in St. Giles' Church, and assistant at worship there, to John Knox. For this service he was granted by the Edinburgh Town Council 100 marks per annum, which was supplemented by occasional collections on his behalf. In 1567, after the murder of Lord Darnley, Bothwell, having divorced his wife, at once "sent to ask his banns with the Queen. The reader, John Cairns, whose office it was, did simply refuse."[1] This John Cairns may have been the John mentioned above, son of the heretic Henry Cairns of Leith. The latter and his family, consisting of seven sons and five daughters, on the confiscation of their goods, were expelled from Leith. It is not unlikely they crossed the Forth into Fife, as a generation or so later we find rather frequent mention of families of Cairns in Fife and as far north as Forfar. As a rule we find them pursuing honourable if humble occupations. Not being landholders, we have been unable to trace a consecutive history of any of the Fife or Forfar Cairnses prior to the time when parish registers began to

1 Spottiswood's History. Other accounts state that the banns were read by John Knox's assistant. This may refer to John Craig, who was assistant reader. For a list of documents from which the above facts have been extracted, see Appendix H, M'Crie's *Life of John Knox.*

be kept systematically, that is to say, early in the eighteenth, and in a few cases, the latter half of the seventeenth century.

By referring to these Parish Registers and to the index of Testaments preserved in the Register House in Edinburgh, we are able to trace the descent of several families of the Fife Cairnses, of whom we may mention the following:—

Parish of Dunino.—Robert Cairns, born about 1670, married 1693, Jean Morton. Their son William was born in 1694. He married, about 1730, Agnes Ritchie, and left a daughter Elizabeth, born 1736, and a son Alexander. He lived at Kingsmuir. On 21st December, 1754, he married Christian Grieve; by her he had issue,

A. JAMES, born 1755.

B. ALEXANDER, born 1758.

C. WILLIAM, born 1760.

D. JOHN, born 1763, and five daughters.

The latter, John Cairns, at an early age entered upon a mercantile career, and settled in Paisley, where in 1788 he married Mary Brown, a name well known in the commercial history of that town. She appears to have been born in Kilmarnock, in 1765, and died 1848. John Cairns died 1834, leaving issue,

ADAM, born 1799. He married in 1819 Margaret Haldane of Paisley (born 1800—died 1870) and had issue,

A. JOHN, born 1821. He devoted his time to art, and became a painter of some repute. He married and left issue JANE, wife of the Rev. Alexander Ritchie of Dunblane Cathedral, by whom she has issue.

B. WILLIAM, born 1832, and five daughters, all of whom married, and had issue,

William Cairns, now residing at Pollokshields, Glasgow, founded the firm of Cairns and Laing, of which he is still the head. He married firstly, in 1857, Elizabeth Graham, who died in 1866, and secondly, in 1868, Janet Bauchop, who died in 1900, and has issue,

A. ADAM, born 1858, now of Ingleside, Newlands, Glasgow, married, and has issue.

B. JAMES GRAHAM, born 1862, married, and has issue.

C. JOHN, born 1866, married, and has issue.

D. WILLIAM, born 1869, now of Riverton, S. Australia, married, and has issue.

E. CHARLES HODGE, born 1871, Physician, married, and now residing in Sheffield, has issue.

F. MARGARET LOCHHEAD HALDANE, married in 1889, the Rev. W. M. Christie, now of Aleppo, by whom she has issue.

In the neighbourhood of Yetholm, in Roxburgh, another branch of the Cairns family has been established for several centuries. We have not evidence to show whether this family springs from the Berwick or Galloway Cairnses. They were established in Yetholm in early the seventeenth century. Of this family was

ROBERT CAIRNS, born at Kirk Yetholm, 1731. He married Alison Rae, who died 1784, and dying in 1802,[1] left issue,

A. JOHN CAIRNS, born 1756, who married and had issue, of whom we have record of five daughters, who died young.

[1] Tombstone in Kirk Yetholm.

B. WILLIAM CAIRNS of Kirk Yetholm,[1] who left issue, besides three daughters who died unmarried, and are interred at Kirk Yetholm, two daughters who emigrated to California, a daughter Mrs. Fox, and several sons,

JOHN CAIRNS of Kirk Yetholm, born 1807. He died 1868, leaving issue,

a. WILLIAM CAIRNS, born 1842. He died in 1898, leaving issue,

1. JOHN CAIRNS, now living at Kirk Yetholm, and two sons and six daughters.

b THOMAS CAIRNS of Kirk Yetholm.

c ROBERT CAIRNS of Galashields, who is married and has issue,

1. JOHN CAIRNS.

2. JAMES CAIRNS.

d. JOHN CAIRNS, now of Bluntys Mill, Kirk Yetholm, who is married and has issue,

1. JOHN CAIRNS.

2. ELIZABETH.

e PETER CAIRNS of Kirk Yetholm.

f JAMES CAIRNS of Bluntys Mill, Kirk Yetholm.

g and *h* CHRISTINA and JANET, unmarried.

C ALISON, born 1768, wife of Thomas Robson. Died 1792.

Close to Yetholm, but over the border, at Crookham, Northumberland, we find another family of Cairns established in the middle of the eighteenth century. We have not evidence clearly tracing the connection between this family

[1] Buried in Kirk Yetholm.

and that at Yetholm, but it seems not unlikely they were of the same stock. The earliest of the Crookham family of whom we have mention is Thomas Cairns, born in 1759. He settled at Embleton, and marrying in 1790 Grace Bairnsfather, died in 1841, leaving issue,

A. ROBERT CAIRNS, died unmarried.

B. DAVID CAIRNS, born 1797. He became a Veterinary Surgeon and settled in Forfarshire, where he married in 1825 Elizabeth Young (who died 1862), and dying in 1865, left issue,

1. THOMAS CAIRNS, born 1828. He entered into business in Sunderland, where he married in 1852 Hannah, daughter of Peter Turnbull, of Sunderland, and dying in 1860, left issue,

a. THOMAS CAIRNS, born 1854 at Sunderland; now of Dunira House, Jesmond, Newcastle-on-Tyne. He has for many years been a prominent citizen of Newcastle, taking an active part in its commercial and municipal affairs. He is head of the eminent firm of Cairns, Noble & Co., shipowners and merchants. He represents Newcastle in Parliament, where he has introduced some most useful legislative measures. He married in 1880 Isabella, daughter of William Dixon, of Newcastle, by whom he has issue,

1. THOMAS RUSSELL, and four daughters.

2. JAMES CAIRNS, died in Forfar, 1904.

3. ROBERT CAIRNS, d.s.p. 1860.
4. DAVID CAIRNS, born 1837. He resided in Dublin, and married in 1869, Jessie, daughter of James Waldie, of Edinburgh, and dying in 1904, left issue,
    - *a.* CHARLES WALDIE CAIRNS, born 1872, now of Newcastle-on-Tyne. He married in 1898, Blanca, daughter of Dr. R. W. Shelly, of Sunderland.
    - *b.* DAVID WALDIE CAIRNS, born 1874.
    - *c.* THOMAS YOUNG CAIRNS, born 1876.
    - *d.* JAMES WILLIAM CAIRNS, born 1878. Married 1906, Queenie, daughter of Captain M'Dermot, of Nice.
5. WILLIAM CAIRNS, now of Queen's Park Collegiate School in Glasgow. He married Anne, daughter of John M'Kinley, and has issue,
    - *a.* DAVID LOUIS CAIRNS, M.D., and gold medallist, Glasgow University, now of Huddersfield.
    - *b.* WILLIAM CAIRNS.
    - *c.* ROBERT CAIRNS.
6. ELIZABETH, died unmarried.
7. GRACE, wife of William White.
8. ISABELLA, wife of John Fairweather.

THE WESTERN CAIRNESES.—In former chapters we have recorded the history of the principal descendants of John Cairnis of Cults, heir of his uncle Alexander, the Provost of Lincluden. For the most part we have only been able to chronicle the history of such of his descendants as held land from the Crown. In many cases the records only mention the name of the eldest sons who succeeded to the property. In some cases we have been able to record the names of younger sons, although they possessed no land, but in such instances we were unable to trace in detail their descendants. The records show that by the end of the sixteenth century there were a good many families of Cairns established in Galloway and Dumfries, all undoubtedly cadets of the Orchardton family, descended from younger sons. It was customary for the smaller lairds in Scotland, whose estates were too small to permit of subdivision among their children, to leave all to the eldest son, and let the others provide for themselves as best they could. We find them becoming merchants, tenant farmers, or even occupying humbler if equally honourable positions in life.

Our difficulty in tracing the descent of various members of the Cairnes family in the Galloway district is greatly increased by the fact that hardly a parish register exists of older date than 1750, and few begin much before 1800. In hardly any part of Scotland have these registers been so badly preserved. We may mention a few families of Cairns in Galloway, whose precise origin is unknown, or if known, whose descendants we have been unable to follow out.

Cairnes of Knocklittle and Barnbachil.—This family descended from Henry de Cairnis, younger son of John, nephew of the Provost of Lincluden. They held the property for five generations, but in no case can we find even the names of any but the eldest son who succeeded as heir.

The last of the family recorded was Richard, who sold the property to Lord Herries in 1572.[1]

Cairnes of Little Spottes.—The first of this family was James, son of the elder William of Orchardton. He had a charter from Lord Herries of these lands in 1529,[2] but we cannot find any record of how long he or his descendants, if any, held this property.

Cairns of Muretoun.—Among the deeds produced at a lawsuit by John Murray of Dundrennan against Robert Cairns of Torr, Hew Cairns of Kipp and John Cairns in Auchingule and others, feuars of land in Dundrennan in 1610, were the following:—

1°. A tack by Henry, Bishop of Galloway, to Edward Cairns, son and heir of the late George Cairns of Muretoun, of the five merk lands of Auchingule, with reversion, failing male issue, to William Cairns of Orchardton, undated.[3]

2°. Confirmation by Adam, commendator of Dundrennan, to the above Edward Cairns and Margaret M'Clellan his wife, of the above lands, dated 1543.

3°. Another tack from the same to the same and his sons John, Bernard and Robert, dated 1558.

4°. A confirmation of the last, dated 1560.

5°. A charter under the Great Seal of the same, dated 1606.

1 Terregles Charters. The names of the succeeding holders of the property are given in various entries in the Registrum Magni Sigilli and the Retours of Sasine. See above, page 57.

2 Recorded in a document in the Terregles charter room.

3 This reversionary clause seems to indicate that George of Muretoun was a son of William of Orchardton. We find in the Registrum Magni Sigilli, date 1524, a confirmation of a purchase by George Cairns of Orchardton and Mariote M'Culloch his wife of lands called the Middlethird of Kilcormok.

7°. An assignment by the above Edward Cairns called a writer in Kirkcudbright, of the above lands to his grandson John, son of John his eldest son, who had predeceased him, dated 1606.[1]

From the above, it will appear that George Cairns, evidently a son of William of Orchardton, had by his wife Mariot M'Culloch an eldest son Edward, who married Margaret M'Clellan, and had issue John, Robert, and Bernard. The eldest son John predeceased his father, and left issue John. Of this family we have no further information.

CAIRNS OF LOCHILL.—The first possessor of these lands of the name of Cairns whom we find recorded is Hugh. He appears to have been a second son of David Cairns of Kipp, and brother of the William Cairns of Kipp who died in 1711. He married Margaret Brown, and died in 1717, leaving sons, John his heir, and James, writer in Edinburgh, and three daughters, Agnes, Elizabeth, and Isobel. In 1726 John had sold Lochill, and is described as of Airds and Burnfoot Croft.[2] We are unable to record his descendants, if any, or those of his brother James the writer in Edinburgh.

The disastrous ending to the insurrection of the elder Pretender in 1715 was the ultimate cause of momentous changes in the circumstances of a vast number of Scottish families. In many cases where the family sentiment was clearly in sympathy with one side or the other, the head of the family, imbued with the caution characteristic of

[1] Acts and Decreets, Register House, Vol. 255.

[2] Hornings and Inhibitions, Kirkcudbrightshire, Vol. X., pp. 222, 241, 326. (Register House).

the race, refrained from taking active part with either side. Where the owner of an estate kept rigidly aloof from joining either side, his property was fairly safe whichever side won. This commendable spirit of caution, however, was no hindrance to the cadets of families joining whichever side they desired without incriminating their chiefs. Whatever happened, the individual cadet only could be held responsible. When the insurrection was over and the day of reckoning came, many a younger son of the old Scottish families deemed it wiser to be out of Scotland. In Ireland, where the people had little sympathy with the rising, the consequences of rebellion were not pursued to such an extent as was the case in Scotland. Hence Ireland, particularly the North, became a harbour of refuge for a number of Scottish refugees. Several families now of eminence in the North of Ireland descend from Scottish settlers who arrived in the years immediately following the '15.

Among the Records at Hillsborough Castle, County Down, are the registers of leases and the rent rolls of the Kilwarlin estate. Among the leases granted at this period is one for three lives to William Cairns, dated May, 1716. It seems not unlikely he was one of the many who fled to Ireland from Scotland in this year to escape the consequences of the rebellion. We have been unable to ascertain with certainty to which of the Galloway families of Cairns he belonged, but there are indications suggesting that he was a younger son of William Cairns of Kipp who died in 1711. He certainly was a contemporary of the two sons of this William whose names are recorded.[1] The Christian names Hugh and William so frequently met with in the succeeding generations of the Kipp family prior to 1715 reappear with equal frequency among the descendants of this William Cairns. In fact, the name Hugh in the Cairns family seems to have been almost entirely confined to the Kipp branch.

The lease to William Cairns of 1716 is of the lands of Magheraconluce, near Annahilt, County Down. He died prior to 1735, in which year his widow appears as the tenant. He left several sons, who became tenants of farms in the neighbourhood.[2] His successor in the lands of Magheraconluce was his son William, probably the eldest son. We have no record of the name of his first wife. By her, who died about 1754, he had issue,

A. JOHN CAIRNS, born 1732, died at Parkmount, Belfast, unmarried, 1794.[3]

B. HUGH CAIRNS, born 1735, died at Parkmount, 1808. By his will he left several legacies to his "kinsmen at Annahilt," and £600 to each of his six sisters. He left Parkmount, which he acquired shortly

1 Inhibitions, Kirkcudbrightshire, IX., 36; X., 67. See above, pp. 188-189.

2 In the old Kirk Register of Annahilt Presbyterian Church, which commences with the year 1780, we find between that date and 1800 the names of fathers of children baptised as follows:—William Cairns of Magheraconluce, Robert Cairns of Edendentrillik, James Cairns of Cabra, and Richard Cairns of Drumlough, all apparently grandsons or great-grandsons of the original settler William. Several of the infants baptised were given the name Hugh. This interesting old Register, and the Kirk Session Minutes of the same period, are in possession of the Rev. Josias Mitchell of Annahilt. They are among the oldest extant records of the sort of this district, and contain many entries of interest to families which have since risen to prominent positions in the North of Ireland and elsewhere. In addition to the families above named residing at Annahilt, another grandson of William of the 1716 lease moved to Newtownards, eventually settling at Cherryvalley, Comber. See below, p. 249.

3 Obituary notice, *Belfast News-Letter*, August 22, 1794.

after the death of William Gregg in 1782, to his half-brother Nathan, whose mother had been a daughter of Mr. Gregg. He states in his will that "most of his property consists of money lent out at interest on security," from which it appears that he was one of Belfast's early private bankers, some of whom eventually amalgamated, thus founding what are now known as the Belfast, the Northern, and the Ulster Banks.

c. WILLIAM CAIRNS, born 1737. The name William Cairns continues to appear as holder of the Magheraconluce property subsequent to his father's removal to Belfast after his second marriage. It appears as if he had remained as the tenant, and that Hugh Cairns' "kinsmen at Annahilt" to whom he left money, namely, William and Robert Cairns, were the sons of this William, and therefore nephews of Hugh. Both appear as fathers of children baptised, in the Annahilt Register, one of the children being called Nathan, evidently after his grand-uncle.

D. MARGARET, E. SARAH, F. COLVILLE, G. ELLEN, H. JEAN (Mrs. Ballentine), J. MARY, who all d.s.p.

William Cairns of Magheraconluce married secondly about 1758, Agnes, daughter and heiress of William Gregg of Parkmount. This estate seems to have passed to Mr. Gregg from the representatives of Thomas Lutford, who had a lease for three lives, renewable for ever, from the Donegalls in 1769. Some time after his marriage with Agnes Gregg, William Cairns seems to have moved with his family to Parkmount, or to a house in Carnmoney.[1] After the termination of the third life in the Parkmount lease, Hugh Cairns obtained the renewal for ever thereof. His father died in 1775, the widow Agnes Gregg[2] surviving him, and dying in 1785. Both are interred at Carmoney Churchyard. By his second marriage William Cairns had issue,

K. NATHAN, born 1759. The name Nathan, hitherto unknown in the Cairns family, was inherited from the Greggs. He became a merchant in Dublin, where he married firstly, 20th June, 1778, Sarah Hutchinson, of the Parish of St. James, and secondly, 9th March, 1787, Margaret Keine, of the Parish of St. Mark.[3] He died at Parkmount, 1819, leaving issue, besides one daughter who died young,

1. DANIEL, born 1784. Became an officer in the 28th and afterwards in the 62nd Regiment, and died unmarried, at Jamaica, 1802.

---

1 In *Belfast News-Letter*, October 17, 1775, both William and his eldest son John appear in a list of subscribers to a testimonial to the Rev. Mathew Garnett, Vicar of Carnmoney. For my references to early Belfast newspapers and some of my information as to the Gregg family, I am indebted to Mr. Isaac Ward, who is probably the greatest living authority on old Belfast History.

2 The Gregg family settled in Belfast in the seventeenth century, and became prosperous in business. In 1700 three brothers, Nathan, Thomas, and John Gregg, were merchants in Belfast. Nathan died 1705, leaving sons John and Thomas, then under age. Thomas had an eldest son Nathan and other children, of whom probably William of Parkmount was one. Nathan mentions these children in his will, also his sisters Elizabeth, wife of James Smith of Belfast, maltster, and Agnes, wife of John Stevenson of Broadisland, Co. Antrim.

3 Book of Grants of Licenses, Dublin, in the Public Record Office, Dublin. In both these entries, Nathan is written Nathaniel, but undoubtedly Nathan was the name. In the first marriage Hutchinson is given as the wife's name, but in a family Bible the name is recorded Hutchins.

2. WILLIAM, of Parkmount, born 1789. He entered the army and became a captain in the 47th Regiment. He married when only seventeen, Rosanna, daughter of Hugh Johnston, merchant of Belfast. During his father's lifetime he lived at Rushpark, near Carrickfergus, and also had a house in Belfast, which stood on the grounds now occupied by the shop of Robinson & Cleaver, Ltd. After his father's death, he removed to Parkmount, which he shortly afterwards sold to John M'Neile, a banker in Belfast.[1] He eventually lived at Cultra, County Down. He married secondly Matilda, daughter of Francis Beggs of The Grange, Malahide, and dying at Cultra in 1844, left issue,

a. NATHAN DANIEL, born 1807. He married 1839, Mary, daughter of Thomas Miller of Preston, and dying in 1844, left issue,

1. WILLIAM M'NEILE, born 1843, late captain 43rd Regiment. Married 1873, Josephine Peray, daughter of

1 A son of Alexander M'Neile of Ballycastle, who was descended from Neill M'Neile, second son of Donald M'Neile, fourth son of Neill M'Neile of Macrihanish and Kintyre, of the M'Neiles of Gigha. Neill of Machrihanish, who came over to Ireland about 1625 with his relatives the MacNaughtens, obtained the lands of Killoquin, County Antrim, where he settled, marrying Rose Stewart of Garry, in that County. John M'Neile of Parkmount, having succeeded to a large fortune as heir of his uncle General M'Neile, purchased Parkmount and a considerable estate at Craigs, Co. Antrim, and became a private banker in Belfast, eventually forming, with others, what is now the Northern Bank. His grandson has recently sold Parkmount, which, as Belfast extended, became a most valuable property. The purchaser is a prominent merchant in Belfast, Sir Robert Anderson, Knt., D.L., who was High Sheriff of the City of Belfast in 1903.

the Rev. P. Bushe, Rector of Castletownshend, County Cork.

2. KATHERINE MARIA.

3. ROSANNA, wife of W. H. Coddington.

b. HUGH M'CALMONT, born 1819. Was educated at the Belfast Academy, then at the corner of Donegall Street and Academy Street, and afterwards at Trinity College, Dublin. His father at first intended that he should take Holy Orders,[1] but his own inclination, backed by the advice of his tutor, the Rev. George Wheeler, decided him to allow his son to enter the legal profession. He obtained his B.A. degree in 1838, and was called to the English Bar in 1844. Though shy and nervous as a speaker in the early part of his career, he advanced rapidly in his profession. He entered Parliament in 1852 as member for his native city; he was made a Q.C. in 1856, and in 1858, under Lord Derby's Administration, was appointed Solicitor General for England, and

1 The Cairnes family since the Reformation were all originally Presbyterians. The Earl's great-grandfather, or some of his family at least, seem to have conformed to the Established Church shortly after their removal to Parkmount. The writer recollects seeing in the *Belfast News-Letter*, date about 1790, an advertisement inserted by John Cairns of Parkmount, offering a reward for the recovery of his watch, which he had lost the previous Sunday between Parkmount and Carnmoney Church. As early as 1775 both John and his father William appear on a list of subscribers to a testimonial to the Vicar of Carnmoney. Benn, however, in his History of Belfast (Supplement) records that two of John's sisters were members of Rosemary Street Presbyterian Church.

SIR HUGH M'CALMONT CAIRNS, FIRST EARL CAIRNS,
and Lord Chancellor of England.

From a Photo.]

received the honour of knighthood. From this date he became a most conspicuous figure in public life, and enjoyed an enormous practice at the bar. His speeches in the House of Commons were masterpieces of oratory, their greatest characteristics being sound logic and remarkable lucidity. On the 14th of May, 1858, in a debate on Indian affairs, he made a remarkable speech of an hour's duration, which Disraeli, then leader of the House, described in his daily official letter to the Queen as "one of the two greatest speeches ever delivered in Parliament, which charmed everyone by its lucidity and controlled everyone by its logic."[1] In 1866 he became Attorney General, and later in the same year a Lord Justice of Appeal. At the same time he was offered a peerage, but declined it on the ground of want of sufficient means to properly support the dignity. In 1867, when the offer was renewed, he accepted it, and was created Baron Cairns of Garmoyle, County Antrim. On Disraeli becoming Prime Minister in 1868, and

[1] Martin, *Life of the Prince Consort*, IV., 411. Probably the most notable of all Lord Cairns's speeches was that made in Parliament in the debate which followed the surrender by Mr. Gladstone to the Boers after Majuba Hill.

again in 1874, he appointed Lord Cairns Lord Chancellor. In 1878 he was created Viscount Garmoyle and Earl Cairns, in the peerage of the United Kingdom. During Lord Beaconsfield's Administration there was no one whose advice he oftener sought and acted upon than that of Lord Cairns; and on his death, there was a strong feeling in favour of his assuming the leadership of the Conservative party, to which Lord Salisbury was eventually chosen. Cairns's great success in life was admittedly due entirely to his colossal ability. In public life it cannot be said that he was widely popular, but this was because he at all times scorned to play to the gallery, directing his actions rather in accordance with his strong and fearless sense of rectitude. To casual acquaintances he is said to have been cold and distant, but to his intimates he displayed a natural and unrestrained charm of manner which cemented some of the warmest friendships. In religion he was a Churchman of pronounced evangelical views, and his personal piety was most sincere. He frequently presided at Exeter Hall meetings, and was a zealous supporter of foreign missions, of Dr. Barnardo's homes, and of the Young Men's Christian Association. He married in 1856, Mary Harriet, daughter of John M'Neile of Parkmount,[1] who survives him, and dying in 1885, left issue,

1. Arthur William, second Earl Cairns, born 1861. He married in 1887, Olivia Elizabeth, daughter of Alexander Augustus Berens, and dying in 1890, left issue,

aa. Louisa Rosemary Kathleen Virginia.

2. Herbert John, third Earl Cairns, born 1863, and died unmarried in 1904.

3. Wilfred Dallas, fourth and present Earl, born 1865. Married in 1894, Olive, daughter of the late John Patteson Cobbold, M.P., by whom he has issue,

aa. Hester Margaret.

bb. Ursula Helen.

cc. Sheila Mary.

4. Douglas Halyburton, born 1867.

5. Lilias Charlotte, who married the Rev. H. Nevile Sherbrooke, and died in 1889, leaving issue.

[1] See above, p. 243, note. John M'Neile of Parkmount married in 1823, Charlotte Lavinia, daughter of Lieutenant-General Sir Thomas Dallas, by whom he had issue—1, the late Henry Hugh M'Neile, D.L., of Parkmount; 2, Alexander John M'Neile; and 3, the present Dowager Countess Cairns, now of Lindisfarne, Bournemouth.

6. KATHLEEN MARY, wife of the Rev. Edward Francis Whately Eliot, vicar of All Souls, Eastbourne.

c. WILLIAM WELLINGTON, born 1828. Entered the Indian Civil Service (Ceylon) 1852, and eventually became Governor of the Straits Settlements (1867). He afterwards held successively the Governorships of St. Kitts, British Honduras, Trinidad, Queensland, and South Australia, which he resigned in 1877. He was nominated C.M.G. 1874, and K.C.M.G. 1877. Sir William Cairns died, unmarried, in 1888.

d. ANNA MARIA, died unmarried 1890.

e. MARGARET, wife of Robert M'Calmont, of Galton Park, Reigate. She died without issue in 1889.

f. ELIZABETH, died unmarried 1845.

g. SARAH ROSANNA, died young.

h. ROSANNA, died young.

j. JANE MONTGOMERY, wife of William Crawford of Dalchoolin, County Down. She died 1899, without issue.

k. MATILDA, wife of the Rev. De la Cherois Crommelin, by whom she has issue,

MAUDE, wife of Pelham Greenhill, by whom she has issue.

l. ROSANNA, married James M'Donnell of Kilsharvan, County Meath,[1] and Murlough,

[1] See "The Clan Donald," by M'Donalds, Vol. III., p. 407.

County Antrim, and dying in 1872, left issue two daughters, Helen and Margaret.

m. and *n.* HELEN and FRANCES, died unmarried.

Of the grandsons of William Cairns the original holder of Magheraconluce, we have mentioned above John Cairns. He was born at Annahilt in 1744. He settled near Newtownards, where he took a farm, and in 1790, on the sale of the Cherryvalley property near Comber, he secured a portion of it and settled there. Cherryvalley had been the home for several centuries of the Gillespie family, of whom the last representative was the celebrated Major-General Sir Rollo Gillespie.[1] John Cairns of Cherryvalley died in 1824, leaving issue,

JOHN, of Cherryvalley. Married Mary A. Robinson, and dying in 1886, left issue,

A. JOHN (The Rev.), now minister of Ballina, of whom later

B. THOMAS ROBINSON (The Rev., D.D.). Born 1845. He entered the Irish Presbyterian ministry, afterwards going to Australia. He is now minister in Ballarat, and (1906) Moderator of the General Assembly of the Presbyterian Church of Victoria, and an honorary D.D. of the Assembly's College (Ireland). He married Alice Hurst.

C. JOSEPH, born 1852. He married Helen

[1] The family of Gillespie, originally M'Gillespicks, are said to have been a branch of the Scottish clan Donald, descended from a Gillespick MacDonald, who settled in Co. Down at a very early date. There were also Gillespies of pure Irish origin, however; the name means "Servant of the Bishop" in Gaelic.

Hackett, by whom he has issue. He now resides near Saintfield, Co. Down.

D. JAMES, now of Cherryvalley, born 1857.

E. HUGH, now of Cherryvalley, born 1861.

F. EDWARD, born 1864, a Physician now practising in Belfast. He married Elizabeth Atchison, and has issue.

The Rev. John Cairns, born 1838, the head of this branch of the family, was minister of Castlebar 1863 to 1879, and is now minister of Ballina. He married M. Jane Steen, and has issue,

A. JOHN E. (The Rev., M.A.) minister of Castlebar, born 1666. He married Edith Robertson, and has issue—

1. STANLEY.
2. ALBERT.

B. THOMAS, a Physician, now practising at Northampton, born 1867.

C. JOSEPH S., a Civil Engineer, and Assistant County Surveyor of County Mayo, born 1871.

D. FREDERICK JAMES, a Physician, now practising in Cardiff, born 1876.

E. ALBERT E., now residing in Dublin, born 1877.

F. WILLIAM B., born 1879.

G. FRANCIS L., born 1884, and four daughters.

CAIRNS OF DUNDRENNAN ABBEY. The earliest record of this family which we have been able to find is in the Parish Register of Kirkcudbright, where under date 14th March, 1766, is recorded the marriage of "Joseph M'Whan, Merchant, and Peggie Cairns." Their only child Stewart

M'Whan, daughter of Joseph M'Whan and Margaret Cairns, was baptised 21st July, 1769. Her marriage is entered 18th October, 1790, "Adam Maitland to Stewart M'Whan." In 1789, Margaret's brother Thomas Cairns acquired by purchase the Abbey and estate of Dundrennan, of which he had confirmation by a charter under the Great Seal, 3rd February, 1789. He subsequently purchased from Mrs. Hamilton, daughter and heiress of Edward Cairns, the estate of Girstingwood.[1] He is described in the Great Seal Charter as "Ex Urbe Londini, Armiger." That he was a native of Kirkcudbright there can be no doubt, and that he was a cadet of the Orchardton family is equally probable. Unfortunately the Kirkcudbright parish registers do not carry us back much earlier than the date of his sister's marriage. The christian name Thomas was unusual in the Galloway family, the only other instance of it that we have met with being Thomas Cairns, merchant and indweller in Dumfries, who in 1710 put Robert Brown to the horn for a debt of 1,000 marks.[2]

Thomas Cairns of Dundrennan and Girstingwood died in 1800 leaving as his sole heiress his niece Stewart M'Whan, wife of Adam Maitland. In the instrument of Sasine he is described as "of Dundrennan, merchant in London." Adam Maitland is designated as of Castle-creavy. He was decended from the Rev. William Maitland, a distinguished Scottish ecclesiastic, who flourished in the

[1] See above, p. 196 The Girstingwood papers which are preserved at Craiglaw include several letters from Thomas Cairns to Mrs. Hamilton relative to the purchase of Girstingwood. They throw no light upon the origin of Thomas Cairns; they are merely business letters, not as if written to a relation.

[2] Inhibitions, Kirkcudbrightshire, Vol. X. p. 204.—Register House.

latter portion of the seventeenth century, and came of a family long settled in Galloway who claimed kinship with the Maitlands of Lauderdale. By his wife, the heiress of Dundrennan, he had issue,

A. THOMAS, born 1792. He entered the legal profession and became Solicitor General in 1840. He represented his native county in Parliament 1845 to 1850, when he was created a Lord of Session with the title of Lord Dundrennan, but died the following year. He married in 1815, Isabella Graham, daughter of James McDowall of Garthland, by whom he left issue,

1. STUART CAIRNS, born 1816. He married in 1841, Margaret Shippen, daughter of Dominick Lynch of Newborough, County Galway, and dying in 1861, left issue.

a. DAVID, now of Dundrennan Abbey and Cumpstone, born 1848. Served as a Lieutenant 74th Highlanders; is a D.L. for Kirkcudbright. He married, 1872, Elinor Frances, daughter of the late Thomas Gray Scott, W.S., and has issue,

1. STUART CAIRNS, born 1873.

2. CLAUDE ARCHIBALD SCOTT, born 1874.

3. GRAHAM M'DOWALL, born 1879, and two daughters.

b. THOMAS, born 1854. Died 1906; and five daughters.

2. George Ferguson, of Hermand. Died 1876.
3. Adam, an adjutant in the 79th Highlanders, died before Sebastopol, 1854.
4. James William, born 1829. Died 1860; and three daughters,

B. Joseph, born 1801. Died 1864.

C. John, born 1807. Died 1835.

D. Edward Francis, born 1809. Entered the legal profession, and like his brother Lord Dundrennan attained great eminence therein. He became Solicitor General for Scotland in 1855, which office he retained until 1862, when he was created a Lord of Session with the title of Lord Barcaple. He died s.p. in 1870.

CHAPTER X.

Armorial Bearings, Crests, and Seals.

THE Cairnes family bore arms from very early times. Sir David Lindsay, who was Lyon King of Arms from 1552 to 1555; and who was one of the greatest authorities on Scottish heraldry in any age, has in his armorial MSS. left a most valuable stock of information compiled by him from the sources at that time at his disposal, regarding the arms of all the Scottish families entitled to bear them. As the result of his investigations as to the Cairnes family of that ilk he records that their arms were "Gules, three martlets or."[1]

It will be borne in mind that the family of Cairnes of that ilk became extinct in the chief male line in the person of Duncan de Carnys who died about 1390, so that we presume Sir David Lyndsay had evidence that the family bore these arms at least as early as the fourteenth century. Sir George Crichton of Carnys, Earl of Caithness, grandson and heir of Duncan, and his descendants quartered the arms of Cairnis 2nd and 3rd with those of Crichton 1st and 4th,[2] though a later reference describes the tincture of the field as "sable," instead of "gules." In all other records referring to the arms, the field is described as "gules," so it seems apparent that "sable' is

1 Armorial MSS. of Sir David Lindsay, Advocates' Library, Edinburgh.

2 Nisbet, Vol. I., p. 279.

SEAL OF WILLIAM DE CAIRNIS
VICAR OF GLAMMIS
1455

THE SEAL OF JOHN DE CARNYS
BAILIE OF EDINBURGH
1482

THE SEAL OF BARTHOLEMEW DE CARNYS
BAILIE OF EDINBURGH
1476

SEAL OF SIR ALEXANDER CAIRNES BART.

THE SEAL OF ROBERT CAIRNES OF KILLYFADDY 1669
ALSO OF DAVID CAIRNES
OF LONDONDERRY AND KNOCKMANY

CARVED STONE AT PILMUIR EARLY 16TH CENTURY

CARVED STONE ABOVE THE DOORWAY OF PILMUIR HOUSE
DISPLAYING THE ARMS OF WILLIAM CAIRNS
IMPALED WITH THOSE OF HIS WIFE AGNES BROWN
1624

here incorrect, especially as further on the family of Crichton of Strathurd, direct representatives of the Crichtons of Carnys, are recorded by Lindsay to have quartered the Cairnes arms 2nd and 3rd with the field "gules."

The earliest Seal of a Cairnes with which we have met is that of William de Cairnis, Vicar of Glammys (Forfar). It is attached to an indenture between Walter and Thomas Ogilvy,[1] dated 25th September, 1455. It was a common custom for an ecclesiastic to unite on his seal his personal arms with those of his benefice, and the seal of the Vicar of Glammys is a pleasing example of this usage. The arms of Cairns are displayed on a broad chief on the shield, while the base, supporters, and crest we presume to be those of the parish or church of Glammys, namely, "a mullet of six points; supporters, two lions sejant gardant; crest, a demi figure of the Virgin with child."

Alexander de Carnys, Provost of Lincluden, had a seal, and in his important position, must have frequently used it, but unfortunately no impression of it can now be found. A curious reference to the provost's seal however occurs in the Register of the Great Seal of date 1420.[2] It reads "This indenture, made at Lauchmabane, ye third day of Feveryhair, MCDXX, betuyx a hee and a mychty Lord Schir Archebald, Eryle of Douglas on ye ta part, and his Squyar Michel Ramsay on tother part . . . . and the said Michel, for he had na sele of hys awn, he procuryt the sele of Mayster Alexander of Carnys, Provost of Lyncludene, to be set to ye part . . . ."

---

[1] This document remains in possession of the present head of this family, Sir Reginald Ogilvy of Baldovan, who kindly facilitated the reproduction of the seal in this work.

[2] Reg. Mag. Sigilli., vol. II., No. 143.

The gravestone of the provost, illustrated in a former chapter, has much interest from a heraldic point of view. Though neither the arms of the college, nor of the provost, are displayed, there is, pendent from a tree, a plain shield, crossed by an uncharged fesse. The latter is of the width usually allowed for fesse bars intended to bear charges, but neither the shield nor the fesse show any trace of ever having been inscribed. The tree however, has an important significance. From a very early period the Cairneses adopted with the several crests borne by various branches of the family, the motto "effloresco." In heraldry, a growing tree is often regarded as an emblem of prosperity, and is associated with the verb "effloresco."[1] On the provost's tomb, while the inscription round the margin has been deeply and distinctly cut, the design in the centre is merely outlined, as if unfinished, and left for completion on the advent of someone versed in heraldic inscriptions. If this theory be correct, the heraldic sculptor came not, and the arms of the college on the shield, and of the provost on the fess-bar were never cut, the outlines and evident intention only being apparent. The inference that a tree was originally associated with the arms and motto of the Cairnses, as suggested by the provost's tombstone, has some support in the seals of Robert Cairnes of Killyfaddy and David Cairnes of Londonderry. The crest of the original Cults family was a "martlet proper," but after the building of the round tower of Orchardton, we usually find the martlet perched on a round embattled tower. This

[1] *E.g.* The arms of Glasgow, a tree efflorescens, with the motto "Let Glasgow *Flourish* by the preaching of the Word."

"Effloresco" "Effloresco"

CRESTS OF THE CAIRNES FAMILY OF ORCHARDTON, MONAGHAN AND TYRONE

"Effloresco"

CREST OF CAIRNS OF PILMUIR.

"Semper fidelis" "Pro deo rege et patria"

CRESTS OF CAIRNS OF TORR.

"Effloresco"

CREST OF THE EARLS CAIRNS

addition to the crest was not however always borne, and in the seals of Robert and David Cairnes we find the martlet perched on the bough of a tree, thus again associating a tree with the shield and crest, over two hundred years after the date of the tombstone.[1]

The Galloway family of Cairnes, and their representatives, the Ulster Cairneses, all enclosed the shield within a bordure, as a mark of difference from the parent family of Mid Lothian from which they sprung. The several branches of the Galloway family for distinction, differenced in the tinctures of the field and charges of their shields, while the Pilmuir family adopted the fleur de lys as a mark of cadency, implying descent from a sixth son of the main stem. Thus the recorded arms of the main branches of Cairnes are as follows:—

CARNYS OF THAT ILK. "Gules, three martlets or."[2]—(1).

CAIRNIS OF CULTS, AND LATER OF ORCHARDTON. "Gules, three martlets argent, within a bordure or."[3]—(2). Crest, "on a round tower embattled, a martlet, ppr.," or "perched on the bough of a tree, a martlet, ppr." Motto, "Effloresco."

CAIRNES OF CULTS, AND LATER OF MONAGHAN. "Argent, three martlets gules, within a bordure or."—(3). Crest and motto as Orchardton.[4]

CAIRNES OF KILLYFADDY. "Gules, three martlets

[1] It is curious to find also in the arms of Glasgow a martlet perched on the topmost branch of the tree. The little etching on the title page of this work shows probably the original manner in which the arms and crest of the Cairnes family were displayed.

[2] MS. of Sir David Lindsay.

[3] Lyon Registers.

[4] Register in Ulster Office. It will be noted that this shield and No. 5 are incorrect heraldry.

within a bordure or."—(4)[1]. Crest, "a martlet, perched on the bough of a tree ppr.," or, "a martlet on a round tower embattled ppr." Motto, "Effloresco."

CAIRNS OF PILMUIR. "Gules, three martlets argent, a fleur de lys of the last, for difference,"—(6). Crest, "a cinquefoil proper;" motto, "Effloresco."

CAIRNS OF KIPP. "Argent, three martlets gules, within a bordure azure."—(7).

THE EARLS CAIRNS. "Gules, three martlets argent, on a bordure of the last, as many trefoils slipped vert."—(8). Crest, "a martlet argent, charged on the breast with a trefoil slipped vert." Motto, "Effloresco."[2]

CAIRNS OF TORR. "Argent, three martlets gules, within a bordure or."—(5). Crest, "a lion rampant ppr." Motto, "pro Deo, Rege, et Patria,"[3] or, "a stag's head erased ppr.; between the attires, a cross crosslett fitchée or."[4] Motto "Semper Fidelis."

Attached to one of the St. Clair charters dated 1460 is the seal of John Cairnis, bailie of Edinburgh This seal displays the three martlets 2 and 1, with a mullet on the chief point, the latter suggesting descent from a third son of the head of the family. It is probable this John Cairnis, whose name appears several times in the register of the great seal as a witness to charters, was a grandson of

1 In the Ulster Office no distinction between the arms of the Monaghan and Tyrone families is recorded. In the family papers I find in the seal of John Elliot Cairnes, who died 1802, the tinctures as above. This may, however, have been more by accident than design.

2 Confirmation of arms, Ulster Office, 1878.

3 Seal of Edward Cairns of Tor about 1780.

4 Torr Family Papers.

ARMS OF THE FAMILY OF CAIRNES OF THAT ILK AND ITS BRANCHES.

1. CARNYS OF THAT ILK

2. CAIRNIS OF CULTS AND LATER OF ORCHARDTON

3. CAIRNES OF CULTS AND LATER OF MONAGHAN

4. CAIRNES OF KILLYFADDY SAVILLE LODGE AND STAMEEN

5. CAIRNS OF TORR

6. CAIRNS OF PILMUIR

7. CAIRNS OF KIPP

8. THE EARLS CAIRNS

9. CAIRNIS (FORMAN ARMORIAL)

10. CAIRNIS (FORMAN ARMORIAL)

William de Carnys the constable of Edinburgh Castle, and therefore a cousin of Orchardton.

The seal of Bartholomew de Carnys appears attached to a document in the Register House, dated 1472. It bears the three martlets 2 and 1, and is charged with a crescent in the fesse point, and a label of three points in chief, from which it may be inferred with much probability that Bartholomew was an eldest son, his father being then alive, and that he descended from a second son of the head of the family. It is probable that he was a great grandson of John de Carnys the elder custumar of Linlithgow.[1]

At Pilmuir are two very interesting heraldic carvings, one above the doorway in the turret displaying the arms of William Cairns impaled with those of his wife's family, Broun, of date 1624. Their son Richard, officially registered his arms in 1672 without those of Broun quartered, so we may infer that his mother was not an heiress. In the register of Richard Cairns's arms, the fleur de lys for difference, crest and motto are also recorded.[2]

The other stone is evidently much older, probably fifteenth or sixteenth century. It shows the Cairns arms, with the initials I.C. and M.V. Unfortunately it is undated. It was most probably carved by an ancestor of William, the builder of Pilmuir House, as an adornment to the family residence which existed long before. A striking feature about this stone is that the position of the martlets

---

1 I am indebted to Mr. MacDonald, the Carrick Persuivant of Scotland, for enabling me to reproduce the seals of John and Bartholomew Cairns.

2 See above p. 258.

is reversed to 1 and 2, the only instance we have met with where this arrangement occurs. Round the stone is a carved border; whether this is merely for ornamentation or is a heraldic bordure for difference we cannot say. Both stones are illustrated here.

The seals of Robert Cairnes of Killyfaddy, 1669, Sir Alexander Cairnes of Monaghan, and David Cairnes of Londonderry, already referred to, are also reproduced. The second only displays the round tower in the crest, and has the badge of a baronet in the fesse point of the shield. From Sir Alexander's crest, the Corporation of Monaghan chose the design for their official arms. In some early instances of the use of the arms of Monaghan the baronet's badge is wrongly included in the shield; as Sir Alexander was created a baronet in 1708, and the baronetcy became extinct upon the death of Sir Henry in 1743, it is probable that the arms of the Corporation were first designed between these dates.[1]

In the armorial MS.[2] of Sir Robert Forman, who was Lyon King of Arms, 1555-1567, are emblazoned several coats of arms of Cairnes, but unfortunately the emblazonments only are given with the surnames, but without particulars as to the individuals to whom they are recorded. One of these is "gules, three martlets argent, quartering azure, three leopards' faces or." (14). The tinctures of the field and charges of the first and 4th quarterings suggest the Orchardton family, though the absence of the bordure render this uncertain. The arms displayed 2nd and 3rd are borne by the English families of Barnes and Moore, but the family of

[1] See Shield No. 18.

[2] Court of the Lord Lyon, Register House, Edinburgh.

M'Ghie of Kirkcudbright bore arms with the same charges on a field sable. It is quite possible this shield is that of William Cairnis the elder, of Orchardton, and that his father, John Cairnis the first of Orchardton, whose wife does not appear to have been mentioned in any of the records, married an heiress of a cadet family of the M'Ghies. In the Forman armorial, though emblazoned on the versos of pages, and therefore apparently added at a date subsequent to that of the MS., are recorded two other Cairnes coats of arms, the identity of whose owners we cannot trace. They are, "or, three martlets azure, on a chief gules, an acorn between two mullets of the field," (9) and, "or, three martlets azure within a bordure engrailed gules." (10).

Thomas Cairns, merchant of London, a native of Kirkcudbright, who purchased the Dundrennan Abbey estate in 1789 was undoubtedly a cadet of the family of Orchardton and Cults; he does not however appear by the records to have borne arms. The Maitland family, who succeeded to this property as his heirs, do not quarter the arms of Cairns, but in lieu thereof quarter a shield displaying a representation of Dundrennan Abbey. The Cairnses, first as tenants,[1] and after the reformation, as proprietors of a considerable portion of the Abbey lands of Dundrennan,[2] and finally as the purchasers of abbey and lands,[3] certainly could claim an association with Dundrennan of very respectable antiquity; but purely from a heraldic point of view, one is inclined to wonder why the armorial artist of

[1] Dating from at least 1530.

[2] See Chap. VIII.

[3] See Chap. IX.

the nineteenth century who was responsible for the illustration of Dundrennan Abbey as a heraldic design, ignored the venerable martlets of Cairns.

It will be noted in shields Nos. 3 and 4 that the families of Monaghan and Tyrone are shown with a difference in the tinctures of their shields. No. 3 only appears in the Register of the Ulster Office as applicable to both families. No. 4 is taken from a beautifully cut seal of very considerable antiquity, in the possession of the Tyrone family. As they more nearly than any other family are the representatives of the Orchardton family,[1] it seems appropriate that they should bear the arms of Orchardton. It may be intentional that the tincture of the martlets is *or* while the Lyon Register shows the martlets in the Orchardton arms *argent*, to record a difference in consequence of the family descending through a female heir.

Modern Quartering. The Tyrone family of Cairnes in the male line is represented by Frederick Cairnes of Killester House, Raheny, County Dublin, as the lineal head of the family through the ultimate failure of the male issue of Lieutenant-Colonel John Elliot Cairnes, K.H., whose son, Lieutenant William John Drew Cairnes, the head of the family, died in 1857. Frederick Cairnes is the heir male of his grandfather William Cairnes of Stameen, next eldest brother of Lieutenant-Colonel Cairnes. His arms

[1] They are the actual representatives in name and seniority of descent in almost unbroken male line. The present head of this family is seventeenth in direct descent from William of Carnys and Whitburn, and only once has the descent passed through a female heir, whose heir assumed her name and arms. The Rossmore family of course descend from the senior or Monaghan branch, but through two female heirs, neither of whose descendants assumed the name.

ARMS OF FAMILIES CONNECTED WITH THE FAMILY OF CAIRNES BY MARRIAGE WITH HEIRESSES, &c.

11. WESTENRA

12. COLONEL MURRAY

13. ELLIOT OF STOBBS

14. CARNYS (ARMORIAL MS OF SIR DAVID LYNDSAY) PROBABLY THE ARMS OF WILLIAM THE ELDER OF ORCHARDTON

15. ARMS OF SIR GEO. CRICHTON EARL OF CAITHNESS AND OF THE CRICHTONS OF STRATHURD

16. MOORE OF GLANDERSTOUN

17. LAWLOR OF KERRY

18. ARMS OF THE CORPORATION OF MONAGHAN

19. MONTGOMERY OF BALLYGOWAN
1ST & 4TH MONTGOMERY OF HESSILHEAD
2ND & 3RD HAMILTON OF CARNESURE

are quarterly "1st Cairnes,[1] 2nd Moore,[2] 3rd Montgomery of Hassilhead, quartering Hamilton,[3] 4th Elliot."[4]

Several families are entitled to quarter the arms of Cairnes through marriages with heiresses of the family. These are;—The representative of the Crichtons of Strathurd;[5]—The representative of Sir Alexander Kirkpatrick sometime of Orchardton;[6]—The representative of the Maxwells of Drumcoltran;[7]—The Westenras, who quarter "1st and 4th Westenra,[8] 2nd Murray,[9] 3rd Cairnes."[10] The head of this family, Lord Rossmore, who married the heiress of the late Richard Christopher Naylor of Hooton Hall, Chester, and Kelmarsh Hall, Northamptonshire, bears also on a shield of pretence the arms of Naylor;[11]—The representatives of the co-heiresses of Captain William Cairnes;[12]—The co-heiresses of Lieutenant-Colonel John Elliot Cairnes, K.H., Katherine who married John Hilliard Lawlor,[13] and her sister Annie;—Dorothy Elliot Cairnes, who as sole heiress of the late Captain William Elliot Cairnes, bears, on a lozenge, the arms of Cairnes as above for the head of the family.

---

1 Shield No. 4.
2 See Appendix IV. and Shield No. 16.
3 See Appendix III. and Shield No. 19.
4 See Appendix I. and Shield No. 13.
5 See pp. 15, 16.
6 See p. 180.
7 See p. 181.
8 Shield No. 11.
9 Shield No. 12.
10 Shield No. 3.
11 See Burke's Landed Gentry under Naylor, Leyland, or Naylor-Leyland.
12 See p. 116.
13 See Appendix V. and Shield No. 17.

APPENDIX I.

Elliot Family.[1]

THIS branch of the old Scottish border family, of Elliot appears to have come over to Ulster at or shortly after the Plantation. According to old family tradition, the founder was a cadet of the house of Stobbs, County Roxburgh. We have several old family papers from which the pedigree is clearly traceable back to William Elliot; he married Margaret, sister of David Cairnes[2] of Londonderry. His son was also named William, and was designated "of Straghan," in the County Fermanagh, in 1689. He appears along with Thomas Elliot of Galoon and George Elliot of Tully, also in Fermanagh, in the list of Protestant gentry attainted by King James's Parliament. In the plantation papers we can only find record of two planters of the name of Elliot. These are Daniel Elliot, who obtained the lands of Tulla-

[1] The author regrets very much that he has not had the time or opportunity to make researches in the Record Office in Dublin or the Register House in Edinburgh, which might throw light upon the identity of the original founder of this branch of the Scottish family of Elliot. He hopes at some future time to investigate the subject more fully. The family tradition that the founder was a cadet of the family of Stobbs in the County of Roxburgh is of old standing. The Rev. John Graham, who enjoyed the acquaintance of the representatives of the Irish Elliots a hundred years ago, in a brief note on the family, in his *Ireland Preserved*, refers to both William Elliot, who was attainted in 1689, and Major William Cairnes, who died in 1789, as "cousins german" of Sir Gilbert (*sic*) Elliot, Lord Heathfield, the hero of the siege of Gibraltar in 1787. Allowing for a certain vagueness in the meaning of the term "cousin german," and even overlooking the fact that Lord Heathfield's Christian name was not Gilbert, but George Augustus, the fact remains that the family tradition that the Irish Elliots were a branch of the Elliots of Stobbs is of considerable antiquity. The tradition that the Irish Elliots and the Elliots of Stobbs were of the same stock has confirmation in the fact that the arms of the Irish Elliots, as recorded in the Ulster Office, are practically those of Stobbs, with an alteration of the tinctures as difference. Elliot of Stobbs in the Lyon Register, Edinburgh, bore "gules, on a bend engrailed or, a baton az" (see shield No. 13, Chapter X.). The several cadets of the house of Stobbs bear as follows:—Lord Heathfield, "Gules on bend arg., a baton az, with an augmentation in chief, commemorative of the siege of Gibraltar"; the Earls of Minto quarter "Gules, within a bordure vair, on a bend engrailed or, a baton azure"; Elliot of Fermanagh, "Argent, on a bend gules, a baton or." (Ulster Office).

[2] David Cairnes's uncle Robert Cairnes of Killyfaddy and Finesker married Mary Elliot, an aunt of William Elliot.

coltier and the precincts thereof, in the County Fermanagh, part of the extensive grant originally allotted to Sir Robert Hamilton[1]; and Sir John Elliot, Knight, Baron of Exchequor, who was allotted the small portion known as the Manor of Kilcronehan, County Cavan. We have no evidence to show whether a relationship existed between Sir John Elliot of Kilcronehan and Daniel of Tullacoltier, nor can we say positively whether the three Elliots in the list of attainders were the descendants of either. It seems probable, however, that they were great grandsons of Daniel Elliot of Tullacoltier, from the fact that some sixty-five years later than his time they held property not far removed from his, and that there does not appear to be record of any other Elliot among the planters in County Fermanagh.

Of the three attainted Elliots, we have further record only of William Elliot of Straghan, near Lisnaskea. In the list of attainders already referred to, he is described as a Lieutenant in the army. He took a prominent part in the defence of Ballyshannon against the forces of James II., and as a captain, fought under King William III. at the battle of the Boyne. He married his first cousin Mary, daughter of William Cairnes of Killyfaddy, and sister of the "Old Captain" William Cairnes (referred to on pp. 112, 113, 156). Of the issue of this marriage we have record only of the eldest son William Elliot of Cloneblagh, who married Elizabeth daughter of Hugh Montgomery of Lisduff, County Longford. (See Appendix II., and for their issue, p. 112 *sqq.*). Lieutenant William Elliot, who married Mary Cairnes, had two sisters, Mary, wife of her cousin Doctor Thomas Cairnes, and Lettice, wife of the Rev. Humphrey Thompson of Monaghan.

The early family burying place of the Elliots of Fermanagh was in the old churchyard of Augherlurcher.[2] Some tombstones recording the family were extant in 1825, but the author has not had the opportunity of ascertaining if any still remain.

---

[1] Inquisitions, Fermanagh, 1623.

[2] Also known as Archerlurcher or Augherlaugher.

APPENDIX II.

MONTGOMERIES OF LISDUFF.

THE first of this family of whom we have been able to find record is Hugh Montgomery, who came over to Ireland with his kinsman Sir Hugh Montgomery of Braidstain, first Viscount Ards.[1] We do not know what was the relationship between Hugh, the ancestor of the Lisduff family, and the laird of Braidstain, but it was probably near, as we find it recorded that he frequently visited the Viscount. Hugh Montgomery held a commission as Colonel in the army of Prince Maurice of Nassau, upon whose death in 1626 he returned home, marrying in the same year. His eldest son was

HUGH MONTGOMERY. He, with his father, fought on the Royalist side in the wars in Ireland. On the execution of Charles I., both father and son migrated to the Continent. The son served under the Duke of Ormonde, and after the Restoration returned to Ireland, where in consideration of his own and his father's services he was granted the lands of Lisduff in the County of Longford. He frequently visited his kinsmen in County Down, where, as there were several Montgomeries of the name Hugh, he was distinguished by the name of *Grave Maurice*, because of his father's service under a Prince of Orange known as "Maurice the Grave." Hugh Montgomery the grantee of Lisduff, married, about 1680, a lady in the household of William Montgomery of Rosemount ("my deare wives gentlewoman") where was born his eldest son,

JAMES MONTGOMERY of Lisduff. Besides James, were three sons and three daughters, of whom ELIZABETH married in 1700 William Elliot of Cloneblagh (referred to above, p. 112, and Appendix I.)

---

[1] Our information of the Lisduff Montgomeries is chiefly extracted from the manuscripts of William Montgomery of Rosemont (edited by the Rev. Geo. Hill), and from pedigree recorded in the Ulster Office, Dublin.

The Lisduff property, consisting of about 600 acres, is situated some three miles from the town of Longford. It became afterwards known as Cartron Garrow. The issue of James Montgomery became extinct in the male line, the last heiress marrying a Mr. Nesbit of Drumconnor, in the County of Monaghan, "who held a highly respectable position, driving his carriage when there were not five carriages in the county;" by him she left issue two daughters, co-heiresses, who married respectively, a Mr. Macauley of Dublin and the Rev. William Henry of Tassagh, County Armagh. The Henry family for a time owned a portion of the Lisduff estate, which until recently, however, seems to have belonged to a Mr. Courteny, also a descendant of the original grantee Hugh Montgomery.[1]

[1] From the MS. notes of R. Cunningham, Esq., of Castle Cooley, County Londonderry, quoted in *The Montgomery Manuscripts*, edited by the Rev. George Hill, pp. 390-391, *q.v.*

APPENDIX III.

The Montgomeries of Ballymagowan.

THE first member of this family to settle in Ireland was the Rev. James Montgomery. His father had been minister of Montrose in the early years of the seventeenth century. We do not know his christian name, but he was one of the nine sons of the laird of Ha'toune or Hall Town in the parish of Newbyle, Forfarshire. This family was a branch of the Montgomeries of Hassilhead in Ayrshire, who descended from Hugh, third son of Alexander Montgomery of Eglinton, who died 1452. The Braidstain Montgomeries descended from a second son, and the Earls of Eglinton from the eldest son of this Alexander.

The Rev. James Montgomery married in 1633, Elizabeth, widow of the Rev. David Magill, minister in Greyabbey, daughter of John Lindsay of the Dundrod family, by Isabel Shaw of Greenock, sister of the first Viscount Montgomery's wife. The Rev. James Montgomery's wife was therefore a first cousin of the second Viscount. He had an elder brother Samuel, a Major in the army, who died unmarried "in Portaferry and is buryd wher Patt Savadge, Esqr has now his seat in ye church; over which there is an hollow place made in the wall, wherein it was designed his arms and epitaph should have been put."[1]

---

[1] *MS. of William Montgomery of Rosemount.* See *The Montgomery Manuscripts*, edited by the Rev. George Hill, pp. 359 and 365—376. It is a pity these arms were not inscribed here, as much confusion has arisen as to the proper emblazonment. Paterson, in *Parishes and Families of Aryshire*, vol. I., p. 292, quotes the *Pont MS.*, in the Advocates' Library, which states that the arms of the Montgomeries of Hassilhead were "azure, two lances of tournament proper between three fleur de lys or, and in the chief point an annulet or, stoned azure, with an indention on the side of the shield on the dexter side." The absurdity of this emblazonment is manifest. Burke's *Landed Gentry* under Montgomeries of Killee, who are the present representatives of these Montgomeries, confuses the arms with those of Eglinton, to which they have no real claim. The arms of Montgomery of Hassilhead in the MS. Register of the Lord Lyon in Scotland are, "Gules, two spears in saltire between three fleur de lys in chief and flanks, and as many annulets in base, or, stoned azure"—(See shield

The Rev. James Montgomery married secondly a daughter of Hugh Montgomery, seneschal to the first Viscount Montgomery, and died in 1647. His widow married secondly one Smith, who treated his younger stepchildren very badly. On the death of his wife he turned them from his house. We do not know their names or ultimate history. By his first wife, the Rev. James Montgomery had issue,

HUGH MONTGOMERY OF BALLYMAGOWAN. He was born in the year 1635. He remained for some years with his kinsman William Montgomery of Rosemount, with whom he travelled a good deal in England and on the Continent. In 1660 he entered the household of the first Earl of Mount Alexander, his second cousin, "being made his Lds Privy Purs filler; his Cashiere and Paymaster to all his servts, shop-keepers, sadlers, harness makers, tailors, &c., his master of his Escoury, giving him authority over all his men servts to command and correct them, committing the hireing and choice of them unto him also . . . . he was deservedly our Lds Favorit, whence he obtained the designation of my Lords Hugh." He became estate agent and seneschal to the second Earl of Mount Alexander. After the Restoration of Charles II., his father's arrears of pay as chaplain to a regiment, and his own services in the army some years before, were rewarded by debentures, in satisfaction of which he obtained some valuable lands, including Ballymagowan and Ballylimp. About this time also he married Jane, daughter and eventual co-heiress of Hans Hamilton of Carnesure,[1] first cousin of Viscount Clanneboye. In 1671 he went to live at Ballymagowan, which about this time began to be known as at present

No. 19. I regret extremely that through my own mistake the field of the Montgomery quartering in this shield appears azure instead of gules. The original proof-sheet of this illustration showed the shield as described in the *Pont MS.* Sir James Balfour Paul, however, very kindly went into this matter and found the Hassilhead emblazonment in the Lyon Register, a copy of which he sent me. In altering the shield on the lithographic stones I stupidly overlooked having this colour eliminated from the blue stone and placed on the red. I only found out my mistake after all the copies had been printed). It does not appear that any of the Ballymagowan family ever registered their arms in the Ulster Office; but the correct emblazonment would have been as above for Hassilhead, *with a difference*, as not representing the headship of the family.

[1] See shield of arms No. 19 in Chap. X., quartering the arms of Hamilton with Montgomery.

by the name of Springvale. His wife died in 1689. Hugh Montgomery died in 1707; both are buried at Greyabbey, where several of his family are also interred. He left issue,

A. HANS MONTGOMERY, of whom later.

B. HUGH MONTGOMERY, "a propper tall gent^{l}, who served in ye army during the warr ag^{t} ye Irish, and then in ye Duke of Ormond's troop of horse Guards in Flanders and England. He is a well bred grave man, of good reading and discours, free he is of all camp or guarison vices. He is now (A^{O} 1702 in May) marryed to a Frenchman's widdow, a good fortune to him." His wife was Elizabeth Howard, widow of Colonel Francis de la Rue, a French officer who served under William III., by whom he was rewarded with the lands of Killee in the County Cork. He died in 1701 leaving a son Wriothesley, who succeeded to the property, which on his death without issue, he left to his half brother George, eldest son of the above Hugh Montgomery. He was the ancestor of the present George Montgomery of Killee, the head of this branch of the Montgomery family.

C. HAMILTON MONTGOMERY, also served in the army, and married in 1700, Grace, daughter of James Ronaine, a gentleman of position in County Cork.

D. JAMES MONTGOMERY, "a pregnant witty scholar, this yeare (1701) is his 4th in the University at Dublin."

E. SAMUEL MONTGOMERY, eventually a captain in the army. Died in 1715 s.p.

and five daughters, of whom Elizabeth married Captain Johnstone, and Catherine, Bernard Brett of Ballynewport.

The above Hans Montgomery, the eldest son, succeeded to the Ballymagowan or Springvale estate on the death of his father. He was born 1668, was ordained priest in 1691, and became vicar of Ballywalter and Greyabbey. In 1709 he married Elizabeth, daughter of Mr. Townley of Townley Hall, County Louth. He sold his estate, investing the proceeds of the sale in securities, which were eventually divided among his four daughters. He died in 1726 and was buried at Greyabbey. His widow was

The Rev. HANS MONTGOMERY
of Ballymagowan,
Vicar of Ballywalter and Greyabbey.

From a Portrait].

JANE MONTGOMERY,
Mrs. JOHN ELLIOT CAIRNES of Killyfaddy.

From a Portrait].

ALICE MONTGOMERY,
Mrs. ALAN BELLINGHAM
of Castlebellingham.

From a Miniature].

living at Drogheda in 1742. He left issue four daughters only, co-heiresses,

MARY, wife of NICHOLAS FORDE of Seaforde.
LUCY, wife of Alderman HARMAN of Drogheda.
JANE, wife of JOHN ELLIOT CAIRNES of Killyfaddy.
ALICE, wife of ALAN BELLINGHAM of Castlebellingham.[1]

[1] See above p. 114, sqq. Alice Montgomery's marriage took place in 1738, and Jane's in 1742.

APPENDIX IV.

THE FAMILY OF MOORE OF MOORE HALL, KILLINCHY.

THE founder of this family in Ireland was William Moore or Mure, a cadet of the family of Mure of Caldwell in Ayrshire. Being connected by marriage with the family of Hamilton of Dunlop,[1] he came over in the following of James Hamilton, first Viscount Clannaboye, who gave him the lands of Ballybrega and other property of considerable extent adjoining, in 1628.[2] In the grant his wife, whose name is given as Janet, unfortunately without the surname, is co-grantee with her husband, and from this it seems not improbable that she was also a relative, or at least a friend of the Hamiltons.

We have no record of the dates of the deaths of William and Janet Moore. We find James, evidently their son and heir, in possession in 1654. He was a captain in the army, and in this year was appointed by the Presbyterian Congregation of Killinchy a commissioner to present a call to the Rev. John Livingston at Ancrum in Scotland. The call was reluctantly declined, but Livingston came over in 1656 on a visit to his old friends at Killinchy, and stayed at Captain Moore's house.[3] The notorious conspirator Colonel Blood in one of his efforts to form a plot among the Presbyterians of the North of Ireland after the Restoration, stayed with Captain Moore at Ballybrega, who suffered arrest and imprisonment as a suspected co-plotter with Blood. He was liberated after almost a year's imprisonment. He was alive in 1689, when we find his name and that of his son

---

[1] The Rev. Hans Hamilton, minister of Dunlop, Ayrshire, was the father of James, 1st Viscount Clannaboye, and of Janet, who married William Mure of Glandestoun in Ayrshire.

[2] Inquisitions, Down.

[3] *Killinchy, or the Days of Livingston*, by the author of *our Scottish Forefathers* (Belfast 1839) p. 123. The author states that the present Moore Hall, then called Ballybrega, was built at this time. For this we cannot vouch, but as Moore Hall is of considerable antiquity it is quite possible it dates from about this period.

Captain James Moore, junior, in the list of Protestants attainted by the Parliament of James II.

The next possessor of Moore Hall of whom we have record is John Moore. He was born in 1711. He was evidently a son or grandson of the younger James Moore in the list of attainders. We do not know whom he married, but we are enabled to reproduce his and his wife's portraits.[1] A family tradition states that the latter was a relative or member of the family of Hamilton of Killyleagh, but we have no evidence of this. John Moore of Moore Hall died in 1780, leaving issue,

A. HAMILTON MOORE of Moore Hall. Born 1750. He appears to have sold the property and fallen deeply into debt. Among the papers of his sister Mrs. Cairnes is a lawyer's bill of costs amounting to over £20 expended in an unsuccessful attempt to serve him with a writ. We do not know whom he married, and we have record only of one son John who died at Hyderabad in 1808.[2] Hamilton Moore died in 1815.

B. CATHERINE, who was married on the 26th September, 1779, at Moore Hall, by the Rev. Dr. Trail, Rector of Killinchy, to JOHN ELLIOT CAIRNES of Savile Lodge and Kilnahussogue.[3] The trustees of the marriage settlement were William Cairnes the eldest brother of the bridegroom, and Gawn Hamilton of Killyleagh. For the issue of the marriage, see pp. 129-141.[4]

We cannot find that any of the Moores of Moore Hall ever had confirmation of their arms in the Ulster Office. We have given in Chapter X (Shield No. 16) the arms of the parent family of Glanderstoun, which would have been borne by the family of Moore Hall with a charge of difference.

[1] See above, facing p. 128.

[2] *Hibernian Magazine*, May, 1808.

[3] *Belfast News-Letter*. 29 September, 1779, Family papers, &c.

[4] The Rev. John Graham in *Ireland Preserved*, p. 318, refers to "a younger sister who married the late Dean of Down (Dickson), father of the late Bishop of that Diocese and ancestor of Sir Jeremiah Dickson, K.C.B.," &c. The absurdity of this statement is evident, as the Bishop was born in 1745. Sir Jeremiah was the eldest son of the Bishop. His youngest son, the Rev. Stephen Dickson, was Rector of Dungarvan. He married secondly Sarah Moore, who died in 1841 aged 52. She was probably a daughter of Hamilton Moore above named.

APPENDIX V.

LAWLOR FAMILY.

WE learn from the Annals of the Four Masters and the Annals of Ulster, that this family, as early as the eighth century, was of considerable importance in the North-east of Ulster. In 707 A.D.[1] at the battle of Dola in Magh Elle,[2] Leathlobhar son of Eochardh and others were slain. We find no further reference to the name until 826, when Leathlobhar son of Loingseach,[3] king of Dal Araidhe[4] won a notable victory over foreigners. He ruled until 871, when it is recorded that he died after a good reign. Donald M'Firbis has preserved the Lawlor and Lynch pedigree, from which it appears that Leathlobhar the first of the name was 13th, and Loingseach, 16th in descent from Fiadra Araidhe, the progenitor of the Dal Araidhe.[5] Leathlobhar son of Loingseach was succeeded by Bec Ua Leathlobhair, Lord of Dal Araidhe, who died 904. Of him the poet has written:—

> "Awful news that now disperses those ships of the sea that have braved many dangers and perils,
> That no longer lives the golden scion, the sage, the beloved, the famed chieftain of Tuagh Inbhir."[6]

He was succeeded by Loingseach Ua Leathlobhair as Lord of Dal Araidhe. In 912 an army was led by Niall son of Aedh Finnliath into Dal Araidhe, in the month of June. Loingseach Ua Leathlobhair attacked it at Glenravel on the Cloughwater, and was defeated, losing his brother Flathrual Ua Leathlobhair. He

---

[1] Annals of the Four Masters. The Annals of Ulster gave the date 708.

[2] The district east of the Bann, near Coleraine.

[3] Loingseach, modernised Lynch. The O'Lynches and O'Lawlors, of Uladh, were of the same origin and closely connected, if not identical. It will be noticed that in the successive chiefs of this district, between the years 826 and 930, the names vary between Lynch O'Lawlor and Lawlor O'Lynch. We cannot discover whether these Lynches are identical with the family of that name so widely spread over Connaught.

[4] The district in County Antrim east of the River Main and south of the Cloughwater.

[5] Reeves, "*Ecclesiastical Antiquities of Down, Connor and Dromore*," p. 343.

[6] Annals of the Four Masters—Tuagh Inbhir was the country at the mouth of the Bann.

was then joined by Aedh, son of Eochagan, King of Uladh, and pursued the invaders to Carnearny.[1] Here another battle was fought, Niall being again victorious, and many on both sides being slain. In 930 occurred the death of Loingseach Ua Leathlobhair.

From this date we find no reference to the Lawlors in this district in the annals. But in a topographical poem by John O'Dugan, quoted by Reeves, and stated by him to be an account of the distribution of Uladh as it existed in the middle of the fourteenth century,[2] occurs the following:—

"Of their nobles, the men of slaughters
Oh-Aidith, O'Eodiagan,
Their plunders are great plunders,
O'Lavrey, O'Lawlor,
O'Lynchy of the proud champions,
&c., &c."

The Lawlors may have remained as chiefs in Dal Araidhe as late as the period mentioned by Reeves, but we have been unable to find any other record confirming this. In the Annals, under date 1053, a Leathlobhar is mentioned as Lord of Oirghialla,[3] and in 1080, Donald Ua Leathlobhair Lord of Fearnmhagh[4] was slain by the Ua Laithens.

The date of their expulsion from the County Antrim is very uncertain. It is quite probable, however, that they were among the native chiefs expelled by de Courcy in the twelfth century. Sir Bernard Burke, in his Landed Gentry, states, under Lalor of Cregg, that "at an early period they migrated with the O'Mores from Ulster to the extensive district of Leix in the Queen's County, of which country the O'Mores became powerful princes, and under them, the O'Lawlors were influential chieftains, possessing considerable landed property between Stradbally and Maryborough. The principal seat of the O'Lawlors was Disert, near the Rock of Dunamaise," the almost impregnable stronghold of the O'Mores. We have no grounds for controverting Sir Bernard Burke's account of the family, and such records as we have met with bearing on

[1] A townland near Ballymena.
[2] Reeves, "*Ecclesiastical Antiquities*," p. 367.
[3] Oriel, the district round Armagh.
[4] Farney, County Monaghan.

the subject all tend to confirm it.[1] For example, we find in 1396, Congal O'Lawlor was a Canon of Leighlin Cathedral,[2] and in 1435 Richard Lachlobr was presented to the living of Killeban, near Stradbally, Diocese of Leighlin.[3] In 1536, William O'Lawlour was presented to the same living.[4] In 1538 several members of the Fitzgerald family of Leinster were indicted for conspiring to instigate Kedagh O'More of Dunamaise and Neal O'Lawlor of Disert to make war upon the Earl of Ormond. In another document the term "make war upon" is modified into "to steal cattle" from the Earl.[5] Subsequent to this date the records available afford a little more information as to the state of this district.

The O'Lawlors were closely allied to the O'Mores, and joined with them in many wild ventures. With them were associated the O'Kellys. Of the latter family, it is related that they were a very savage and barbarous people, much addicted to robbery and plunder.[6] If this account is to be taken as correct, we fear these ill behaved O'Kellys had a very bad influence on the conduct of the O'Lawlors. No less than fifteen times between 1556 and 1600 did they break out in open rebellion against the English.[7]

That they had reason to be dissatisfied with their treatment is also certain. In 1556, or thereabouts, the Lord Deputy Bellingham, on instructions from the English Court, granted to certain English families the lands which had belonged from time immemorial to the O'Mores and O'Lawlors and others, forming therefrom the King's and Queen's Counties. A sanguinary battle was fought between the

[1] Unfortunately we have not had opportunity of examining such records as may exist which might throw more light upon the date of the settlement of the Lawlors in Disert. They were evidently firmly settled there by the fourteenth century or earlier.

[2] Calendar of Papal Registers, vol. iv., p. 529.

[3] Calend. Rot. Pat. Canc. Hib. vol. i., part i., p. 256.

[4] Calendar of the Patent and Close Rolls of Chancery, vol. i., p. 29, no. 50.

[5] Fiants of Henry VIII., No. 171, and Calendar of State Papers, 1509-1573, vol. vi., No. 55.

[6] Calendar of the Carew MSS., 1515-1589, p. 437.

[7] Calendar of State Papers, 1611-1614, p. 480. The term rebellion in the Irish State Papers of this period seems to have a most comprehensive meaning. As a rule, any attempt on the part of an Irish chieftain to keep what belonged to him was rebellion, and any attempt on his part to recover what had been stolen from him by the Saxons was classed as robbery and plunder. In most cases the punishment was much the same, fire and sword.

old possessors and the English invaders at Stradbally Bridge, but although the latter lost heavily, being reinforced from Dublin, they remained in possession of their newly acquired territories.

After forty years of continual unrest, the Lord Deputy, Sir Arthur Chichester, organised an expedition to quell the disturbances in the Queen's County.[1] With fire and sword he spread devastation through the lands of the unfortunate Irish chiefs. Miserable as their lot had been during the years of oppression before this expedition, it was by it made tenfold more so. With relentless cruelty the English burned their dwellings and crops, and drove them,[2] in many cases naked, into the woods, or slew them in cold blood. In their wretched state they presented a petition to Lord Salisbury in 1607, setting forth the shocking treatment they had received from the English, particularly Patrick Crosbie.[3]

The Rev. John Crosbie, who had married the daughter of Jeremiah O'Lawlor of Disert, and had been appointed Bishop of Adfert in 1601, seems to have had some influence in arranging a *modus vivendi* between the English settlers and the Irish of Leix. He was a brother of Patrick Crosbie. In addition to being the grantees of the Dunamaise and Disert property in Queen's County, the Crosbies had been granted extensive estates in North Kerry. In 1608, as an upshot of the petition to Lord Salisbury, a formal treaty of peace was duly drawn up and signed, between Patrick

[1] Calendar of the Carew MSS., 1589-1600, p. 430.

[2] It appears as if some of the Lawlors at this time submitted to the Lord Deputy, independently of those who made the treaty with Crosbie, and remained in possession of lands at Disert, as we find, in 1641, a Jeremiah Lalor, said by Burke (Landed Gentry under Lalor of Cregg) to have been a grandson of Jeremiah Lawlor, the father-in-law of Bishop Crosbie. We cannot tell whether he was the head of the family, or the son of a younger son. His descendants have always borne arms without any charge of difference denoting descent from a younger son, whereas the Kerry family have from an early date borne a crescent in the dexter chief. If this may be taken as evidence, it would show that the Kerry Lawlors descend from a second son of the chief Jeremiah, whose daughter married Bishop Crosbie, of Ardfert, and that the Jeremiah of 1641 was the lineal head of the family. He was, according to Burke, born in 1626, but the same authority states that he took a prominent part in the defence of the Castle of Dunamase against the Parliamentarians in 1641, and was then a Major in the Irish forces, and it seems difficult to reconcile both statements. He received extensive grants of lands in the neighbourhood of Templemore, after the restoration. He was the ancestor of the families of Lalor of Cregg and Power Lalor of Long Orchard, County Tipperary.

[3] Calendar State Papers. Ireland, 1606-1608—p. 195.

Crosbie on the one hand, and the chiefs of the O'Mores, O'Lawlors, and Dowlings[1] and three others. By this Patrick Crosbie "swears never to revenge upon any of the Septs any anger or controversy that happened between them heretofore. . . . . That he shall give the six ploughlands of Tarbert to the six persons subscribed, and to their heirs, they paying him and his heirs £6 sterling as chief rent—and for the rest of the Septs he shall place them in the Abbey O'Dorney, Coishcassan, and upon the Plountain in his other lands, and shall divide among them twelve ploughlands upon long leases, giving them such freeholds as shall be set down by the Bishop of Kerry (Crosbie, as representing both Patrick Crosbie and the O'Lawlor Sept) and John M'Murtagh O'More."

In return for these favours, the Septs were to swear loving and faithful allegiance to Patrick Crosbie and his heirs, as their chieftains. The treaty was signed by Patrick Crosbie, John M'Murtagh (O'More), Teig O'Lawlor, Robert Dowling, and others. Thus were removed to the County Kerry the chiefs of these ancient Irish clans, with many of their followers, as subordinates to their Saxon conquerors.

Under the Crosbies the Lawlors received much consideration, and acted for many generations as estate agents or middlemen, holding large tracts of land on lease, and extorting as much as they could from the native tenants. By Winifred O'Lawlor, the Bishop had sons, Sir Walter Crosbie, Bart., and David Crosbie, governor of Kerry in 1641, and was ancestor of the present Crosbies of Ardfert and Ballyheigue.

We are unable, from lack of correct data, to trace in detail the descent of the Lawlors of Kerry from the family of Jeremiah, the father of Winifred. They appear occasionally in the records available to the author[2] as resident at Ardfert and Ballyheigue, usually connected with the Ballyheigue or Ardfert estates. Though doubtless the Bishop's wife conformed to the Established Church, we find one Jeremiah O'Lawlor a captain in the Irish Roman Catholic army of 1641, leading a band against Lord Kerry. He stormed

[1] Calendar State Papers, Ireland, 1606-1608—p. 465. This document is in the Public Record Office, Dublin.

[2] No parish or other local records of a nature likely to produce information seem now to be extant in the Record Office. It is probable the rent rolls or family papers at Ballyheigue or Ardfert would throw light upon the genealogy of the family were one to investigate them.

and burned his castle near Ardfert, and we have no doubt committed atrocities so common at the time.[1]

In 1731 occurred the celebrated robbery of the Danish silver from the ship "Golden Lyon," wrecked in Ballyheigue Bay. Evidence is not forthcoming that this particular ship was one of many said to have been enticed on to the rocks of Kerry by false lights, but rumours to that effect existed. The treasure, amounting to nearly £20,000 in silver, was rescued from the wreck and safely stored at Ballyheigue Castle, where it lay for some months. The good people of Kerry naturally thought that so much money would be useful at home, and a widespread conspiracy was formed to capture it. It was arranged that if the robbery was successful, the money was to be distributed in fixed proportions between Lady Margaret Crosbie, the gentry of the neighbourhood, and those who committed the robbery. The details of the plot were ably carried out by David Lawlor of Ballyheigue and others, acting under the advice of the Rev. Francis Lauder, Archdeacon of Ardfert. A strong band was got together, and under the leadership of Lawlor stormed the castle and captured the silver. Four chests were left for Lady Margaret, and eight put on carts kindly lent for the occasion by the Archdeacon. Of these, three were opened at the cross roads, and the contents distributed in hatfuls to the people, one was sent to Tralee for friends there, and the remainder safely deposited in the Archdeacon's barn for division among the gentry.

The Danish Government made an urgent appeal to England on behalf of the owners of the silver, and the Irish law officers of the Crown caused several arrests to be made. Among those arrested were the Archdeacon of Ardfert, Arthur Crosbie of Tubrid, David Lawlor, Thomas Crosbie, Thomas Cantillon,[2] and others. The

[1] Smith's History of Kerry, 1756, p. 204.

[2] Cantillon—This family were of great antiquity in Kerry and possessed the Ballyheigue estate for centuries prior to the arrival in Kerry of the Crosbies. In an inquisition held at Killarney in 1622 the following appeared:—"That Thomas Cantylone died 2nd February, 1613, seized of the lands of the three Ballyheigues or Heyston, Toneriegh, &c., &c., . . . and being so seized, demised Toneriegh to Timothy Lawlor. Said Thomas Cantylone's son and heir Richard was aged twelve years at his father's death. Honora Lawlor, wife of said Thomas, Morris de Courcy and Daniel Lawlor were in receipt of the profits of said lands. After the death of said Thomas, said Honora Lawlor married Morris de Courcy without the license of the King." The Cantillons intermarried with the Crosbies and remained lords of

first four were tried at the Kerry Assizes, 1732 to 1734, and were all acquitted by the juries. The Castle authorities, seeing that no jury in Kerry would convict their friends in this conspiracy, brought Cantillon for trial to Dublin, where the jury, utterly void of any feelings of Kerry justice, found the prisoner guilty, the only man of the hundreds implicated who was convicted.[1]

The last of the descendants of Captain Jeremiah Lawlor to hold lands under the Crosbies seems to have been Jeremiah, who died about 1750. The leases by which he held expired either at his death, or shortly afterwards, and the then proprietor of the estate, probably to save the middleman's profit from the sub-lettings, refused to renew them. Jeremiah Lawlor left issue, of whom Michael, we believe the eldest son, came to reside in Tralee about 1760. There he married Mary, daughter of Richard Dowling, by whom he had issue,

A. RICE LAWLOR, who was drowned at sea unmarried.

B. MICHAEL LAWLOR, who had issue, one of his sons being a doctor in Queenstown.[2]

C. JEREMIAH LAWLOR, a physician of Tralee. Born January, 1772. He married in 1808 Catherine, daughter of Robert Hilliard,[3] of Listrim, by his wife Mary, daughter of

Ballyheigue until 1649, when they appear among the forfeited Papist proprietors. The Ballyheigue property was granted to Crosbie of Ardfert, and though some of the Cantillons remained as holders under the Crosbies, the heads of the family migrated to France. A descendant of one of the emigrants became a distinguished officer in the Grand Army of Napoleon, and underwent trial for an attempt on the life of the Duke of Wellington after 1815. He was acquitted, and in the will of Napoleon was left a considerable sum. (Hickson, Old Kerry Records ii., p. 50.) The representative of the Cantillon family, le Chevalier Antoine Sylvain de Cantillon, was created Baron de Ballyheigue by Louis Philippe. Thomas Cantillon, who was convicted of participation in the silver robbery, was, so far as our information goes, the last descendant in Kerry in the male line of this ancient and noble family.

[1] For a most detailed and well authenticated account of the Silver Robbery, see Hickson, "Old Kerry Records," ii., pp. 45-100; but for a more interesting and amusing, though inaccurate and misleading account, see Froude, "English in Ireland," i. pp. 477-498.

[2] We regret that we are unable to chronicle the descendants of Michael Lawlor. In the days before railways and the penny post were established, many near relationships were forgotten, and we have no knowledge of the representatives of this branch of the family.

[3] The representative of a very old and well-known Kerry family, who descend from Robert Hilliard, a Captain in the Parliamentary Army. He was a son of Robert Hilliard, second son of Sir Robert of Partington, in Yorkshire, 1st Baronet. The Baronetcy became dormant on the death of the 4th Baronet in 1814, the title passing *de jure* to the representative

Robert Hewson of Castlehewson, Co. Limerick. Jeremiah Lawlor, his wife, her sister Mrs. Sealy, and his niece Miss Dillon, who were on a visit, died at his residence in the Square, Tralee, of cholera, on the 5th of August, 1832. Jeremiah Lawlor left issue,

1. MICHAEL LAWLOR, physician, of 3 Day Place, Tralee. Born 1809, married Lucy, daughter of David Morphy and his wife Barbara,[1] daughter of Arthur Herbert of Brewsterfield, d.s.p. 1880.
2. ROBERT HILLIARD LAWLOR, d.s.p.
3. WILLIAM LAWLOR, of 8 Day Place, Tralee. Born 1814; graduated in T.C.D., where he took out his M.D. degree. He afterwards became a distinguished physician in Tralee, being medical officer to the county asylum and gaol. He married Elmslie, daughter of Captain Roy, R.N., and died s.p. in 1883.
4. JOHN HILLIARD LAWLOR. Born 1819, of whom later.
5. EDWARD LAWLOR. Born 1820. Became a solicitor, and practised in Dublin. He married, 1850, his cousin Ellen, daughter of William Lawlor, collector of H.M. Customs in Barbadoes. He was a son of a younger brother of the Michael Lawlor who came to Tralee about 1760. Edward Lawlor died in 1898, leaving one surviving daughter Frances, who has since died unmarried.

of the Parliamentarian Captain. This was the above Robert Hilliard, of Listrim, who had neither the ambition nor the means to pursue his claim. His mother was Barbara Mason, of Ballydowney, County Kerry, daughter of John Mason, and first cousin of Robert Emmet. Besides Catherine, Robert Hilliard had issue, (1) William, of Listrim, who married Miss Herbert, of Brewsterfield, ancestor of the present Hilliards, of Cahirslee. (2) Robert, d.s.p., 1801. (3) George, married Miss Giles, d.s.p. (4) Christopher, married Miss Collis, of Barrow, and had issue, John, who married Miss Creagh, and Elizabeth, wife of the Rev. John Kerin. (5) John, married, 1824, Miss Hickson, and had issue, Catherine, wife of Captain Oliver Day Stokes. (6) Henry, a distinguished Peninsular and Waterloo officer, married Miss Taylor, leaving an only daughter, the present Mrs. John George Hewson, of Tubrid. (7) Barbara, wife of Samuel Sealy of Maglass, d.s.p., 1832. (8) Elizabeth, wife of the Hon. Edward De Moleyns, a son of Lord Ventry, by whom she had issue.

[1] A sister of this lady, Frances Herbert, married Philip James Somers, whose eldest son, Philip Reginald, succeeded as 5th Lord Somers; he was thus a first cousin of Mrs. Lawlor of 3 Day Place. Another sister was Mrs. Hilliard of Listrim.

D. CATHERINE, wife of A. Spring, a member of an old Kerry family.

E. MARY, wife of Captain Dillon, an officer in the army.

Another branch of the Lawlors of Kerry settled in Killarney, and several ancient monuments erected to members of the family are in Mucross Abbey. Of this family was Martin Lawlor, of Grenagh, Killarney, whose only daughter and heiress, Ellen, married about 1800 Denis Shyne, and had an eldest son and heir, Denis Shyne, who assumed the surname of Lawlor in addition to his own. Denis Shyne Lawlor was a D.L. for Co. Kerry, and High Sheriff 1840. He married in 1840 Isabella, daughter of Edward Huddleston of Sawston, Cambridgeshire, and had issue, the present Denis Alexander Shine-Lawlor-Huddleston of Castle Lough, Co. Kerry, and Sawston, Cambridgeshire.

The above named John Hilliard Lawlor was an official in the old Agricultural Bank of Ireland, which merged in the Provincial Bank of Ireland in 1837. As manager of the branch in Ballymena, he lived to be the oldest official in the Bank. He was murdered on the 31st of May, 1889. In 1847 he married Catherine, daughter and heiress of Lieutenant-Colonel John Elliot Cairnes, K.H.,(the head of the Tyrone family, who survives him. By her he had issue—

A. JOHN ELLIOT CAIRNES. Born 1850. District Inspector of the Royal Irish Constabulary. He died, unmarried, 1899.

B. WILLIAM HAMILTON. Born 1852. He married in 1882 Mary Ellen, daughter of the late Robert Martin of Kilbroney, Co. Down, by whom he has issue.

C. HUGH JACKSON. Born 1860; educated at the Diocesan School of Armagh, and Connor at Ballymena. He entered Trinity College, Dublin, and after a distinguished career, graduated B.A. in 1882 as Senior Moderator in Mathematics and in Mental and Moral Science, and University Student. He subsequently took the degrees of M.A., B.D., and D.D. He is now Beresford Professor of Ecclesiastical History in Dublin University, Precentor of the Cathedral of Saint Patrick, Dublin, Honorary Chaplain to the Lord Lieutenant, and Examining Chaplain to the Bishop of Edinburgh. He is the Author of several Works on Ecclesiastical History and Biography and on Palæography. He married 1stly Kate Anna Helena, daughter of the late Arthur Samuels of Langara, County Dublin, sister of Arthur Warren Samuels, K.C.; and 2ndly Leila Mary, daughter of the late John Haslar Samuels of Beaufort, County Dublin.

D. THOMAS HAMILTON JONES. Born 1865, now residing in Lifford, County Donegal. He married in 1902, Leonora Josephine, daughter of John Cochrane of Edenmore and Combermere, County Donegal, by whom he has issue.

E. ARTHUR CAIRNES, now of 3 Anna Mount, Kingstown. Born 1868. He married in 1895, Margaret Alice, daughter of the late John Wingfield King, of Ballygrehan, Co. Sligo, and Grove Lodge, Windsor, D.L., Captain 5th (Northumberland) Fusiliers, and has issue.

F. HENRY CAIRNES. Born 1870, the author of this work. He married in 1893, Beatrice Kathleen, daughter of Alexander M'Donald of Glenarm, only surviving son and heir of the late Colonel Donald M'Donald, C.B., of the 92nd Gordon Highlanders, who led that regiment at Waterloo, and heir presumptive in the male line of the M'Donalds of Dalschosnie and Dunalistair, Perthshire. He has issue.

G. KATHERINE HILLIARD, wife of David Ellis, of Creeve House, near Newry, County Down, now living in Australia, by whom she has issue.

H. SUSAN MARY, wife of the Rev. Josiah Nicholson Shearman, B.A., Rector of St. Matthew's Parish, Belfast, by whom she has issue.

I. ANNIE CONSTANCE GWYNN, died unmarried 1875.

K. LUCY ELIZABETH CAIRNES.

L. & M. GEORGE HILLIARD and FRANCIS HEWSON, died in infancy.

ARMORIAL BEARINGS.—Like many of the ancient Irish families who long withstood the English suzerainty, the Lawlors were by force of circumstances compelled to accept what we may call subordinate positions under the Saxon invaders. The Lalors of

Tipperary, whom we may assume, from want of contradictory evidence, to be the chiefs of the ancient family of Disert, Queen's County, formerly Lords of Dal Araidhe, bear the arms, for Long Orchard, "Or, a lion rampant guardant gules"; crest, "an arm embowed, vested gules, cuffed vert., the hand ppr., grasping a short sword, ppr.," motto "Fortis et Fidelis"; for Cregg, Arms, "Vert, a lion rampant or"; crest and motto, as Long Orchard. We do not know the earliest date of which there is record of these arms being borne by the Tipperary family. The earliest instance of the Kerry branch bearing arms with which we have met is in the seal of Michael Lawlor of Tralee (circ. 1750). It displays in tinctures or and gules, the arms as Cregg, with a crescent of the second for difference, in the dexter chief[1]; crest as above, with the motto, "Virtute et Valore."

The armorial bearings of the Lawlors of Kerry do not appear to have been officially registered in the Ulster Office: having, however, been borne by them in direct descent for at least 150 years, an official grant of the arms is unnecessary, a confirmation, should any representative of the family desire to establish his undoubted right to the arms, being now all that would be required.

[1] See above, page 276, footnote, and shield No. 17, chap. X.

INDEX.

THE END.

R. CARSWELL AND SON, PRINTERS AND LITHOGRAPHERS, BELFAST.

FOR RECORDING ADDITIONAL INFORMATION

Printed in Great Britain
by Amazon

58255536R00220